ILLUMINATING SHADOWS

ILLUMINATING SHADOWS

THE MYTHIC POWER OF FILM

GEOFFREY HILL

Shambhala
BOSTON & LONDON
1992

Shambhala Publications, Inc.
Horticultural Hall
300 Massachusetts Avenue
Boston, Massachusetts 02115

Shambhala Publications, Inc.
Random Century House
20 Vauxhall Bridge Road
London SW1V   2SA

"*Little Shop of Horrors:* The Battle between Heaven and Earth" first appeared in *The San Francisco Jung Institute Library Journal* 9, no. 1 (1990).

The photographs on pages 67, 68, 114, and 116 are used courtesy of the Museum of Modern Art Film Stills Archive. Other photo sources: pp. 47, 50, 45: Avco Embassy Pictures; 88, 93, 185, 189: Island Pictures; 140, 157: The Danish Film Institute; 144, 153: Miramax Films; 165, 178: The Geffen Film Company; 200, 203, 210: Embassy Pictures Corp; 214, 221: De Laurentiis Entertainment Group; 230, 232, 247: Expanded Entertainment; 267, 268, 273: Hot Weather Films; 283, 286: Columbia Pictures; 290, 294: Universal City Studios; 300, 305: Tri-Star Pictures.

Figures 1–10 on pp. 238–245 are from the *Rosarium philosophorum, secunda pars alchemiae de lapide philosophico* (Frankfort, 1550).

9   8   7   6   5   4   3   2   1

First Edition

Printed in the United States of America on acid-free paper

Distributed in the United States by Random House, Inc., in Canada by Random House of Canada Ltd, and in the United Kingdom by the Random Century Group

Library of Congress Cataloging-in-Publication Data

Hill, Geoffrey Michael, 1950–
    Illuminating shadows: the mythic power of film/Geoffrey Michael
Hill.
        p.   cm.
    Includes bibliographical references.
    ISBN 0-87773-645-6 (pbk.)
    1. Motion pictures.   2. Popular culture.   3. Myth.   I. Title.
PN1995.H48   1992   91-53098
791.43—dc20   CIP

To Professor Beatriss, on whom truth and beauty
are equally bestowed

June 9, 1992

Dear Betty,

I give this book to you as a
sign of my affection and regard, and as
a request that we always remain
friends.

Best always,
Jeremy Bricker

CONTENTS

CONTENTS

PREFACE

Each of the films written about in this book has much wisdom to offer the open-minded viewer. True to the nature of good art, they have each affected me in a very positive way. I offer these essays to share with others some of the beneficent impact each film has to offer.

I recommend that the reader view each film before reading its respective essay; if you have not seen the film for a few years, do view it again before reading the essay. (Fortunately all of the films are available on videocassette.) Actually, each essay can be easily followed even by someone who has not seen the film to which it pertains. But the film themselves are paramount. Watch the films with the anticipation of receiving insight, as each is enlightening in its own way. Then read each essay to add to your own interpretation. Enough exposure to good art can change one's life.

ACKNOWLEDGMENTS

I would first like to extend my appreciation to the gracious people who participated in the Cinema Club dialogue group wherein the foundations of the enclosed film analyses were first tested. The monks at Saint Andrew's Priory in Valyermo, California, especially Fathers Werner, Gregory, and Anselm, are also to be gratefully acknowledged for inviting me to deliver some of the same material in their monastery-sponsored workshops. For the use of their cabin in which to hide away and write, I thank my parents, William and Harriet Hill. For his encouraging support I am grateful to David O'Neal at Shambhala Publications. Finally, I am especially indebted to John Beebe, who, more than anyone else, believed in the project from the beginning.

PART 1
INTRODUCTION

FROM CAVE SHADOWS TO THE SILVER SCREEN

THE WISDOM OF CINEMYTH

As ironic modern worshipers we congregate at the cinematic temple. We pay our votive offerings at the box office. We buy our ritual corn. We hush in reverent anticipation as the lights go down and the celluloid magic begins. Throughout the filmic narrative we identify with the hero. We vilify the antihero. We vicariously exult in the victories of the drama. And we are spiritually inspired by the moral of the story, all while believing we are modern techno-secular people, devoid of religion. Yet the depth and intensity of our participation reveal a religious fervor that is not much different from that of religious zealots.

I didn't see Frank Capra's 1946 film *It's a Wonderful Life* until the mid-1980s. My first viewing of this timeless classic at an art theater caused me to weep profusely. Every time I have seen it since, tears have flowed down my face. When I saw *Field of Dreams* for the first time at the theater, I cried. When I saw it again on video, I sobbed convulsively. *Repo Man* made me laugh continually throughout the film. And many others have moved me profoundly. But besides the emotional impact these films have on me and others, there is something deeper about

3

them that changes our lives. Our participation in these cinemyths helps alter the consciousness of society, either for good or ill, depending on the myths portrayed.

This participation in the cinema commands as much spiritual devotion as any religion. In India, a country noted for its variety and wealth of religious practice, the cinema is one of the largest industries, daily pulling in literally millions of unemployed devotees to its thousands of cinematic shrines, even during matinee. During the days of the cinematic "dream palaces" of the 1920s, the American grand movie houses rivaled and surpassed contemporary temples and cathedrals in both elegance of design and popular attendance. The cinema has become to the modern world the collective cathedral of primitive *participation mystique*. It is the tribal dream house of modern civilization.

Our participation in the cinema is our participation in myth. While the names, times, and styles have changed, the myths that were familiar to our ancestors are the myths on the silver screen. The purpose of this book is to show how the cinema is a modern manifestation of myth, both in the ancient and modern varieties.

Myth is not, as popularly conceived, something that is not true. To the contrary, the scholar of religion Ananda Coomaraswamy reminds us that myth is actually "the nearest to absolute truth that can be expressed in words" (Dooling, 2–3). Rafaele Pettazzoni says that "myth is not fable, but history, 'true history' and not 'false history.'" Mircea Eliade, Bronislaw Malinowski, and others also suggest that myth, as something held to be sacred by the believers thereof, is considered true (Eliade 1949, 174; Malinowski, 21, 43, 124).

Roland Barthes and Claude Lévi-Strauss suggest that myth is both language (Barthes 1957, 11 & 109; Lévi-Strauss 1963, 209), and, according to Lévi-Strauss, something simultaneously different from language. This idea itself could warrant volumes of philosophy. The idea of myth as language suggests that myth carries the consciousness of humanity on the carriage of words and symbols, which is what the cinema does. Northrop Frye goes so far as to say that "mythological thinking cannot be superseded, because it forms the framework and context for all thinking" (Frye 1990, xvi).

However we may feel about myth or however we may define it, myth is a collective cultural expression of the sacred mass consciousness. As used herein, the term signifies a traditional tribal numinous story, usually with significant spiritual import. Even in a secular culture, much more is sacralized than we would care to admit. Often even our political ideologies and media heroes are mythicized.

All cultures have myth, even if they consider themselves thoroughly modern and secular. The popular definition of myth as "something that is not true" itself indicates that our culture is in a state of mythic denial, especially when one looks at the significant history of mythic participation in Western culture. Of course the more something is denied the more that which is denied is revealed as viable.

Myth is a religious cultural expression, religion being defined here as a collective set of beliefs, attitudes, practices, rituals, and behaviors that are held passionately and from which a feeling of transcendence is derived by the members of a particular culture. In a secular society, the function of religion may be fulfilled by something other than what is traditionally thought to be religious or sacred. The phenomenon of football, for example, can be thought of as a sacred institution. Zealous devotees congregate in their inspirational stadium to passionately roar and support their mythic heroes for the common good of their respective community tribes. Here, true believers spend inordinate amounts of time, money, and energy in an activity that enriches a priestly caste and religiously inspires the devotees to passionate fervor, sometimes even to zealous violence. Certainly in terms of passion, football would seem to rank higher than the participation in modern western "religion." But in terms of the promotion of collective ideologies, the cinema serves this religious purpose more adequately than football.

MODERN MYTH

While we might assume that myth is something with only ancient dress and application, myth has always been around, changing its costume for every culture and mode of thought. Archetypes remain

5

the same, but the manner in which they appear will differ with each generation. Depending on the time and culture, the archetypal fool may appear as the knight's squire, the court jester, the trickster god, the vaudeville buffoon, or the stand-up comic. The hero will be the dragon slayer, the giant killer, the army hero, the courageous Young Turk, or the race car driver. The witch doctor will be the magician, the sorcerer, the mad scientist, the priest, or the psychotherapist. The dragon will be the ancient regime, the avaricious merchant, the bad father, the wealthy cattle herder, or the school principal. Hades will be a nefarious gravedigger, an underground wizard, or a Mafia chieftain.

So while each generation demands a new skin, the archetypes of the ancient myths remain the same through the ages. The more modern and the more removed we are from ancient mythic participation, the less recognizable will be our myths. That is why every generation has had interpreters of contemporary mythic forms. In the Renaissance, for example, scholarly humanists revealed the classical mythic archetypes as found in the visual arts of the day. So also today, the mythic archetypes of contemporary cultural expressions are sometimes unrecognizable to the general populace. Hopefully mythic interpretations of today's contemporary art forms will teach us not only how connected we still are to myth, but how *sophia*, or wisdom, can be gleaned from such mythic awareness.

THE THREAD OF MYTH

It is easier to understand the vantage of myth in film if we look back to trace myth through cultural expression from ancient times up through and including the cinema. Outlined here is a rough sketch of the threading of myth through the various stages and varieties of human expression. This outline is not meant to be a dogmatic assertion of the history of myth. To prove any exact outline of this would indeed be beyond the scope of this project, and will be left to the scholarly specialists in the histories of mythology and consciousness. This outline is meant to serve merely as a suggested picture of the thread of myth-religion that runs through the sociohistoric expression of human numinosity. This thread of mythic expression runs roughly thus:

Consciousness → Dream → Myth → Religion → Art →
Drama → Literature → Cinema

As to exactly which of these comes specifically in which order is open to debate. Besides, the exact order is not important. What is important is that we see a common thread running from the primeval religious consciousness down through modern cultural expression. These stages obviously overlap regularly, and no doubt one of these expressions might come before another in one culture and after it in another culture.

Consciousness/Dream

It is suggested that myth and religion begin with human consciousness itself and with dreams, our spontaneous inner expression of consciousness. Joseph Campbell says that "dream is the personalized myth, myth the depersonalized dream" (Campbell 1949, 19). Certainly many of our collective myths must have originated in dreams. Some primitive tribes have been known to share their dreams communally, to interpret them as a group, and even to find communal guidance from them (Hall; Stewart). Could this be what moderns do with literature and the cinema, although possibly in a subconscious way?

Plato called art a dream for wakened minds, recognizing the connection between inner consciousness and art. Whatever originates in the primitive, the secretive, and the personal eventually finds its way into the modern, the expressive, and the public. Whatever was in the primeval mind and whatever is in our contemporary collective subconscious mind eventually shows up in the public collective expression of shared myths. Parker Tyler has said that "Hollywood is but the industrialization of the mechanical worker's daylight dream ... extended ritualistically into those hours reserved by custom for relaxation and amusement" (Tyler 1944). German filmmaker Werner Herzog, in *Burden of Dreams*, the film about the making of his *Fitzcarraldo*, says, "I make films because I learned nothing else, and I articulate my dreams in my films. It is my duty. That is the basis of every art—whether painting, music, or filmmaking. That's the only difference between you and me. I articulate my dreams." Indeed, the filmmaker is a recorder of dreams that are not much different from the dreams of most people.

All peoples dream, and all peoples have myths. When our personal consciousness blends into the collective consciousness of our respective tribes, such cultural expressions become the established myths of the culture, because all individuals within a given culture have a shared consciousness with the rest of that culture, and all peoples have a need for cultural myths that act as guiding lights for the motility of the collective soul. In ancient and primitive societies, common dreams were and are shared with the community and become the property of the tribe. These stories either remain as mere stories and are added to the collective folktales of the tribe, or, if the stories are profound and numinous enough, they take on a higher status and become the myths of the culture.

Myth/Religion

When a society develops a written language, the communal stories are recorded for posterity. Written myths are the oral tradition of a civilized tribe taken to the next stage of human expression. Along with written myths come organized religion, religious drama, and formalized tradition. Through all the changes occurring in human spiritual expression, collective myth continues to assert itself like a river flowing through the topographically variant wilderness. The land will change over time, and the river may divert into new courses, but the river will continue to flow through time, perpetuating the cycle of nature. Likewise, whatever may happen in human civilization, with its changing ideologies, theologies, and worldviews, myth will always be threaded through the cloak of human expression in any medium that happens to be available at the time. Like dreams on the personal level, myth on the social level supplies the signs and symbols that help the human spirit resolve its dilemmas and transcend above the indignities of the temporal plain. C. G. Jung said that religious myth "is one of man's greatest and most significant achievements, giving him the security and inner strength not to be crushed by the monstrousness of the universe" (Jung 1952, 231).

Eventually the collective myth is formalized into a systematized body of ritualistic religion, and the myth is enacted in rite and ceremony (although some would say that rite comes before myth). With this formalization comes a certain amount of sterility and stasis. While the rites and ceremonies preserve a certain freshness in the religion, they also tend to make the myth stationary, thus creating a need for ever-new ways of expressing the ancient truths, such as through various art forms.

Art (and Artists)

Besides stories that become the myth of culture, various other art forms have always been used to depict subjects of myth. From ancient cave paintings with elements of sympathetic magic to modern performance art, art has always served its culture as a carrier of myth. The ancient Assyrian bas-reliefs carried the dignity of that culture's religion into public display. Likewise, Greek statuary, Egyptian pyramids, and Gothic cathedrals have served their respective cultures as bearers of the collective myth.

The artist has traditionally stood between the public culture and the hidden elements of numinous phenomena. Ezra Pound thought of the artist as "the antennae of the race" (McLuhan, x). Many luminaries have thought of the artist as the prophet of society's spiritual secrets. The artist has always seemed to be aware of phenomena of which many others are quite unaware. It is as if some artists have a sixth sense, enabling them to "tune in" to seemingly invisible mysteries of the universe. It is as if they are able to pick up signals surrounding the human culture and translate them into a language meaningful enough to the masses. The artist is a seer; as Aldous Huxley says: "What the rest of us see only under the influence of mescalin, the artist is congenitally equipped to see all the time. His perception is not limited to what is biologically or socially useful" (Huxley, 33).

The artist sees and hears things that others do not see or hear, as if through invisible and inaudible signals. And where do these invisible signals come from? Who knows? Master storyteller Ruth Sawyer says, "Creative art is the power to be for the moment a flash of communication between God and man" (Sawyer, 162). And so it seems to be with myth, and so it is with myth expressed in art. Art has always been the transporter of culture's myth. But this is not to say that all artists are necessarily priests or prophets. Quite the contrary. Some of them are mere commercial prostitutes, or bohemian fad-addicts at best. Others, however, carry the torch of enlightenment that elucidates the higher path of the human spirit.

But we don't have to look to the artist for prophecy. Our dreams are prophetic enough. As Werner Herzog reminds us, the only difference between him and somebody else is that he records his dreams. The artist who does this is merely heralding what most people could gather, if they would only listen to their own dreams.

Unlike traditional Freudian psychoanalysis that looks at art as a symptom of a sickness, and unlike Ernst Kris, who sees art as "regression in the service of the ego" (Kris, 177), art is something grander and higher than a neurotic touch of divine madness. As Jung said, "If a work of art is explained in the same way as a neurosis, then either the work of art is a neurosis or a neurosis is a work of art" (Jung 1966, 67). Art has often been thought of as the imitation of divine art (Plato, *Laws*, 667–69, *Statesman*, 306d; Eliade 1954, 32). This is how the primitive viewed art, and likewise the modern artist still carries within this feeling of divine creative imitation, even if it is at the subconscious level.

Recognizing the spiritual element in art, William Blake called the Bible "the great code of art," which later inspired the title of one of Northrop Frye's books of literary criticism (Frye 1982, xvi). While the mythic or spiritual view of human expression might have been forgotten by the modern mind, the artist throughout the generations has not lost sight of it. Thomas Mann also recognized this truth. He said that the artist's eye has a "mythical slant upon life" (Campbell 1959, 21). C. G. Jung, known for his avid acknowledgment of the spiritual in human expression, recognized this mythical slant:

> It is therefore to be expected that the poet will turn to mythological figures in order to give suitable expression to his experience. Nothing would be more mistaken than to suppose that he is working with second-hand material. On the contrary, the primordial experience is the source of his creativeness, but it is so dark and amorphous that it requires the related mythological imagery to give it form. (Jung 1966, 96)

It is as if the artist, whether or not he or she recognizes it, carries the historic mythic torch which illumines for all generations the participation of *in illo tempore*, or the sacred time as outlined by Mircea Eliade (Eliade 1954, 20). The artist, along with the other sages of civilization, is also the forge in which myths are wrought into new shapes for each succeeding generation. Northrop Frye says of the artist as mythmaker; "Every society is the embodiment of a myth, and as the artist is the shaper of myth, there is a sense in which he holds in his hand the thunderbolts that destroy one society and create another" (Frye 1963, 147).

Since we no longer believe in "myth," the hero of myth has jumped out of the mythic play and has become the artist-hero of a modern "mythless" culture. Hence, for a society that prides itself on modernity, or postmodernity we cannot avoid the hero in whom we pretend not to believe.

Drama

From the most ancient times drama has had its roots in myth and religion. Primitive peoples have always enacted their religious devotion in song, dance, and play. As civilization advanced, so too did theater. In the golden age of Greek drama, the poets, actors, and directors were all considered ministers of religion during the drama festivals. The plays were designed to interpret life rather than escape from it. After Rome conquered Greece, drama turned into a form of escapism, an attitude that unfortunately has been with us far too powerfully to this day. If that weren't enough of a deterioration of drama, the church officially dismantled the theatre during her Roman conquest. It was eventually revived about a thousand years later in the Middle Ages as morality plays designed to teach the gospel to the illiterate masses. And it has fortunately been a live and mythic institution ever since.

Literature

Society with a written language inevitably produces fictional literature. Here one might think that secular literature is indeed "secular," that is, removed from the religious element of society. But the mythic and religious influence in human consciousness is merely transformed into new forms via literature. From the oral tradition, myth is manifested in plays, religious ritual, and eventually literature. Whatever mythic dramas are enacted on stage eventually find their way into written literature.

Northrop Frye says that "literature is a reconstructed mythology" (Frye 1963, 38). He is not the only thinker to equate literature with things mythical or religious. Philosopher Georges Bataille also sees a clear connection: "Following upon religion, literature is in fact religion's heir. A sacrifice is a novel, a story, illustrated in a bloody fashion" (Bataille, 87).

From the earliest literature the ancient themes and archetypes of myth are present. The Book of Job, the Homeric epics, the Attic tragedies, and the Mahabharata are all literary works that are considered myth. Much medieval literature, such as that of Dante and Chaucer was no doubt written with the same motivation as earlier "mythic" literature, that is, to inspire religious sentiment, and to enlighten the readers. But because of their later dates of composition, medieval works are usually categorized as literature rather than as myth. If the *Divine Comedy* had been written several hundred years earlier, we would probably now consider it myth instead of "mere" poetry. Likewise, we are not in the habit of considering modern novels or films as myth.

Even when serious literature seems completely secular, as in Melville's *Moby Dick* or Hemingway's *The Old Man and the Sea*, traces of religious mythic import are almost always evident. Instead of Jonah and the fish, or Job and Leviathan, or David and Goliath, or Christ and the Devil, or Moses and Pharaoh, we have Captain Ahab and the white whale, or the old man and the eternal struggle with the impossible. The setting and names change, but the same primordial issues play out in ever-present narratives through "secular" literature.

Some secular writers of the modern world purposefully base their narratives on mythic origins. Joyce's Steven Daedalus and Hesse's Narziss and Goldmund are obvious references to mythic characters of old. But even when modern secular novels are not intentionally based on mythic origins, such as the works of Dostoyevsky and Tolstoy, their content is often ripe with the rich material of medieval morality plays, inspiring religious thought and provoking moral, philosophic, and psychological questions at sublime levels of contemplation.

While Raskolnikov in *Crime and Punishment* wrestles with his own philosophical demon of ethics, we read Dostoyevsky's novel with a modern mind, seeing mainly a moral dilemma played out on the stage of the modern world. We need to remind ourselves, however, that Raskolnikov's demon is Daniel Webster's Devil, which is Faust's Mephistopheles, which is Everyman's tempter, which is Saint Augustine's Faustus, which is Job's Satan, which is Adam's serpent.

Northrop Frye, who has always seen the connection between literature and myth, even so much as calling literature the direct descendent of myth (Frye 1982, 34), cannot avoid analyzing literature as myth. He says, "In literature, whatever has a shape has a mythical shape" (Frye 1963, 38). When one studies literary plots, depending on who is counting, there might be only one plot (the hero-redeemer) or thirty-six (as counted by Goethe). All of them are mythical in origin. Arthur Koestler (354–57) lists seven major archetypal patterns:

1. The Promethean striving for omnipotence and omniscience (The Tower of Babel, The Flight of Icarus)
2. Individual against society (Oedipus)
3. Polygonal patterns of libidinous relations (Vulcan-Venus-Mars triangle)
4. The War of the Sexes (Amazon myths, Simone de Beauvoir)
5. Love Triumphant, or Defeated (Song of Songs, Tristan and Isolde)
6. The Conquest of the Flesh (from Buddha to Aldous Huxley)
7. The Puppet on Strings, or Volition against Fate

Of course all of these patterns have their origin in myth. Aristotle saw literature and drama as the highest forms of learning, no doubt because they have the capacity to bring the highest human ideals down to the lowest recipient and they bring the participant back up to the lofts of religious sublimity.

Cinema

One of the most recent manifestations of myth in human expression is the cinema. It was not mere technical brilliance nor narrative intrigue that brought devotees of the *Star Wars* trilogy to camp out in front of the box office for several days before tickets went on sale. The mythic nature of the human spirit compels such science fiction aficionados to religious devotion and heightens an altered sense of anticipation during this modern phenomenon of mythic hero worship.

To mine this mythic element in film it is necessary to dig deeper into numinosity than what would normally be done in film criticism. According to analytical psychology each of us has stirring within us the symbols, archetypes, and myths of a vast collective unconscious borrowed from ancestors of the distant and recent past. Through a familiarity with symbols, religion, and mythology, mythic connections can be found in even the most secular films, as in the most secular psyches.

Plato wrote a metaphorical story of some cave dwellers chained to

14

the floor of their abode, only being able to see shadows projected onto the wall before them. Being released from this colorless bondage, one is able to see brilliant varieties of colors and patterns in a whole new world of illuminated existence.

Similarly, the first slide projector, called the magic lantern, hints of its numinous characteristic of being able to project illuminated brilliant images onto a screen in a dark room, and thus into the human soul. In England, the cinema house was originally called the bioscope, signifying the viewing of life. Indeed, the cinema is the theater of life, the screen of human existence casting illuminating shadows onto the wall of tribal participation.

Film is an excellent medium for conveying myth, whether intentionally or not. Marshall McLuhan points out that film transports the viewer to another world:

> Whatever the camera turns to, the audience accepts. We are transported to another world. As René Clair observed, the screen opens its white door into a harem of beautiful visions and adolescent dreams, compared to which the loveliest real body seems defective. Yeats saw the movie as a world of Platonic ideals with the film projector playing "a spume upon a ghostly paradigm of things." This was the world that haunted Don Quixote, who found it through the folio door of the newly printed romances. (McLuhan, 286)

Some mythic content is rather obvious and intentional such as in films like *Jason and the Argonauts*, *Hercules*, *The Robe*, *The Ten Commandments*, and *Samson and Delila*. These films were quite popular during the days of the prudish Hayes Code, which from 1930 to 1966 all but outlawed sex on the screen.

There are other genres that also intentionally portray myth, at least in the first version or two. For example, the filmic adaptation of George Bernard Shaw's *Pygmalion* was an intentional copy of the Greek myth of Pygmalion. *My Fair Lady* was an intentional musical adaption of the original movie. Over the years, there have been many versions of the same basic story of the man of stature "creating" a lady of culture out of earthy raw material. Filmic versions of this story would include *Educating Rita*, *Mona Lisa*, and *Pretty Woman*, among several others. The Greek myth of Pyramus and Thisbe has been transposed into many versions over the centuries, most notably in Shakespeare's *Romeo and Juliet* and in Franco Zeffirelli's film version of the play, in the stage and film versions of *West Side Story*, in *Love Story*, *Torn Apart*, and other films with the same general story line of a young couple kept apart by family barriers. This remaking of myth in newer forms is nothing new. Long before film came into existence, there were over nine hundred versions of the myth of Cupid and Psyche found on various continents of the world (Grant and Hazel, 3).

Then there are films that focus on religious issues and characters that are not intentionally based on ancient myths, yet carry obvious and powerful spiritual import nonetheless: *Elmer Gantry*, *The Night of the Hunter*, *Tender Mercies*, *Chariots of Fire*, *Places in the Heart*, *Gandhi*, and others.

Intentionally and obviously mythic (though not as much as *The Ten Commandments*) are films of another category. This genre includes the *Star Wars* trilogy, created with the help of Joseph Campbell's structural outline of the hero myth; *Peter Pan*, based slightly on the god Pan and on the Greek principle of the *puer aeternus*, or eternal youth; *Splash* and *The Little Mermaid*, both based on Hans Christian Andersen's tale and on mythic stories of sirens and sea nymphs.

There are even cine-mythic films about film, such as *The Purple Rose of Cairo*, *Apartment Zero*, *Cinema Paradiso*, and *The Icicle Thief*, all focusing on the mythic power of cinema.

While the films of this study have been picked particularly for their mythic content, it must be acknowledged that most films have some mythic import. Contrary to our general conception that myth is usually created only at the inception of a particular civilization, myth is created and re-created perpetually throughout the history of all civilizations. With a synthesis of ideologies, worldviews, and attitudes, myths that are not generally recognized as myth find their way into the folkways, literature, foreign policies, and films of their respective cultures.

When myths are manifested in film we see the emergence and continuation of particular genres that promote mass participation in each respective myth. One such mythic genre is the western, which has done well to promote the mythic ideals of and justifications for such cultural ideologies as westward expansion, manifest destiny, racism, rugged individualism, and puritanical capitalism. The films of the early Russian Revolution similarly promulgated the ideologies of state Marxism, a revulsion for czarism, agricultural and industrial collectivism, and a reverence for and redemption of Mother Russia. Likewise, the films of the Third Reich mythicized the Fatherland, a revivication of Teutonic mythology, the exaltation of the white race, anti-Hebraiism, and nationalist exclusivism. And no differently, the Rocky/Rambo genre promotes a contemporary myth that will hopefully lose its need for existence with the demise of the Communist threat. This mythic genre serves to justify reactionary attitudes at both the personal and national levels.

But none of these genres are the subject of this study. The films discussed in this book are usually not intentionally mythical at all, and are not obviously mythic to most viewers. The films written about herein are largely mythicized at the subconscious level. After writing the analysis of Little Shop of Horrors contained herein, it was given to Charles Griffith, the screenwriter of the original 1960 version. His reaction was one of great complimentarity that I liked his film so much, and total surprise that I saw so much mythic content in his simple story that he had no intention whatsoever of including. And so it is with many filmmakers. While they might not be aware of their mythic participation, they nonetheless convey significant mythic import.

The films of this study are what I would categorize as secular religious films, unintentionally mythic films, subconscious numinous films or cinema sophia—in essence, numinous films from which wisdom can be gleaned. Certainly some of the makers of these films had some mythic or religious ideas in mind. But the mythic import is believed to be largely unintentional and therefore mostly unconscious in its delivery.

Since the films in this collection are mostly of the western mind, it is only natural that the mythological archetypes would be derived mostly from a Western religious mythology.

It is assumed that the films of this genre arise from the same sphere as do dreams, from the collective unconscious. And the interpretation of these films is done in a similar fashion as depth psychology would analyze dreams.

PARTICIPATION

Samuel Taylor Coleridge suggested that in order to enjoy drama and literature, we as moderns had to effect a "willing suspension of disbelief." This is something the primitive never had to do. It is only with a rational, skeptical mind that we must purposefully will our soul into participation. But participate we do. It is always humorous to hear sophisticated filmgoers complain about the director being too heavy-handed, manipulating the audience's emotions. This is like complaining that a magician tries to trick his audience. We, as sophisticated filmgoers don't want to admit our participation. An emotional involvement with the cinema is for naive filmgoers, we might assume. But the fact we consider ourselves film buffs belies our denial of participation.

Film wouldn't be a successful transporter to other worlds if it weren't for the fact that filmgoers have this natural tendency to "participate" in the mythic process. Following Lucien Lévy-Bruhl's concept of *participation mystique*, we can view the filmgoer as one who intimately and spiritually involves himself or herself in the magic of the cinema. We can say that the cinema is actually a modern form of shamanism. While the primitives have their rituals, possessions, medicines, and incantations (which we also have in various forms) we as moderns have our movie house.

When missionaries show films to indigenous peoples who have never seen such white man's magic before, the primitives don't see the images as we do. They see shadows, colors, abstract figures, and a convoluted mixture of moving yet unrecognizable blotches on a flat two-dimensional screen. It is only with repeated exposure to film that primitives can train their eyes to see what we see, and probably only much later that their naturally participatory minds can participate through our modern medium of film. The more modern and technical the medium of participation, the more work it seems is required to elicit the spirit of participation. When cultures climb up the ladder of technical sophistication, there is less outward exhibition of participation and less inward willingness to suspend disbelief.

When sound motion pictures came into existence, Soviet filmgoers had a difficult time with them. They could readily accept moving pictures, and could easily participate with them. But when sound was introduced, that addition to an already novel medium of moving pictures caused a temporary backlash and decline in Soviet film attendance. Leading Soviet film directors, Sergei Eisenstein and Vsevolod Pudovkin, reasoned that in order to be effective, sound in film must be used symbolically rather than realistically (McLuhan, 287). They no doubt intuited that in order to capture the participatory nature of the filmgoer, the primeval medium of abstract symbolism was more religiously relevant than straight realism, which is often more devoid of mythic elements.

Film scholar Robert Ray aptly points out that the enormous success of the film industry, particularly its Hollywood form, was a result of the industry becoming "intuitively Lévi-Straussian: the American film industry discovered and used the existing body of mythic oppositions provided it by the local culture. In effect, the great Hollywood czars became naive, prodigious anthropologists" (Ray, 13). If Marshal McLuhan is correct in arguing that each of our media is an extension of ourselves, and that the medium is the message, then his argument would support the contention that film is but an extension of our most inner and ancient consciousness. After epochs of civilization, through a long and circuitous route, the numinous soul extends itself through film, and the spiritual element endemic in film conveys human expression at its most primitive state, in spite of the various media of highly sophisticated technology.

When we allow ourselves to be fully taken in by a film, we experience all of the emotions the primitive goes through during his or her ceremony with the witch doctor. The witch doctor in our case is the filmmaker, under whose spell we willingly surrender. In our modern trance state, we feel elated. We feel scared, threatened. We become horrified. We anticipate psychic healing and receive it. We call up the ghost of a cosmic hero. We vicariously benefit from the heroic exploits of our totemic ancestors. We are wooed, comforted, and romanced, all within the space of one hundred minutes. In essence, we allow ourselves to be taken over by a spell that is as real and potent as the trance state of the primitive. We become possessed with the spirits of good and ill according to the enchanting magic of the celluloid shaman. While we have largely left the formal rituals of possession and trance states behind in our modern denial of religion, we have not killed the numinous powers that haunted our religions of yore. In fact, the more we try to eliminate the religious ghosts of our "naive" and primitive past, the more those ghosts will overwhelm us.

The movie house is the perfect place for such haunting. The dark cavern of the cinema is reminiscent of a ceremonial sweat lodge, an initiation pit, the dark night of the soul, the belly of the fish, the alchemical grave, or the wilderness of the night journey. The movie house is the tomb of our rational consciousness and the womb of our conversional rebirth. It is the communal meeting place where tribal strangers of like mind meet to explore the inner reaches of the soul. It is the baptismal font where our skepticism is drowned in the motherly sea of awe and wonder. It is the renewal of Plato's cave, where instead of seeing only shadows, we find illumination in the dark. It is revelation out of the depths of dramatic pathos, where we are allowed a glimpse of the other side. It is our temple, our shrine, our house of worship, and our prayer room. It is a psychoanalytic depth chamber, and a tribal rallying hall.

Depending on our level of suspended disbelief, we all participate at different levels, but we all participate. The primitive and naive participate in the witch doctor's magic wholeheartedly, and the modern sophisticates participate with guarded mind and denial. But we all participate.

Participation is a powerful phenomenon for the primitive, and it has never lost its power and hold on the modern mind. It has been pointed out that Richard Nixon repeatedly viewed the film *Patton* directly preceding his bombing of Cambodia in 1970 (Carpenter and Seltzer). Certainly some who have given themselves over to selfish power will be further empowered through their participation in certain ideological myths, but likewise for modern seekers of enlightenment, if they too are willing to participate, they surely will find some jewels of wisdom and beneficent power in the depths of the tribal theater.

FROM FORMALISM TO CINEMASOPHIA

FILM ANALYSIS

S everal years ago I organized a fortnightly Cinema Club at which I showed films and led analytical discussions. This group lasted for more than two years. We analyzed films from several angles: philosophically, psychologically, economically, politically, literarily, mythically, and, as we joked, sometimes even cinematically. There are several valid schools of film interpretation, to some of which I owe a debt. But throughout the duration of the discussion group, and throughout the analysis of the films in this book, the mythological method has predominated. To provide an understanding of the method of analysis used in this book, a brief and elementary overview of the major schools of film criticism is warranted.

THEORIES OF FILM ANALYSIS

Formalism

One of the first methods of film criticism was the strict formalist tradition begun by Sergei Eisenstein and others that saw cinema as an art machine confronting nature. Seen most graphically in Eisenstein's strong use of montage, the single shot was considered the basic building block of film from which other blocks formed montage, their foundation for film art. What was originally thought of as a tool to enlighten consciousness eventually turned into a mere machine for propaganda through Stalin's socialist realism.

Realism

Opposed to formalism were the realist film theorists who, instead of seeing cinema as a means of constructing montage building blocks, saw the cinema rather as a lens through which to see the glories of nature. Both Seigfried Kracauer and André Bazin, having a strong interest in organic nature, emphasized the earth as an entity that will naturally radiate her own wisdom if the cinema is used as a conduit of her natural beauty.

The Auteur Theory

The school of *auteur* theory, placing the emphasis on the director as the main author of the film, has been well represented by the writers of the French journal *Cahiers du Cinéma* many of whom became filmmakers themselves, such as François Truffaut, Jean-Luc Godard, Jacques Rivette, Claude Chabrol, and Eric Rohmer. Critics of the *auteur* theory argue that it places too much emphasis on the monolithic dominance of the director.

Structuralism and Semiology

The two most prominent schools of thought in contemporary film theory are structuralism and semiology, related methods of studying the signs and symbols of cinema. Both entered the world of film theory in the 1960s and '70s mainly as a result of the void of *auteur* theory felt by some critics.

Both structuralism and semiology are attempts to make an exact

23

science of specific signs. While structuralism tends toward practical criticism, semiology is more theoretical in nature, and more specific in its analysis of signifying codes. While semiology focuses on single codes in various structures, structuralism studies how those codes operate within a given structure such as within a single film.

The main proponent of film semiology has been unquestionably Christian Metz, a linguist and former student of psychoanalyst Jacques Lacan. He has devoted his efforts to dismantling the previous schools of thought in order to construct a new, comprehensive system of understanding exactly how a film signifies, that is, how it communicates meaning to its audience.

Critics of semiology have argued that the system is too top-heavy, that it is far too specific, and too weighted down with minute details and terminology, and that it is too logical, somewhat ignoring the film itself and replacing it with a microscopic look at signifying slices of the film. If these criticisms are valid, then it may also be valid, according to semiotician Roland Barthes, that "semiology is . . . perhaps destined to be absorbed into a trans-linguistics, the materials of which may be myth, narrative, journalism, or on the other hand, objects of our civilization, in so far as they are spoken (through press, prospectus, interview, conversation, and perhaps even the inner language, which is ruled by the laws of imagination)" (Barthes 1964, 11). This is a noble and quite remarkable statement coming from a noted semiotician, especially in light of his emphasis on "inner language, which is ruled by the laws of imagination," a rather unscientific terminology, to say the least.

If there is a serious challenge against the scientific method today, it is found within phenomenology.

Phenomenology

As a less popular but nonetheless viable voice, the school of phenomenology is trying to gain its own place in the world of film theory. The phenomenologists were influenced by the philosophies of Martin Heidegger, Jean-Paul Sartre, Maurice Merleau-Ponty, and Mikel Dufrenne. Carrying phenomenology into film, its first two leaders, André Bazin and Amédée Ayfre, sought to put limits on scientific logic, choosing rather a higher priority on art over art theory. Picking up after the deaths of these first two prominent film phenomenologists, Henri Agel has carried the torch in his opposition to the strict logic of structuralism and semiotics. Phenomenology emphasizes experience, sense, and the unveiling of natural truth, as opposed to the rigorous logic of science. The phenomenologist sees cinema (and nature) in much the same way that the early romantics saw art, through a participatory involvement with it. According to Bazin, one of the earliest heralds of cinema phenomenology, art unveils a beautifully radiating world of nature that can be experienced only through the senses, and that remains hidden to the sterile world of logical analysis. According to Ayfre, there are many kinds of truth that can't be reduced to mere logic. The phenomenologist would seek to "unveil" certain truths in nature, rather than "codify signifiers" in a schema of scientific examination. Just as the realists dethroned "King Montage," so too do the phenomenologists seek to dethrone the god or goddess Reason. Rather than seeing cinema as a collection of signs signifying meaning, the phenomenologist sees the cinema, like nature, as something naturally radiating sense impressions. Agel refers to Gaston Bachelard as saying that nature (rather than man) is the mother of images.

Ideology

Somewhat related to mythology in film are those who have written significant work on film ideology, such as Robert Sklar, Robert Ray, and Michael Wood. Sklar (1975) has traced the dominant ideological trends in American cinema, which are essentially the traditional American beliefs in the virtues of deferred gratification, hard work, and perseverance. Robert Ray (1985), besides examining the ideological trends of the Hollywood cinema, which are very politically connected, also shows the "corrected" forms of ideology, which essentially are newer, more progressive ideologies replacing older, more conservative modes. Michael Wood (1975) draws heavily on the work of the classicist G. S. Kirk, a mythologist who in turn has employed the binary structuralism of Lévi-Strauss.

Psychoanalysis

There are many psychoanalytic studies of film, which open up the cinema to a richer psychological understanding (e.g., Munsterberg, Arnheim 1932, Wolfenstein and Leites, Greenberg). The Freudian analytic journals and several other film journals have had a good share of orthodox interpretations of films over the years.

Dream Screen

Then there are writers who have approached film as dream analysis, such as Bruce Kawin (1978), Marsha Kinder (1980), Jane Feuer (1982), and Robert Eberwein (1984). As we saw earlier, film is an extension of dream, so it is only natural to interpret film as dream material.

Mythology

There are a few works that have specifically set out to analyze myth in cinema. But rather than focus on actual ancient myths, most of these works are good social commentaries on modern sociological myth. Parker Tyler (1970), Richard Maynard (1974), Yvette Biró (1982), and Rita Parks (1982) have all written excellent analyses of such modern film mythology, which is somewhat similar to the ideological studies mentioned above.

26

Writing from a different perspective, John Beebe, psychoanalyst and editor of *The San Francisco Jung Institute Library Journal*, has consistently delivered excellent Jungian interpretations of film in his various essays.

Religion

There have been several books written on religion in the cinema, most of which focus on theological issues, morality, or social commentaries on the overt religious themes found in films (van der Leeuw, Gibson, Butler, Hurley, Cooper and Skrade, Ferlita and May, Thomas Martin, Campbell and Pitts, Malone). There are a few that stand out as exceptional in this area. James M. Wall, currently the editor of *The Christian Century*, has consistently written thought-provoking film reviews in his publication. Paul Schrader, best known for his screenwriting and directing, is also a film scholar of note. His book, *Transcendental Style in Film* (1972), is an excellent religious analysis of three directors' works: Ozu, Bresson and Dreyer. Ronald Holloway's thought-provoking book, *Beyond the Image* (1977), invites the reader to discover religion in the secular pulpit of the cinema.

METHOD OF PRESENT ANALYSIS

Previous and simultaneous to studying film, I had also been studying religion, mythology, anthropology, and symbology. So naturally, my interest in these areas has influenced my interpretations. It was only after I had already analyzed many films that I studied semiotics, structuralism, and other current and more academically respectable trends of film analysis. But the mythological or anthropological influences have predominated.

In this book, we will be using such tools and ideas as cyclical analysis, the concept of time, archetypes, symbology, numerology, names (the sounds as well as the meanings), and the signification of places, colors, movement, and opposites—especially masculine and feminine. To understand the meaning of these elements in film yields a greater understanding of the film, but more than that, of the human soul, in the same way that symbols in dreams yield a greater understanding of one's life. Throughout the films of this book, we will be analyzing the nature of the collective soul, since public art is a reflection of the societal soul.

Cyclical Analysis

An important part of the current analysis is the concept of cyclicality. The works of psychoanalyst C. G. Jung, scholar of religion Mircea Eliade and literary critic Northrop Frye will help illumine our path. All of these thinkers have developed cyclical models of analysis, which I have borrowed and somewhat reformulated in my own analysis of film.

C. G. Jung

Our first theorist of cyclicality in our film analysis is C. G. Jung. Jung spent many years studying ancient alchemy, among his many interests. The alchemists were fond of drawing quaternities, sectoring the world into four quarters such as the elements:

air

fire water

earth

or the seasons:

summer

spring   autumn

winter

The alchemists worked out various formulae to give them a better grasp of nature, such as:

summer
red
fire

south

spring		center		autumn
blue	east	black	west	yellow
wood		earth		gold

north

winter
white
water

The purpose of the quaternities was to help the alchemists map out the formulations of their *magnum opus*, or great work. Relying on ancient wisdom and laws of nature, these quaternities helped the alchemists see a clearer picture of their work.

29

In conceptualizing the human condition, Jung would draw his own quaternities as a map to help integrate opposite elements in human nature, as in his quaternity for the human personality:

thinking

sensation   intuition

feeling

Jung also used quaternities and mandalas to configure the psychological process of individuation, or wholeness, with the idea being that the reconciliation of opposites brings a peaceful marriage of polar extremes in the soul. Jung's quaternities, and those of the alchemists, are clockwise cycles of nature. To follow these quaternities in a clockwise direction is to follow the motion of life.

Mircea Eliade

In *Cosmos and History: The Myth of the Eternal Return*, the book he considered his most significant, Mircea Eliade expounds in depth the grand cycle of eternity as it effects human consciousness. As his title implies, Eliade explains the difference between cosmos and history or mythic time and temporal time, as they both relate to the myth of the eternal cycle. He illustrates how, as moderns, who insist that we are connected only to history, we are able to create only in temporal, historical time. Archaic traditional people, on the other hand, are free from historical time, and as they participate in cosmogonic time, *in illo tempore*, in the Age of Gold, they are free to create more fully, and to luxuriate in eternity, because of their full participation in the eternal cycle, in the cosmic rhythms of the eternal return.

Eliade suggests that some artists of modern times are connected to mythical time, and therefore create with a more primeval and cyclical bent: "It is worth noting that the work of two of the most significant writers of our day—T. S. Eliot and James Joyce—is saturated with nostalgia for the myth of eternal repetition and, in the last analysis, for the abolition of time" (Eliade 1954, 153).

Northrop Frye

Northrop Frye explains a cycle that he says he borrowed from Jung and Sir James Frazer (although he does not specifically cite the sources) in his excellent book *Fables of Identity: Studies in Poetic Mythology* (1963, 15–16):

> The myth is the central informing power that gives archetypal significance to the ritual and archetypal narrative to the oracle. Hence the myth *is* the archetype, though it might be convenient to say myth only when referring to narrative, and archetype when speaking of significance. In the solar cycle of the day, the seasonal cycle of the year, and the organic cycle of human life, there is a single pattern of significance, out of which myth constructs a central narrative around a figure who is partly the sun, partly vegetative fertility, and partly a god or archetypal human being. The crucial importance of this myth has been forced on literary critics by Jung and Frazer in particular, but the several books now available on it are not always systematic in their approach, for which reason I supply the following table of its phases:
>
> 1. dawn, spring, birth, comedy*
> 2. noon, summer, marriage, romance
> 3. sunset, autumn, death, tragedy
> 4. darkness, winter, dissolution, satire

While Frye doesn't draw out a circular diagram, he does provide four quarters of a circle that are roughly equivalent to the ancient

---

* Actually, most printings of *Fables of Identity* place comedy in the summer quarter and romance in the spring. But this is inconsistent with Frye's earlier and more comprehensive work, *Anatomy of Criticism*, where he places the genres as I have.

alchemical quaternity. The most valuable part of Frye's circle is his inclusion of the four major genres of literature (and therefore of cinema as well).

Now, when we borrow elements from each of these sources and place them in our own structural quaternity, it revolves clockwise as follows:

noon
summer
south
youth
romance
yellow/gold
growth/fruit
eros

dawn		dusk
spring		autumn/fall
east	center	west
birth/rebirth	timelessness	maturity
comedy	spacelessness	tragedy
pastels	still point	brown/red
blossom		harvest/planting
laughter		passion

night
winter
north
old age/death
satire/irony
white/black
dormancy
mourning

Spring/Morning/Comedy/Birth/Rebirth

Following our quaternity around in a clockwise circle, we begin at the left, in the true beginning of the new year, in springtime, the season of comedy. When Abraham and Sarah were pregnant with Isaac, they were very old. The idea of new life coming from somebodies old and near death became a joke to them, and they therefore named their child Isaac, which in Hebrew means "laughter." Notice that we have also included seasonal colors in our quaternity. The fool traditionally wore multicolored costumes, as does one of his modern heirs, the clown, befitting his connection to dawn and springtime. After a black, wintry death comes a fresh new beginning, a colorful twist of life. A resurrection is a comedic, ironic reversal of a tragic death, just as Jesus Christ is depicted as a clown in *Godspell*, and just as Saint Paul encouraged believers in the resurrection to be "fools for Christ's sake." Spring and birth are times of rejoicing, just as Ulysses' rosy-fingered dawn is a sign of new hope after his ordeals with horror. The emotion of the first quarter is laughter, the emotion of childhood.

Summer/Noon/Romance/Youth

Following our circle around to the second stage, at the zenith, we find Romance, which belongs appropriately to summer, noon, and youth. The end of comedy is romantic union. The clown usually ends up with the girl, befitting the end result of comedy. The jester receives the baton from the grim reaper of winter and hands it over to the Cupid of romance. The protagonist of romance is in the youthful noon of life. The ideals of the hero are romanticized in his prime. The illuminating light of the sun shines brightest at its zenith, at noon, when the sun god kisses Mother Earth most passionately. The hero or heroine is never more splendid than in this romantic noon of life. Summer romances and heroic quests are stirred to their highest sublimity when the young hero is at the summit of human perfection. While the hero spends his childhood playing and laughing as children do, eventually he becomes romantically inclined. The emotion stirred at this quarter is eros, or romantic love, leading to a union. But eventually the romanticized hero falls from grace.

Autumn/Dusk/Tragedy/Maturity

Usually the fall of tragedy separates the hero from his or her loved one. Just as noon falls into dusk, summer falls into autumn, and youth falls into middle age, so too must the hero of myth fall into tragedy. The romantic receives the baton from the jester and hands it over to the tragic bearer of bad news. The autumn winds metaphorically bring in their wake the tragic consequences of natural life. After the honeymoon is over, we are confronted with real life, including all of the pain and agony of this temporal existence. After hovering for a while in the stratosphere of romantic ideals and universal essentialism, the hero eventually plunges, like Icarus, into the depths of biospheric existentialism. This is the midlife crisis, the appearance of the beast, the kidnapping of the maiden, the threat of an avaricious banker, or the vicious dominance of an institutional monster. Whatever appearance it takes, it is the attempt on the part of the Grand Inquisitor to castrate, dismember, or altogether eliminate the promising young hero. The emotion of this quarter is passion which, contrary to its modern usage, literally means "to suffer," as in the passion of Christ. The end of tragedy, of course, is death, either literally or figuratively, which brings us to the next stage in our quaternity.

Winter/Night/Irony/Satire/Death

When the hero falls, he or she is beckoned to the depressive underworld of chthonic introspection, to the last and lowest quarter of our quaternity. Sometimes the hero's death is a literal martyrdom, destined to give inspiration to a cause. One way or another, the hero is symbolic of the orbic seed, which is planted in the earth to be reborn as new fruit. As the gospels attest, "a corn of wheat must go into the ground and die before it can bring forth fruit." Moses has to go into his own dormant wilderness before he can lead the children of Israel out of Egypt. And the children of Israel themselves must endure forty years in the wilderness before entering into the promised land. The winter death is Jonah's three days in the belly of the fish. It is Jesus' three days and three nights in the tomb. It is Persephone's wintry captivity in the house of Hades, and Luke Skywalker's wound and separation from Princess Leia. Winter is Gandhi's and Martin Luther King, Jr.'s assassinations, and Ingmar Bergman's heroic knight handing the baton over to Death in *The Seventh Seal*. The low quarter is Saint John of the Cross's dark night of the soul, and King David's broken and contrite heart. It is Joseph being thrown into the well and into Potiphar's jail, and it is Job's ash heap. The dark of night is Shane's temporary victimization, America's Civil War and Great Depression, and General William Tecumseh Sherman's near-insane depression. It is Vincent Van Gogh's depression and death, and Benjamin's exile from his true love in *The Graduate*. The emotions associated with this low quarter are sadness, mourning, or horror. And just as each of the other seasons of life inevitably ushers in a new season, so too does winter ironically turn into springtime.

Satire and irony are both placed in the dead of night and in the grip of winter because it is by their reversals that death is transformed into life. Here also, reside paradox and ambiguity, their mysterious sisters. It is through the ironic twist of winter that we learn that life is death and death is life. It is through the sardonic eyes of the satirist we learn that extremities reveal the opposite. It is through *The Book of the Dead* that we learn the secrets to life. As the mad officer in *Apocalypse Now* observes, it is through horror that peace is attained. It is through the abstract and otherworldly secrets of satire and irony that the mysteries of the other side are revealed. It is through the valley of the shadow of death that the hopeful light of the new morn is conceived. It is by embracing the terror of the tomb that we reap the fruit of the womb. And so life goes on in its perennial cycle, as winter twists into spring, as night glistens into morn, as biting satire leads the way for light comedy, as the reaper hands the baton to the jester, starting the eternal cycle over again.

Time

As we can see in our structural diagram of cyclicality, and as we shall further see in the analyses of cinemasophia, the theme of time plays an essential part in most of these films, be it a demonic speeding-up of time, a slowing down of time, or an emphasis on transcending time. This emphasis on time is no mere coincidence. Claude Lévi-Strauss suggests that the thing that gives myth an operational value is that "the specific pattern described is timeless; it explains the present and the past as well as the future" (Lévi-Strauss 1963, 209).

The protagonists of the stories, as mythic pilgrims, must deal with time as the gnawing monster that it is, since they are in essence our ambassadors in the realm of mythic time. Their dealings with time and eternity are representative of our own timely negotiations in a time and space dimension, while we intuitively believe in a "time" beyond time. Their successful negotiations with temporal and primordial time become vicarious victories for those of us still stuck in normal time. And while the characters within the various plots have some interesting twists on time, so too do the filmmakers in giving us a mythic handle on time. The filmmakers, as cosmic time travelers, as makers of cinemasophia, have transcended historical time to some degree and have intuitively participated in the eternal return. As they participate in mythical time, their creativity takes on a primeval quality, evoking numinous stirrings that provoke sublime reflection in the participants thereof. If we view our cinematic protagonists as religious time pilgrims, and if we willingly suspend our disbelief enough to participate in the magic, we too can attain some of the mythic wealth of the Golden Age in the form of *sophia* rather than the traditional academic goal of mere knowledge.

PART 2

MASCULINE MONSTERS

This section examines the masculine dragons which reflect our current age of patriarchy. While all of these cinemyths show an overcompensated masculinity, they each offer a different solution to the problem of evil—with the exception of *The Sailor Who Fell from Grace with the Sea*, for which we can hopefully find our own solution. Not all the dragons are easily recognizable as they are in *It's a Wonderful Life*. The dragon in *The Seventh Seal*, contrary to what may be assumed, is not Death, but rather a more subtle and pernicious foe. Likewise, the monster of *A Year of the Quiet Sun* is not easily recognized.

The traditional heroic fight is absent in *The Sailor*, which indicates that the demon, like the one in *Shane*, is not necessarily *without*, but *within* the personal and collective soul.

THE SAILOR WHO FELL FROM GRACE WITH THE SEA

THE RELIGION OF THE NIETZSCHEAN
SAMURAI WARRIORS

Lewis John Carlino's 1976 film, *The Sailor Who Fell from Grace with the Sea*, is a macabre story of murderous childhood based on the novel of the same title, by Yukio Mishima, the Nobel-nominated Japanese novelist and playwright. While all artists are mirrored in their work to some degree, Mishima's image is hauntingly reflected in graphic and ghostly fashion. The novelist's life was an unusual one, in which he developed a philosophy of life and death that was tellingly authenticated by his own dramatic suicide, which to him, was a logical extension of, and the grand culmination of his art. A knowledge of the novelist will yield better understanding of his art.

YUKIO MISHIMA

Yukio Mishima was essentially stolen from his mother by his paternal grandmother and raised at her sickbed under her ever-present, ever-dominant and ever-doting mothering. Feeling disappointed in her min-imally successful son (Mishima's father) the grandmother felt it was her personal responsibility to raise her grandson with a more significant destiny as the goal. He was a sickly but precocious child. While she raised him his first few years as a little girl, she simultaneously instilled within him a strong belief in the feudal samurai spirit. As a child, Mishima developed fascinations with the young male dying hero and with blood, sweat, muscles, soldiers, and white gloves, all of which became literal fetishes in his adult life. Excruciating forms of death with copious amount of blood were sources of erotic fantasy for him.

Several of Mishima's earliest childhood memories are recorded in Henry Scott Stokes's book *The Life and Death of Yukio Mishima.* His earliest memory was of the sweaty night-soil man carrying a bucket of excrement through the street. Mishima distinctly remembered the man's tight-fitting trousers, and his occupation gave him a sense of tragedy "in the most sensuous meaning of the word."

Another distinctive memory was of the smell of the sweat of soldiers who passed his house on their way back from maneuvers. In a Western art book in the Mishima household was Guido Reni's painting of Saint Sebastian. Like most of the versions of Saint Sebastian, this one depicts the saint martyred with piercing arrows. Young Mishima recalls being enthralled over this picture. He became so stimulated by it, that it was the source of his first masturbation and ejaculation.

Throughout his prolific literary career—he wrote forty novels, eighteen plays, and twenty volumes of short stories—Mishima was consumed with the theme of the death of the heroic young man. The act of *seppuku*, or *hara-kiri*, was the common form of death of several of his heroes, and Mishima considered it the crowning act of one's life. He even acted out this ancient ritual of disembowelment on several occasions, playing the lead roles in some of his own plays. He became obsessed with muscles, and once he discovered weight lifting he spent inordinate amounts of energy attempting to sculpt his body into muscular perfection. Mishima's all-consuming allegiance was to the ancient and all but extinct samurai spirit. He believed that Japanese culture had grown soft and decadent by abandoning the samurai code of hardness, militarism, and sacrificial honor. In the last few years of his life, his income as a successful writer enabled him to hire and richly uniform his own private army of about one hundred men sworn to the samurai code of feudal times.

He agreed with the American anthropologist Ruth Benedict, who wrote in her book *The Chrysanthemum and the Sword* that there was a significant difference in Japanese culture between the chrysanthemum (the arts) and the sword (the martial tradition). He felt strongly that Japanese culture emphasized the former to the detriment of the latter.

Along with his obsessive fascination with the dying hero, Mishima developed a philosophy about the worth of youth contrasted with the uselessness of old age. He wrote in the postscript to the *Ni Ni Rocu Incident* trilogy: "Among my incurable convictions is the belief that the old are eternally ugly, the young eternally beautiful. The wisdom of the old is eternally murky, the actions of the young eternally transparent. The longer people live, the worse they become. Human life, in other words, is an upside-down process of decline and fall."

Mishima's life and death was a combination of Japanese and Western ideals. Being well versed in the philosophy of Nietzsche, he developed ideas close to the *Übermensch* philosophy. He was also fully enveloped in the samurai philosophy of *bunburyodo*, which is the idea that the samurai knight is to practice the dual arts of literature (*bun*) and the sword (*bu*) in equal measure. Mishima was disgusted with the fact that this practice had been all but forgotten in Japanese culture.

At the age of forty-five, when he felt that he could go no further in the perfection of his body and his art, he knew it was time to take his samurai code to its ultimate conclusion. Having planned his own suicide far in advance, he marched into a military compound with some of his most trusted soldiers one day in 1970; he held the commanding general captive and demanded to speak to the soldiers of the compound. He was granted this request, and preached about patriotism and honor to a disgusted audience of military personnel. Having spoken from the balcony of the general's office, he then disemboweled himself in the general's office and was beheaded by one of his soldiers, who in turn disemboweled himself and who was in turn beheaded by a third soldier, all according to Mishima's design. Adhering to the ancient Japanese belief that one's sincerity resides literally in one's entrails, Mishima's death was the culmination and authentication of what he preached in his life.

THE SEVERE STORY

The film version of *The Sailor Who Fell from Grace with the Sea* transposes Mishima's Japanese story to an English setting. Filmed on the south coast of England at Dartmouth, the story concerns a group of public school youths led by a harsh boy who lords his stern authority over his club mates. One of the members of this secret boy's club is Jonathan (Jonathan Kahn), who vacillates in his allegiance to the leader. Jonathan is the son of a widowed mother who owns and operates a local antique shoppe. Both mother and son elatedly exult in the newfound friendship of the second mate of a large ship that pulls into their harbor.

The leader of the boy's club is called Number One, or the Chief. Each of the other four boys is sequentially numbered according to his respective rank in the secret society. Number One, as the center of this story, chastises his subordinates for their childishness. He condemns adults for their lack of authenticity, and he obsesses over a need to break all rules, to live a life of authentic hardness, and to find the pure and perfect order of life, found literally in one's exposed, beating heart.

Because they misunderstand the severity of the chief's philosophy, it takes a while for the other boys to be brought around to the truth of his philosophy. Being boys, they laugh at pictures of couples making love and exhibit all of the normal playfulness of children. But Number One does not allow himself nor them such trivialities. He maintains an austere posture, punishing his mates for their childishness and lecturing them on the pure and perfect order of things.

To demonstrate this pure and perfect order, he drugs Cedric the cat and cuts him open in order to show his pupils the beating heart, which he considers the core of life. He insists that Cedric, being a pampered, milk-lapping creature of comfort, is just a cat posing as life. Real life in the pure and perfect order of things would demand that Cedric revert to his natural order of hunting in the wild. There are no heroes in the chief's philosophy, only adults posing as such. The normal life of families, convention, and society is decadent and meaningless. Real life in Number One's world is a reversion to natural chaos and hardness.

When Number One has finally convinced his followers of the truth of his philosophy, and when he gets disgusted enough with the sailor having left the life of the sea, he orders the ritualistic killing of the sailor. During the ceremony Jonathan places out two maritime flags, a blue one, signifying the beginning of a voyage, and a red one, meaning that there is danger ahead. The sailor tells the story of the dangerous storm to the boys just before his demise. (Incidentally, the field where the murder scene was filmed is actually called Willful Murder because of a real killing that took place there.)

THE CHARACTERS

Now, to help expose the heart of this story, let us focus a little closer on each of the main characters, beginning with the one the furthest removed from Number One, and the only female in our line-up.

Anne Osborne

Jonathan's mother, played by Sarah Miles, represents the softness of civilization, as opposed to the chaotic hard side of life. Hers is a life of bourgeois comfort, or civilized cushiness. While she mostly personifies such softness, she herself has lapses of character and periodically resorts to moments of chaotic hardness. When she catches her son Jonathan vouyeristically spying on her and the sailor through a hole in her bedroom wall, she lashes out in harsh violence toward him. She asks her housekeeper if she might be too hard on Jonathan, only to be told that she is not hard enough. During her civilized British tea ceremony, while showing off her new sailor friend, she allows herself to be masturbated in public, as the sailor instructs her to act natural and enjoy it. Along with Jonathan, she is fascinated with ships, muscles, and stories of storms at sea. But her predominant trait is that of softness and sedate civilization.

The Sailor

Jim Cameron, the sailor, played by Kris Kristofferson, is a man who has had two conversions in his life. Originally, growing up on a farm in Kansas, he left the tranquil pastoral life with boundaries and pursued his calling as a sailor. He says that the land never changes, but the sea, by contrast, always changes. After reading Jack London and Joseph Conrad novels, he took out to sea and devoted his life to the thrill of the dangerous calling. He also speaks of his shark, which represents the ever-present danger of life at sea.

When he meets and falls in love with Anne Osborne, all of his romantic ideals about the unknown change. He no longer sees his shark after falling for her. He tells her that after his time away from her at sea, he missed her silkiness. Thus he falls from grace with the sea and converts from a life of dangerous chaos to one of civilized order. He proposes to marry her, and the two of them plan for a life of land-based order together. While at the tea shoppe with Anne, he makes a sarcastic remark about the shoppe being a great place for a funeral, not realizing that his own death is close at hand. When Anne announces to her housekeeper that Jim will be staying with them, the housekeeper responds by saying she had better call the butcher.

Jonathan

Like his fellow club members, Jonathan starts out with normal boyish curiosity and innocence. He initially idolizes the sailor, then, as a result of being punished and demoted for this sin by Number One, he eventually undergoes a conversion and betrays his friendship with the sailor for acceptance by his superior. His conversion is woefully authentic. At home he draws a picture of an anchor on his chest and writes of his heart as a stainless steel anchor that cannot rust. Thus, we witness a genuine change of heart in this once normal boy. He buys into the grim philosophy of his group leader.

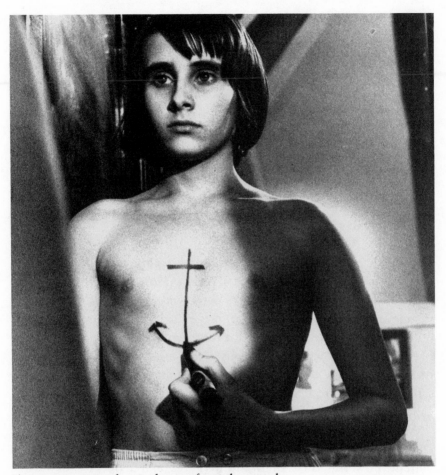

A superman must have a heart of stainless steel.

Number One

If anybody in the story represents Mishima's philosophy, it is of course the chief of the boy's club. With his obsessive emphasis on pure and perfect order, on hardness, severity, natural chaos, rule breaking, and ritualized authentication of the core of life, this austere boy is the epitome of one positively dedicated to a life of stringent truculence. While others in the story might waver in their allegiances and attitudes, this grave boy is glaciated in a permanently rigid stance of sternness. His is a life of cold seriousness, hardened by an unyielding philosophy of assumed strength. His mission is to convert his followers to his grim view of life, which he eventually does, through practical and theoretical lessons of direness. If one of his disciples falters, punishment, humiliation, and demotion await the unfaithful backslider. He says at one point to his band of disciples that they have a long way to go before they are "ready," no doubt implying the ultimate participation for which he is preparing them.

OPTIONS OF SEVERITY

The sailor, being the ultimate victim and experimental guinea pig of the chief's rigorous designs, has several options from which he can choose, from the least to the most severe. Just as the sequential numbering of the club members represents degrees of severity, so too do options presented to the sailor represent such degrees.

Number One in Severity. Obviously the most severe of the sailor's options is the one chosen for him by Number One. Like Cedric, the sailor who falls from grace with the sea meets his pure and perfect calling in his murder and subsequent cardioectomy.

Number Two. The next severe option would be for the sailor to continue to be a sailor, to put himself at risk with his shark, to wrestle with the powerful forces of the storms at sea, and to operate his life in a hardened determination to marry the perfection of chaos.

Number Three. Next in degree of severity would be for the sailor to vacillate between the sea and a comfortable domestic life. He certainly does this for a while before making a hard decision for the softest of alternatives. Jonathan and his compatriots also vacillate for a time in their decision to commit themselves to the chief's pure and perfect order. Anne Osborne vacillates regularly, depending on outward circumstances like Jonathan's behavior, or whether or not she is having her needs met by a man.

Number Four. The least severe option, to abandon the chaotic sea for tranquil domesticity, is the one the sailor actually chooses. Ironically, it turns out to be the most severe option. Since in the Chief's mind the sailor tampers with perfection by leaving his calling to the sea, he has to be rescued from his backsliding and brought back to severity through dissection.

RITUALISTIC CYCLES

Each of the four options of severity, just like the four main characters, represents a different ritual of nature and a different speed of cyclical existence. This is where the story takes on a more religious or mythical significance. Ritual plays an important part in the drama. The most

By choosing the soft option, the sailor becomes subject to the hard option.

obvious ritual is the dissection of Cedric the cat, which is a precursor to the same ritual later performed with the sailor. Others are the British tea time observed by Anne Osborne and the boys' meetings at the stone edifice. Mrs. Osborne's nostalgic reflections with her dead husband's picture are a ritual recalling of the bygone magic of "once upon a time." Jonathan's and Mrs. Osborne's visiting the ship is a ritualistic search for excitement and a more stimulating life.

The character with the greatest sense of ritual is obviously Number One, and the one with the least is Jonathan's mother. Next to this woman of soft culture, especially after his fall from grace, is the sailor. In fact, even when Jonathan's mother begins acting out her rage on Jonathan, the sailor intervenes on his behalf and interrupts her severity. During her time of rage, she no doubt is operating in the pure and perfect order, like a cat hunting in the wilds, or like a shark attacking a sailor, or like a sailor risking his life in order to authenticate himself.

Following the sailor in degrees of ritual and severity is Jonathan, who after his conversion is closest to the ritualistic severity of Number One. It is he who invites Jim Cameron to the grand ceremony.

Now if we look again at each of the four ritualistic options, we can easily see four different cycles of nature, each with a different level of severity, and each with a different speed of revolution.

Number Four. The fourth and seemingly safest option is a conventional cycle: getting married, having babies, growing old, dying naturally, etc., etc.—perpetuating a normal, relatively slow cycle of civilized existence. At the beginning of the film the camera pans from the rocky coast to the Osborne house, signifying the contrast between the severity of the chaotic ocean and the serenity of domestic life. Anne Osborne is the representative of this slow cycle.

Number Three. Cycle number three, that of vacillating between bourgeois comfort and the pure and perfect chaos of the sea, could be as slow as the fourth, or faster, depending on the oscillations of one's wavering spirit. The sailor is the representative of this cycle. Of course, he ultimately chooses the fourth and softest option over the faster and more severe.

Number Two. More severe, and predictably shorter in duration than the slower cycles, is option number two: the sailor going to sea, the cat hunting in the wilds, the mother lashing out in rage, the shark eating its victim or the amoeba eating its victim. The ingredient of natural danger speeds up the cycle of life. Instead of living a long and comfortable life, the person opting for this cycle faces the ever-present possibility of premature death. Certainly the little chief would have been somewhat satisfied with the sailor, had the sailor opted for this cycle, the more severe and shorter of the sailor's cyclical choices. This option allows the sailor sexual union in port towns but forbids him to settle down into the normal life of inauthentic matrimony. But even a romanticized idolization of the sailor in this option is condemned by Number One. As he says, there are no heroes, only adults posing as such. Ultimately, in his unwavering allegiance to his narrow view of authenticity, Number One can be satisfied only with option number one.

Number One. The number one cycle in terms of severity and shortness, is the only choice that is not given to the sailor. This option is chosen for him because of his having chosen the wrong cycle, according to the chief of the clandestine tribe. In essence, Number One, having seen Cedric and the sailor both fall from the grace of the pure and perfect order, short-circuits the cycles of both in order to redeem them from civilized decadence. The feline had become a pampered fat cat posing as life; the sailor had become an inauthentic man posing as life. In order to redeem their authenticity, it is necessary to expose the core of their sincerity, the heart.

The tight, ritualistic cycle of Number One is a quick, compulsive, demonic speeding up of the natural cycle of life. To authenticate the sailor by showing his core is to catapult him off into the cycle of eternity, saving him from the slow decadence of the normal cycle of life. This demonic cycle is actually an imitation of cosmogonic or eternal time. While the latter revolves in a more graceful natural cycle, the former either obsessively speeds up or compulsively repeats more of the same demonic monotony.

49

THE NIETZSCHEAN SAMURAI WARRIORS

Number One's philosophy is Mishima's philosophy, which is Nietzsche's philosophy, which is also the samurai's philosophy, but of course, carried to an extreme. The concepts of hardness and severity, which Number One, Mishima and Nietzsche all use almost obsessively, provide the overarching energy behind our story. Nietzsche felt that the person who could single-mindedly endure the hardness of life for the longest period of time is the truly strong person, the *Übermensch*. The sea is the mythic Leviathan, the harsh chaos of life apart from ordered civilization. The sailor is the hard, strong man who comes to terms with the Leviathan and thus is the superman of the drama, until he falls in love and falls from grace. According to the chief samurai of

Number One, as his dour countenance reveals, is the severe *Übermensch*.

our drama (Number One), carving out a cozy harbor and civilizing the chaos represents lifeless decadence. So Number One must maintain the posture of being the one hard thing that can survive the chaos. This union of severe hardness with uncontrolled chaos represents the pure and perfect order of things.

The ironic problem with such an inexorable philosophy is that the system does not recognize the hardness of an overlooked soft principle. Neither Number One, nor Mishima, nor Nietzsche can truly be the *Übermensch*. At best, each can be only a prophet for the hard thing. Each was raised in a comfortable, bourgeois, civilized culture. Each was pampered, protected from chaos, enculturated with all of the sensitive, soft aspects of his culture, and each despised his comfortable existence. The principle that the philosophy does not recognize is that of *enantiodromia*, the cataclysmic reversal of opposites. To deal with hard chaos with hardness guarantees more chaos and hardness, which eventually will overwhelm the perpetrator of the hardness.

Mishima, having grown up in girl's clothes, pampered by his doting grandmother, overreacted to the smothering softness by trying to create a life of demonic hardness. His obsession with hard muscles, hard soldiers, and hard steel weapons that disembowel one's soft entrails was a reaction against the motherly softness in which he felt smothered as a child. His ideal was to die young as a hard man of steel. To live long enough to become a soft, contented old person would have merely reminded him of his fat-cat childhood. Such a long, slow, soft cycle was anathema to this hard, ritualized breaker of decadence. In reality, each of these three prophets of the *Übermensch* was a highly sensitive, enculturated softy who tried desperately to deny his softness. To acknowledge such softness was more than each could bear. Their only option was to tenaciously hold to the position of Number One: in severity, in coldness, in denial of enculturation, and—much to their own detriment—in being overtaken by their own obsession of hardness.

Mishima's private army can be seen as a tragic symbol of developmental purgatory. Instead of fulfilling a purpose that was meaningful to more than its members and their commander, it was merely an adult child's toy army commissioned to compliment the fledgling ego of a child victimized by the hard tyranny of motherly softness. Thus Number One, as a projection of Mishima, is a soft thing that has denied its softness and deluded itself into believing that hardness is the only authentic option for true living.

Like Mishima, Nietzsche also despised his poetic, learned encul-turation. The son of a Lutheran minister, Nietzsche considered Chris-tianity a slow, decadent, controlled way of death. He felt that marrying hardness was his only option, for to marry civilization would be tantamount to philosophic suicide. For such an iron-fisted thinker, severe strength was the only authentic affirmation of life, though it may have contributed to his madness.

While the obsession with hardness is considered modern, secular, and devoid of religious significance by its practitioners, it is actually the most fanatically religious of spiritual practices; for that which is most harshly denied is most tellingly revealed. While donning the macho mentality of the modern strong secularist, Number One might assume that his philosophy is the epitome of strength in a spiritless dimension of time and space. In reality, the excessive speed of the cycle reveals the greatest participation in eternity (albeit in a demonic style). For the greater the severity and tightness of the ritual, the greater is one's longing for eternal time. After all, ritual, being an imitation of the natural cosmogonic rhythm of nature, is designed to transport the participant into the grander cosmic natural ritual.

One of the pictures that fascinated Mishima as a child was of a glorious knight on a white horse with a mighty sword held aloft. He was devastated to learn from the housekeeper that his hero was actually not a man at all, but a woman, Joan of Arc. Mishima felt that the heroic death could be meaningful only if it came to a hard man, not a soft woman.

While hardness is an attempt to deny and overcome the soft femi-nine principle, it actually reveals the feminine in ways that would be most embarrassing to its deniers. What men ritually connected with muscles forget is that an obsession with the body is actually a feminine trait. The overmasculinized hardness in our samurai trinity reveals terrorized little boys running in fear from soft mothering.

The pure and perfect order would be to die with no children, as a Saint Sebastian, as a martyr for the faith in the religion of demonic masculinity. Mishima's eroticized obsessions, Nietzsche's icy hardness, and Number One's despotic rules designed to break rules are all symptoms of a nonreligious religion. Our atheistic trinity of Nietzsche, Mishima, and Number One is a romanticized triad of nonromantic religious fanatics, gravely bent on denying that which their neuroses most ironically reveal.

The gospel of the pure and perfect order is the ideal of the samurai knight being catapulted into a heaven called Hard and Severe. Such a religion is not much different from that of the modern samurai warriors, the kamikaze pilots of World War II. And it is not much different from the Nietzschean influenced Aryan soldiers who so ritually rallied behind the Number One Madman of the Third Reich. And it is not much different than the mass fanatical support of a military-industrial-media complex in the name of a new world order. In each of these cases, whether as Shintoist martyrs for the emperor, or as Wotanish warriors of the master race of the fatherland, or as Jewish and Christian zealots for "democracy," they prove that the overmasculinized rituals of extremism merely perpetuate more extremitism. A post-war revival of the same spirit on Mishima's part, or anybody else's part must be met with something other than blind allegiance to the deified hard phallus.

The redeeming symbols found in the film are several. The ship sailing into the harbor, the fascination with the pistons in the cylinders of the ship's engine, and the gender-ambiguous stone edifice on the hill all signify that a union of polarities might offer a workable alternative to harsh extremities.

THE SEVENTH SEAL

A MORALITY PLAY OF THE FEMININE PRINCIPLE

In Ingmar Bergman's *The Seventh Seal*, Max von Sydow plays a fourteenth-century knight in a plague-infested return from the crusades. He asks timeless questions about God, faith, death, and eternity. Using the backdrop of the fourteenth-century black plague, Bergman's film is thought-provoking to the modern mind. True to Bergman's style, it is a film of contrasts, theological questioning, and philosophical speculation, in spite of the fact that Bergman does not consider himself an intellectual filmmaker. As in many of his other films, Bergman weaves his characteristic themes—the agony of the couple, an equivocal God, death, time, a journey, fear, and the perennial search for God—into the fabric of this medieval tapestry.

When Bergman first presented a proposal for *The Seventh Seal* to Svensk Filmindustri, it was rejected. Then, with the critical success of *Smiles of a Summer Night* in 1955, he finally got approval to make it. Much to the delight of the producers who originally rejected it, the film won the Grand Prize at the Cannes film festival in 1956.

CONTRASTS

In characteristic Bergmanian fashion, contrasts propel *The Seventh Seal* toward a search for resolution. The most pervasive and striking contrasts are those between the knight, Antonius Block, and his squire, Jons:

KNIGHT	SQUIRE
idealistic	realistic
pious	ribald
mystical	empirical
Platonic	Aristotelian
abstract	concrete
metaphysical	physical
straight	sardonic
ascetic	hedonistic
essentialistic	existentialistic
speculative	pragmatic
questioning	answering
tolerant	intolerant

While Antonius Block searches for ultimate meaning Jons cares more about immediate causes and effects. While the knight prays for divine direction and salvation, his squire is content to sing vulgar songs of carnal lust. While the knight shows signs of inner agony, his squire revels in temporal pleasures. The polarization of these two men poignantly dramatizes the separation of the upper and lower stories of life.

Several of the film's other polarities can be described in terms of yin and yang:

YANG	YIN
light	dark
white	black
life	death
good	evil
God	Devil

aggressive masculinity	passive femininity
sublimity	absurdity
religious fanaticism	pastoral tranquillity
comedy	tragedy
romance	death
love	hatred
words	silence
levity	solemnity
war	peace
integrity	hypocrisy
eternity	temporality

At every turn of the road we are faced with another contrast. The knight's serious talk with the confessor priest (Death) is contrasted with the squire's drunken blasphemies exchanged with the church muralist. The squalid atmosphere of the inn is contrasted with the pristine peace of the country. The light comedy of the secular stage is contrasted with the solemn procession of flagellants.

Most of the characters are contrasted either with another part of their own nature or with another character in the story. Raval, the seminary professor turned renegade robber of the dead, is starkly divided within himself. Once a teacher of divinity, he becomes a deplorable rascal of the streets. He is a bully to those weaker than him, but a wincing coward before those stronger than him, such as Jons. The patrons of the inn are crude, carnivorous, and animalistic contrasted with the gentleness of Jof and Mia, especially as seen during their conversation with the knight. The actor Skat is a comedic, deceptive character of illusion, as compared to the rene-gade minister Raval, a tragic, openly sinful character of blatant evil. Jof and Mia, a rather innocent, benign couple, are contrasted with Plog and Lisa, the crude smith and his unfaithful wife. The knight's rationalism is contrasted with Jof's intuition. And Raval is denied water at his death, whereas the condemned witch is given water at hers.

These psychological, social, philosophical, and spiritual contrasts point to consummational inevitability. When we see such stark differences between people, within individual souls, and between external and internal forces, reconciliation is not far away.

THE CHARACTERS

Skat

The self-assured director of the drama troupe, while he prides himself on his ability to trick others, is done in by Death after his grandest illusion, a mock suicide. The final joke is on him, as an Everyman reminder that "pride comes before a fall." His death produces no sound, in contrast with the squirrel we hear eating the sawdust of the tree stump—an apt image of the insignificance of life, in comparison to the grand scheme of existence.

Raval

The former seminary professor turned scoundrelous knave is a bully on the surface, a coward at heart. It was he who encouraged the knight on his crusade, as a representative of the most high. It is also he who receives the wrath of the realist squire Jons, and ultimately the wrath of the plague. Raval, the only grossly evil character in the story, is the only named character we know to actually die of the plague, as if to show that there is divine justice in the world after all.

Tyan

We don't know much of this young woman's life, apart from a few circumstances surrounding her condemnation and execution. Accused and convicted of having carnal knowledge of the Devil, she is blamed for the plague that is devastating the land. This alleged witch is most likely an innocent sacrificial victim of society's reaction to the epidemic. Like many women in Bergman's films, she is passive, compliant, and subjected to the unfair violence of a patriarchal society. She is the innocent lamb slaughtered for the vicarious atonement of society.

Plog and Lisa

The smith and his wife are representative of an absurd, unworkable combination of male and female. She is a wanton wench, vacillating in her loyalties with each change of psycho-social weather. He is ignorant and vengeful.

While the act of cuckoldry is being performed onstage, the smith is being cuckolded offstage, a telling dramatic act signifying a real live act. Meanwhile, a cosmic act of cuckoldry is being played out on a grander scale. Interrupting the players' levity is a procession of flagellants, a religious act of mass fear and morbid solemnity. Here Bergman stages a grand cinematic scheme of exponentially multiplying upstaging. The actors are upstaged by the hecklers of the audience. Plog the smith, as a member of the audience, is upstaged by one of the actors for the affection of his unfaithful wife. Then audience and actors are both upstaged by the procession of flagellants, as if to say that, lest we think we are immune from spiritual cuckoldry, the god called fear will steal our affections.

The Unnamed Silent Woman

Saved from the potential rape of Raval by Jons the squire, the figure of the silent young woman speaks of loud silence. Ultra feminine, this silent, pretty woman, true to the Bergmanian canvas, is painted in passive, receptive colors that follow behind the more aggressive dominant colors of masculinity. Though saying not a word throughout the narrative, when Death beckons the pilgrims at the end of the story, she speaks three telling words: "It is finished,"—Christ's last words on the cross—as an honest acknowledgment of the inevitability of the dark reaper. Her symbolic counterparts are found in two animals and a corpse. When Jons asks for directions from a man sitting by a rock, he discovers that the stranger is dead. When the knight asks what the man said, Jons merely says, "He spoke most eloquently." At the dead man's side is a dog, silent as well, but speaking profoundly of the shortness of life. The squirrel that takes the place of the terminated Skat is another spiritual cousin to this silent young woman, not verbalizing, yet speaking loudly of the inevitable.

SECULAR SAINTS

The rest of our players each represents a Christian mythic archetype.

Jof and Mia

Bergman has acknowledged in interviews that the juggler-actor and his wife are loosely representative of Joseph and Mary, the parents of the Christ Child. Their son could have been named Immanuel, but the symbolism would have been too obvious. So he is named Mikael instead. Michael is the heavenly archangel spoken of in the Hebrew Bible, the counterpart to Lucifer, the fallen archangel. Jof prophesies that little Mikael will grow up to do the impossible trick, that of keeping a ball suspended in midair. And the knight prophesies that the child will grow up to make his parents very happy. Thus the child will be a miracle worker, defying the laws of nature, perhaps even overcoming death itself.

Jof, Mia, and Mikael, as signifiers of the holy family, also have to flee the threat of death in a night journey, and as with the children of Israel, the Angel of Death passes over them, saving them from the maw of mortal termination.

It is Jof who has visions, seeing things that nobody else can see. His first vision, prophetically, of the Holy Virgin and her child, points in the spiritual direction of the drama. He is also the only character to see Death and not die, hinting that there can be some victory over death after all.

Jons

This earthy, realist squire personifies pragmatic existentialism. Experienced, wise, worldly, and strong, he represents the profane almost at the complete exclusion of the sacred. While he bears a biblical name (John, meaning "God is gracious"), he is almost the antithesis of the man of faith. Though his is an almost antireligious attitude, his personality somewhat resembles that of John the Baptist in his roughness, in his defiance of authority, in his resolute protest against death, and in his role as a herald against hypocrisy. When he looks into the eyes of the dying witch, he sees the intensity of fear and dread, much like John the Beloved.

Karin

The long-suffering, faithful wife of the knight signifies another saint. Her name, Karin, is derived from Catherine. The story of Saint Catherine, a fourth-century martyr who was broken on a wheel before being decapitated, was brought back to northern Europe by the crusaders from the Holy Land. Karin exemplifies saintly virtues in her Penelope-like patience while waiting for her husband's return from the holy war, and in her brave welcoming of Death into her home.

Antonius Block

The Saint Anthony of this morality play is Antonius Block. Saint Anthony was a third-century Egyptian ascetic whose cult was popularized throughout Europe with the returning crusaders. He was the patron saint of swineherds. An account surrounding his sainthood concerns the story of a pestilence that broke out in the eleventh century. When people made intercession in his name, the plague was said to have stopped. One of the most common artistic depictions of Saint Anthony is that of his temptation.

In several respects Antonius Block typifies Saint Anthony. Certainly he is an ascetic. He is tempted, like Job, to deny God. Like Anthony, the patron saint of swineherds, Antonius Block is seen as a protector and advocate of those associated with the pigs. The two places of the busiest social intercourse in the film are the stage scene and the inn scene. In both of these places pigs roam about freely, doing what pigs do. Antonius Block invites a select group of people to leave the piggish atmosphere of the plague-infested world to follow him through the forest to his castle. Although they all die but Jof, Mia, and Mikael, they at least die with dignity, at the knight's castle. And it is through Antonius's tricky intervention that Jof, Mia, and Mikael are saved from their plight.

THE SEVEN SEALS OF JOHN'S REVELATION

The Seventh Seal is loosely based on the opening of the seven seals in the Book of Revelation. Like the seven seals that allow various curses to inflict humankind in the Book of Revelation, Death shows up seven times in this religious tragedy before claiming his captives.

The first seal opened in Revelation releases a rider with a white horse, who is given a crown and sets out to conquer. Antonius Block is a figure of this first rider. Fate appropriately gives him white in his chess game with Death. As a knight, he is a nobleman trained for royal mounted combat and raised to honorable military rank and to the order of chivalry. The irony here is that what he originally considered a noble cause, the crusades, becomes a spiritual stumbling block to him. At Death's first appearance, the knight is given a temporary reprieve, so that he may attempt to accomplish a meaningful act.

The opening of the second seal reveals a rider on a red horse, who is permitted to take peace from the earth, so that men should slay one another all in the name of God. The crusades are correlative with this curse. At a more personal level, Antonius Block confesses his own lack of personal peace to Death, disguised as a confessor priest at his second appearance. At the same time, we hear the squire's realistic depiction of the crusades as a complete travesty of religion.

The third seal reveals a rider on a black horse with a balance in his

No strategy can be used to avoid Death's inevitable victory.

hand. At Death's third appearance, he takes Antonius's knight and places him in check. Death makes this move knowing Antonius's secret combination of the bishop and the knight. Being tricked on this one, Antonius keeps secret the preparation of the night journey.

The fourth seal reveals a rider named Death on a pale horse, followed by Hell. They are given power to kill a fourth of the people of the earth with sword, famine, pestilence, and wild beasts. The fourth entrance of Death shows him disguised again as a man of the cloth, as a witness to the execution of the witch, the woman blamed for the pestilence. The witch is even tied to her stake as to a cross, and her hands are broken, as if signifying crucifixion. The sacrificial victim signifies the innocent, martyred minority slain for truth's sake, for the naive benefit of the superstitious, sacrifice-hungry masses.

The opening of the fifth seal reveals the souls slain for truth, for the word of God. Each of these innocent souls is given a white robe and told to rest while the remaining numbers of their kind are to be killed.

During Death's fifth appearance, he saws down Skat's tree after joking with him about terminated contracts and canceled performances.

The opening of the sixth seal reveals an earthquake, the sun turning black, the full moon becoming like blood, the stars of the sky falling to the earth, and the sky vanishing like a scroll. Slaves and free all hide in caves, calling out to the mountains to fall on them, to end the threat of violence. Raval, the wicked priest, dies of the plague in inner anguish, as if calling out to the mountains to fall on him.

Death strikes the knight's queen, jeopardizing the knight's last remaining strategies. This hints at another, more significant queen in jeopardy. But the knight manages to distract Death long enough at the chess game so that Jof, Mia, and Mikael can escape, since Jof can see Death at this point. Thus the meaningful act planned by the knight is accomplished after all, even with death and dying all around. Other meaningful acts of his would include giving water to and easing the pain of the witch that was to be executed, and providing safe passage of his guests to his castle.

Part of the narration of the seventh seal is read by Karin, after the safe arrival at the castle: "And when the Lamb broke the seventh seal, there was silence in heaven for about the space of half an hour. And I saw the seven angels which stood before God; and to them were given seven trumpets. And another . . ." Then there is a knock at the door. Jons goes to answer the knock, but nobody is there. Karin continues reading, ". . . and the third angel sounded, and there fell a great star from heaven, burning as it were a torch, and it fell upon the third part of the rivers, and upon the fountains of waters; and the name of the star is called Wormwood. . . ." At this point, His Majesty, Death himself enters the room and is immediately and mournfully recognized by all. This is his seventh appearance. All of them make their comments to him, fitting to each of their personalities and spiritual figurations.

The eighth time Death is seen is in Jof's vision of Death leading the members of the night journey in the *danse macabre*. And here the eighth appearance represents what eight often does—new beginnings, or eternity, as Jof, Mia, and Mikael have been saved from death in order to start anew with the promise of a divine, redeeming child.

A MODERN MORALITY PLAY

The Seventh Seal was released in 1956, not too long after the end of World War II, in the midst of the Cold War. Certainly many were disillusioned and doubted the existence of a just God—feelings and thoughts similar, no doubt, to those after most wars.

The film depicts a small band of actors on their way to a saint's festival to perform a morality play—the play within a play. The film itself is done in the style of a morality play, with common archetypes contrasting the opposing elements of the universe in a medieval dialectic, forcing the need for a peaceful synthesis between the uncomfortable antitheses. Cold War audiences no doubt identified with the archetypes and received some syntheses in their time. Now, many years after its release, the story still bears significant spiritual import, still operating as a morality play, forcing the audience to react, if not consciously, at least subconsciously to the moral of the medieval story.

Bergman sees his films as dreams put to celluloid. He also sees them not as literature on film, but rather as music. An accomplished pianist and organist, Bergman carries an innate sense of the musical, and it is evident in his films. He is prone to make statements like "art lost its creative drive the moment it was separated from worship" (Bergman, xxii). Yet, while Bergman does not consciously decide to make moral, intellectual social commentaries through film, he nonetheless makes films infused with the numinous muses, genii, and furies floating gracefully in the world of dreams and music—the world of subconscious numinosity.

If we were analyzing *The Seventh Seal* merely from a psychodynamic point of view, we could see the film as largely the personal workings out of Bergman's own childhood trauma and religious angst. And certainly there are many of these elements therein. But the film is more than that, if we consider that dreams, including Bergman's dreams, are also the dreams of one's culture and collective unconscious.

The leitmotif in this celluloid morality dream is the human soul stuck in the eternal conflict between the archetypal divisions of male and female, heaven and earth, high and low, life and death. Seeking to reconcile these oppositions, the soul employs various tools designed to remarry an estranged cosmic father and mother. In the midst of this seemingly futile act of reconciliation, God is silent, or at least he's not letting the soul know too much of future events at one time. Death is the awesome reminder that a permanent separation of opposites terminates the game.

So in frustration, the soul tries to employ a combination of bishop and knight in the chess game with Death. Surely this combination is bound to break the threat of Death; sacred and secular powers together seemingly have a better chance against the forces of final termination. But, crafty devil that he is, Death learns the secret of the contender's arsenal and puts the soul in checkmate. Certainly the same combination is employed every time the soul goes to war, in the geopolitical arena as well as in intrapersonal battles. We always find religious reasons to fight our political wars, and we often blame our personal psychic conflicts on political problems.

Perhaps a replacement of knowledge over faith, as the knight prays, will be the key to unlocking the death grip of the opponent's dark tactics. But of course this has been overused to the soul's blind detriment. The god of scientism and the goddess of reason have merely replaced the old deities of faith, without any greater success. But still Death threatens to perpetuate the Grand Divorce throughout eternity.

The knight, as the soul, thinks, maybe if I just meet the Devil himself, surely he knows God, then I'll get closer to God through him. It is written, "Even the demons believe, and tremble." Perhaps, but just as the condemned witch reveals, even many that claim to have intimate knowledge of the Devil are led to this belief through a mass indoctrination of the fanatical masses perpetuated by the religious leaders, also seemingly appointed at times by the master of deception himself, thus adding more confusion to an already convoluted situation.

Certainly one of the soul's most common tactics is the erection of the god Fear. It is precisely this deification that causes our wars in the first place. Either we flagellate ourselves in our own scornful humiliation or we place the blame of our problems on somebody equally worthy of abuse. One way or the other, the sacralization of paranoia, especially if instituted in a propagandistic regime, either secular or religious, will perpetuate the violent cycle of flagellation. Even when the soul is convinced that it is immune to the plague of violence, the soul is fooled by it in a grand drama of upstaged cuckoldry.

So where do we go from here? It seems that the soul has exhausted its higher resources of secular and religious authority, knowledge, and proscribed punishment. Perhaps there are areas that the soul has overlooked. In *The Seventh Seal*, there is only one place where the knight seems to have peace, and that is when he is talking to Mia in the open field. In their conversation, several symbols of hidden and valuable wisdom are suggested by the muses of dream time as possible clues to a way out of the soul's troubles.

Mia offers milk and wild strawberries to the knight as a meal to be eaten with her family, out on the open hills. Here, as the knight partakes of this natural meal, it is as if he is participating in communion. Instead of bread and wine, symbolizing a broken body and spilt blood, we have a eucharist of a less violent symbology, indicating more of a suckling of the feminine, rather than the violence of the masculine. For the violence has already been done at the cross, and it is continuing to be done, as in the scapegoating of the witch.

Mia mentions on two occasions the sense of smell, in reference to the strawberries and to her baby. Here the soul is led to its lower nature. After having soared in our higher nature, almost at the exclusion of the lower, the soul at this juncture of the morality play is led directly down to the basic visceral instincts. Smelling is symbolic of discriminating what is beneath. It is intelligence directed downward. The only other creatures in our story that we witness smelling are animals. But their noses are almost on the ground. While the human nose is far from the ground, the soul must be reminded to smell in order to regain the sense of wisdom from below. This is where Mia leads the knight. When the higher, knightly nature has exhausted its strategic weapons against the Grand Divorcer, the soul must reach downward, to the feminine.

If the soul is prepared to learn from below, then it is ready for the night journey through the dark forest. Here, another symbol of the feminine beckons the soul to quiet reflection in the uncultivated wildwoods. Shrines to the feminine were mostly erected in the forest, signifying the most natural place of her abode. The forest is also the abode of the subconscious, the dark place where the soul can find strength and wisdom for the game of life. The caravan of pilgrims are led through the forest by the knight after his rekindling of the feminine, an appropriate pilgrimage for the soul's descent into lower wisdom. While Antonius prays for knowledge, a masculine trait, it is not until his tutelage with Mia that he learns wisdom, a feminine trait.

Jof's first vision is of the crowned Virgin Mary, the Christian version of the mother goddess. Significantly, when Death takes the knight's queen, Jof suddenly sees Death for the first time. So while Mia operates in the feminine quite naturally, through her visceral and emotional

Instead of a broken body and spilt blood, Mia offers the knight a feminine communion of milk and wild strawberries.

Death is not the wrathful Lord of the Plague, but rather, the joyful Lord of the Dance.

life, Jof participates in the feminine through his intuitive visionary gift. The royal feminine is something very dear to him, and it is at the point of the queen's capture that he moves his family out of harm's way, just as Joseph fled the wrath of patriarchal death in his family's night journey.

And while the holy family escapes the slaughter of innocents in the forest, coming through unscathed in the passover of the Angel of Death, the women who meet Death at the castle seem to welcome him with the wisdom of uncontested surrender. While the knight pleads in anguish at the last moment, and while the squire grudgingly accepts Death only under protest, Karin and the silent woman relinquish any possible rights they may have to Death. For they know intuitively that Death is also the inevitable feminine, claiming her rightful bounty, so that the womb may issue new life from the tomb. And thus, in his eighth appearance Death is not the wrathful Lord of the plague but rather the joyful Lord of the dance, signifying new birth as a result of a reunion with the lower feminine nature. As Mia says, springtime is her favorite.

IT'S A WONDERFUL LIFE

SAINT GEORGE AND THE DRAGON

O n the surface, Frank Capra's 1946 classic *It's a Wonderful Life* projects obvious moral and religious motifs: love, sacrifice, heaven, angels, the theme that each person's life touches many others. But at the same time, deeper mythical qualities touch us at more primal levels. An obvious mythical element is Jimmy Stewart's characteristic David-and-Goliath role, similar to his roles in *Mr. Smith Goes to Washington* and *The Man Who Shot Liberty Valance*, for instance. An analysis of the film's archetypes can reveal other, less obvious, mythical elements.

THE CHARACTERS

The Beast

What is a good myth without a powerful enemy? The bad guy in our story is found dramatically in the cantankerous and miserly Scrooge, played by Lionel Barrymore. He is the monster that threatens to devour the life of the community. This Behemoth, Henry Potter, who keeps a skull on his desk, who has no wife or children, and who always dresses in dark clothes, savors his wartime role as the head of the local draft board by lustily sending dozens of 1-A classified community sons off to their potential destruction in the war machine. His first name, Henry, means "home ruler," signifying the role he sees most fitting to his avaricious personality. This home ruler acts as a personification of the Devil in this archetypal struggle between good and evil. He can easily remind us of the biblical home ruler—Satan is called the temporary "ruler of this world."

George's kid brother, Harry, was originally appointed as the *good* home ruler. His name is derived from Henry and carries the same meaning. But college and a marriage to Ruth Daycon take him away to work for his father-in-law's glass factory in Buffalo. Ironically, instead of ruling at home, he goes off to become a war hero, saving the lives of men on a transport ship, men who we might imagine were sent off to die by the monster at home.

Saint George

In lieu of Harry's rulership at home, George Bailey (James Stewart) is the designated ruler, or at least the combatant of the Evil One, a mission he reluctantly accepts. George's mission, among other things, entails killing the beast through his benevolent and sacrificial giving. In the fourth century a Roman tribune named George was martyred for his faith in Christ; he was later canonized as Saint George, the patron saint of England. Stories surrounding this sacrificed hero depict him killing the Devil, which was later pictorially represented as the good knight slaying the dragon. In *It's a Wonderful Life* George Bailey becomes the Saint George of Bedford Falls.

George receives his mantle, or the symbolic authority for his saintly calling, from his father, Peter Bailey. Perhaps deriving from Frank Capra's Catholic upbringing, are papal implications of this inheritance of authority. Saint Peter, of course, according to Roman Catholic theology, was the first pope, who received his authority from Jesus and who in turn handed down the same spiritual power to succeeding popes and priests. The name Peter means "rock." And just as Saint Peter is believed to be the rock and foundation of the church, likewise, Peter Bailey is considered to be the bedrock of Bedford Falls, at least in the eyes of his son, George Bailey. As Henry Potter ironically testifies,

"Peter Bailey *is* the Building and Loan," a phrase suggesting his foundational role in the saga of Bedford Falls.

George prophetically quips about his own saintly, Christ-like calling when he mentions his "last supper in the old Bailey Boardinghouse." He never fully catches on to his true calling until the end of the story, however, when he learns his valuable lesson from the insipid yet naively insightful angel Clarence.

Mary

Like other heroes, George sacrifices his own plans in order to fulfill his mission. But as is also common among sacrificial heroes, he kicks against the barbs of his calling, as did Saint Paul and Moses. A crucial element in St. George Bailey's mission is to team up with a wholesome hometown girl, Mary Whatcha, played, appropriately, by Donna Reed. George's mother intuitively knows that Mary is the girl for her son; she suggests to her resistant dreamer-child, "Mary will help you find the answers."

Torn between his dreams of seeing the world and the magnetism of Mary, George vacillates in his decision toward her. Her not revealing her wish (to marry George) at the Granville house makes it come true. George's immediate telling of his wish (to see the world) eliminates the magical power of his wish. We are reminded here of how Mary, the mother of Jesus, keeps her secret of the divine union between herself and God which results in the birth of Jesus. George's mystical promise to Mary paints her in the guise of the Blessed Virgin. He boasts that he is going to lasso the moon for her, and that after she swallows it, the moon beams will radiate from her hair, hands, and feet—a verbal picture similar to Catholic iconographic images of Mary, the Mother of God.

DIVIDING THE RED SEA AND MERGING THE OPPOSITES

George Bailey makes a slow but steady pilgrimage toward sainthood. Like Moses, he is destined to lead his people out of Henry Potter's Egypt and into the Promised Land. But instead of Pharaoh's horsemen

71

getting drowned in the Red Sea, George himself is baptized in it, when the floor of the high school gym opens during his dance with Mary. The multiple irony here is that what is meant for evil by Mary's frustrated suitor turns out for good, as the crowd (including the culprit) joins George and Mary in this pool of redemption.

Pharaoh's army was never resurrected from their Red Sea immersion, but George and Mary's dunking symbolizes their baptism, a necessary precursor to the redemptive work to follow. George never makes it to his own promised land of adventure because of his divine calling: he is destined to deliver the residents of a potential Pottersville into their promised land.

Saint George needs the androgynous buffalo gal to fulfill his mission.

After their Red Sea baptism, while walking home in make-do dry clothes, Mary breaks out in spontaneous song, echoing the jubilant response of Miriam, the sister of Moses and Aaron, after their victorious crossing of the Red Sea. (The name Mary is actually a derivative of Miriam.)

Here Mary sings her theme song, "Buffalo gals, won't you come out tonight . . . and dance by the light of the moon." The song, particularly as sung by Mary, hints at her androgynous nature. Though the song apparently refers to a woman of Buffalo, New York, an association with the animal is natural. On one hand, a buffalo is a masculine creature, and a buffalo gal connotes a woman with gutsy, masculine persistence, which Mary possesses in full, as is seen in her psychological lassoing of George. On the other hand, the symbolism of the moon connotes femininity and mystery, which are also reflected in Mary's nurturing character. The androgynous blending of male and female in Mary and her theme song speaks poetically of the major metaphor of the story, the union of male and female, which in turn is a metaphor of the union of heaven and earth.

THE HUSBANDMAN

Besides its allusion to George the Dragon Slayer, the name George means "farmer" or "husbandman," one who plants his seeds in Mother Earth and reaps the life-giving bounty. George Bailey fits this imagery in more ways than one. First of all, there is the seed-bearing connection to Mary. Mary's last name is Whatcha, which can be interpreted at least two ways. If it were pronounced with a silent *h*, it might symbolize Mary's premarital yearnings for George, connoting the idea that she was *watching* him. But strangely, it is pronounced with a silent *w*, the first syllable being the same as *hatch*, as in to hatch an egg. When Mary hints of her pregnancy, George appropriately asks her, "Are you on the nest?"

When George and Mary move the large Martini family into their new home, George blesses them with bread, wine, and salt as Mary leads a goat by the horn, signifying hints of communion and fertility rituals. George and Mary personify both the virtues of virility and fertility and the life-creating blending of male and female. The promised land in gospel parables is depicted as a farmer planting seeds in the earth, the farmer being the Son of God. Similarly, in ancient fertility cults a sacrificial sun god is killed and planted in Mother Earth to insure fertility. George as the husbandman and Mary as the good Earth Mother symbolize this union of heaven and earth.

Uncle Willie's crow symbolizes the birds spoken of in the parable of the sower. The birds represent the evil one who snatches away the seeds of the husbandman. The crow always pops up in the narrative whenever there is trouble (which is almost every scene at the building and loan). The crow is a constant reminder that the pall of death emanating from Henry Potter might snuff out the spirit of those working to produce and preserve life.

THE TEMPTATIONS OF SAINT GEORGE

To be proved in his sainthood, George must pass through the obligatory temptations of the calling. First of all there is Violet Bicks (Gloria Grahame), Mary's lifelong competition for George's heart. Instead of falling into a union with the "bad woman," George lifts her up out of her problems and sets her on higher ground, as Christ did with Mary Magdalene, the woman caught in adultery, and the woman at the well.

Violet represents the paradoxical and precarious balance of redemption. There to tempt the redeemer, she herself is redeemed. Redemption wouldn't be redemptive without fallenness to redeem. She is there as a reminder that the balance between good and evil can lean in either direction while the people wait for their hero. Her name, Violet, recalls the flower worn by the followers of Napoleon while they awaited their hero's return from exile.

The temptation to explore the world is a lingering one for George. But the death of his father, the marriage of his brother, and the run on the building and loan keeps him forever frustrated, at home in Bedford

74

Falls. His references to his mother's cooking the fatted calf for his brother's homecoming indicates his position as the faithful son to Harry's prodigal nature.

Then there is the temptation to go into the plastics business with Sam Wainwright, his old classmate who made it big in New York. Sam is a forerunner of the plastics business tempter of the 1967 film *The Graduate*. Like Benjamin (Dustin Hoffman), George doesn't budge on this one.

But the offer made by Henry Potter himself is more tempting, especially in that it is more similar to the Devil's material temptation of Jesus ("I'll give you all the kingdoms of the world, if you will just follow me"). George almost falls for Potter's offer of twenty thousand dollars a year with a three-year contract. But upon shaking hands with the evil one, he suddenly feels dirty and walks away from the spider's web, as he calls it, wiping his hand clean.

Saint George confronts the dragon.

On December 24th, when absent-minded Uncle Willie misplaces eight thousand dollars and the bank examiner poses a threat to the very institution that is preserving the life of the community, George Bailey despairs for his life. In fact, Mr. Potter makes him realize that, financially speaking, he is worth more dead than alive. That's when he faces his last temptation, to throw away "God's greatest gift to man," his own life.

THE FARMER AND THE JACKASS

Of course, this is where Clarence Oddbody, AS2 (Henry Travers), enters the picture. His superior in heaven says that "he has the brains of a rabbit." But this is obviously the part of the gospel where "God uses the foolish things to confound the wise." This embarrassing excuse for an angel happens to be a Mark Twain fan. He carries a copy of *Tom Sawyer* around with him like a Bible. Clarence is the name of the hero's sidekick in *A Connecticut Yankee in King Authur's Court*, an insipid yet loyal devotee whose blunders turn out for good, like Clarence Oddbody and like Uncle Willie.

When a suicidal George Bailey wishes he had never been born, Clarence seems to recognize a parallel with the book he is carrying. Tom Sawyer, like George, has visions of going off on exciting adventures, but instead stays in town, has a relationship with Becky Thatcher, and fights the forces of evil in the local community. Tom Sawyer also attends his own funeral and gets a chance to see what things are like without him. It would seem that Frank Capra and his co-writers (Frances Goodrich and Albert Hackett) were also influenced by Mark Twain. It is interesting that Twain himself was sidetracked on more than one occasion by marriage and family commitments from his dreams of seeing more of the world. Mark Twain, like George, was also a great humanitarian, fighting in his writings and in his life, for the dignity of his fellow human beings and against the oppression of humanity.

Clarence Oddbody's celestial classification, AS2, is supposed to

Clarence Oddbody, AS2, the jackass of heaven, with a disbelieving Saint George.

stand for "angel, second class." But the symbols don't quite match. *A* is definitely for Angel. *S* and 2 could both stand for "second"; but that would be redundant. It seems rather that AS2 signifies "ASS", with the 2 a double of the *S*. In other words, Clarence, with the brains of a rabbit, a bumbling fool who has not yet earned his wings, is sort of a jackass in heaven. Two other characters, Sam Wainwright and Uncle Willie, offer parallels. Sam Wainwright always enters and exits with a donkey's "hee-haw!" as if to say to George, "Don't be a jackass like your foolish Uncle Willie by staying in this town. Come work with me and I'll make you successful!" Uncle Willie is the kind of character we might imagine Clarence to have been as a human on earth: forgetful and well-meaning but always doing things the wrong way—in short, a mindless jackass.

George's Christmas Eve troubles are caused by the earthly jackass, Uncle Willie. When he prays for a way out, he gets stuck with none other than a heavenly jackass! But as "God uses the foolish things to confound the wise," we should be reminded that the disobedient prophet Balaam was spoken to by a jackass. Sam Wainwright's hee-haws can be a thorn in George's side unless he has enough intuition to hear the voice of God through the jackass. Part of the irony here is that the name Sam means "heard from God."

Uncle Willie, as the earthly jackass of the narrative, is cinematically painted as the farmer's cultivated order reverting back to natural chaos. When Henry Potter's accountant talks about Bailey Park (the order brought out of chaos) he says, "There were once rabbits and squirrels there" (natural chaos). After Uncle Willie's blunder, Willie bows his head in shame, and his pet squirrel climbs up on his shoulders, as if he were a stump in the undeveloped wildwoods. Later, in George's real-life vision, he goes to Bailey Park only to see a cemetery. This reinforces the pastoral notion that the hero-husbandman is needed to cultivate the land.

THE WOUNDED HEALER

The major difference between the protagonist, George, and the antagonist, Henry Potter, lies in the one thing they have in common: their woundedness. There is often a certain mythical power, enveloped in a woundedness such as these two powerful men possess. Potter is crippled, and George has a damaged left ear. In primitive tribes the shaman is often a person with a grave infirmity. This affliction sets him or her apart as a "special person" of the community, one marked by the gods to possess certain incantational abilities. Mythical literature also provides many examples of this phenomenon. Hephaestus is the despised, limping god of the Greek pantheon. Jacob receives a wound in his fight with the Angel of God. Moses has a speech impediment. Oedipus has a swollen foot.

We are not told how Potter became crippled, but we do know how George received his wound. When he jumps into a frozen lake to save his brother's life, his ear becomes infected. And for saving a customer's life from Mr. Gower's incorrect prescription, he has his bad ear slapped, worsening the damage. Potter's wound is a curse to him, for which he selfishly tries to overcompensate. George's wound, which he receives in his self-sacrificial lifesaving, is a curse that becomes a blessing.

Hearing- or sight-impaired people often seem to develop extrasensory gifts to compensate for those areas in which they lack. What George cannot hear physically, he eventually hears psychically. When George is able to hear all in the Pottersville sequence, he is horrified at the sounds of a town without a George Bailey. After coming back to Bedford Falls, he is ecstatic over the reappearance of another wound, a cut lip from a sock in the mouth, which he receives as an answer to a prayer. Thus, his wounds are signs of healing, easily misunderstood in a society under the mistaken belief that suffering and pain are merely evil sores to be sedated. George intuits that suffering, or woundedness, rather than being a disease to be treated, is actually medicine itself with healing and wisdom-procuring properties.

His wanting to take his life, even though destructive, also recalls Abraham laying his son Isaac on the sacrificial altar. In the biblical account, God provides a sacrificial ram just in the nick of time. In George's case, Clarence is the sacrificial jackass whom George jumps over the bridge to rescue, thus ironically turning the curse of his compassionate nature into a blessing again.

The major difference between George and Potter therefore lies in a polarity between potency and impotency. Potter is crippled, which in art often signifies impotency. We see his psychological impotence in his obsessive and selfish efforts to assert his power over the town. The biographies of real-life megalomaniacs reveal similar examples of such overcompensation. Symbolically and otherwise, George is painted as the most virile, potent, and fertile man in town. Even as a child he has visions of having "a couple of harems, and at least three or four wives." As an adult, he bemoans to Mary, "And why do we have to have all of these kids, anyway?" As George the husbandman, he plants a lot of seeds and produces a lot of life, in more ways than one.

Potter is most often seen holding in his mouth and hand a large, phallic cigar. George is seen smoking on three occasions. The first time, he smokes a cigarette on the front porch at his brother's wedding party while feeling flaccidly dejected, throwing away his travel brochures. The second time, looking rather small in Henry Potter's chair, he smokes one of Potter's huge cigars while being tempted by Potter's compensatory vision of wealth and power. The third time, he casually and confidently smokes a pipe in front of the bank examiner, in the midst of trouble. Each smoking cameo signifies a different stage of his growth from youthful spiritual impotency, through midlife ambivalence, to self-assured maturity.

Potter uses the power of his woundedness to clobber the town into submission under his scepter of authority. Conversely, George uses the power of his own woundedness to produce life, freedom, prosperity, and joy.

POTTERSVILLE/POTTERSFIELD

The myth of the Fisher King can also be seen here, in that the old king's land is becoming sterile because of his impotency. A young prince is needed to revivify the kingdom. Young King David must take the throne of the old, impotent, and cruel King Saul. Without the new lifeblood of the virile prince, the region becomes a wasteland. Such is exactly the picture in George's nightmarish vision of Pottersville, a town lacking a redeeming prince. In his vision, Bailey Park, the embodiment of George's saving the townspeople from Potter's slums, becomes Potter's Field, a cemetery. Life is swallowed up in death under the rule of the evil one.

God is spoken of in scriptures as a potter, having made vessels of flesh. And the Devil is spoken of as an imitator of the creator. By analogy, Henry Potter's days as an imposter creator are numbered. A potter's field is a refuse dump, a field where the potter throws his broken pieces of pottery, a useless tract of land. During his troubles, Job sat on such an ash heap, scraping his wounds with a broken clay potsherd. Like Job, George evolves through gain, loss, and regaining.

After Judas Iscariot sold Jesus for thirty pieces of silver, he threw the money back at the chief priests and went out and hung himself. The priests decided they could not put the money in the treasury because it was blood money. So with the silver, they bought the potter's field in which strangers were buried. This field was thereafter called the Field of Blood (Matthew 27:1–10).

In Frank Capra's film, when the people of Pottersville die, alienated from one another and especially from George, a complete stranger to them, they are buried in Potter's Field, a cemetery for strangers. In contrast, Clarence's note to George, on the cover page of *Tom Sawyer*, reads "No man's life is worthless if he has friends." Potter, emotionally alienated from the people, causes them to be strangers to one another. But George befriends those Potter calls the "riffraff," the "garlic eaters," and the "charity cases"; he inspires them to befriend one another and, in turn, him. The rub is that people who were originally strangers, become friends, and as friends they become "strangers in a strange land."

GEORGE AS THE PRIEST AND GOOD SHEPHERD

The biblical parallels in the narrative are fulfilled when George exercises his role as the priest and good shepherd of the people. His priestly role is evident when he and Mary give bread, wine, and salt to the Martini family as they move into Bailey Park. The eucharistic symbolism of the body and blood of Christ is apparent, and salt is a biblical symbol of preserving the good in the land. Another sacramental element is George's image of Mary swallowing the moon he has lassoed. The moon, viewed two-dimensionally, looks like a communion wafer. Mary metaphorically eats the body of Christ to be at one with the redeemer.

When George and Mary begin to head off on their would-be honeymoon, Ernie the cabby notices what looks like a bank run. Mary insists, unsuccessfully, that George not go to the rescue. But after she arrives she has a conversion experience, giving up her two thousand dollars of honeymoon money for the sake of the tottering building and loan. This is the spiritual consummation of her marriage to George.

The sacrificed money becomes the manna from heaven for the children of Israel in the wilderness, another prototypical symbol of the body of Christ. After the withdrawals are paid out of the two thousand dollars, only two single bills remain, which George appropriately dubs Mama Dollar and Papa Dollar. The two dollar bills are sacramentally placed together in a basket and put in the safe to reproduce. And reproduce they do, as the heavenly infection of George and Mary continues to spread. It eventually erupts into a climactic outburst of giving in the Baileys' living room. The number two in both monetary sums is symbolic of two entities coming together as one, the principal theme of the story.

THE MARRIAGE OF HEAVEN AND EARTH

The harsh vision of Pottersville forms a black-and-white contrast between Henry Potter's hypothetical rule and George Bailey's actual influence (an effect woefully diluted, by the way, in the obscene colorized version). Pottersville, where an overcompensated masculinity has gone awry, shares the physical attributes of a potsherd: hardness, sharpness, and worthlessness. Bedford Falls, on the other hand, has a softer, warmer sound to it. A bed is where a river lies. A ford is a flowing body of water. And falls are elements of water penetrating and blending with another body of water. Pottersville is a degenerative, phallic-oriented village, incapable of reproducing life because the anima, or feminine element, has been excluded. Bedford Falls, on the other hand, speaks of a harmonious blending of once-isolated entities brought together to generate life. In the story of Bedford Falls, salvation is found in the union between George and Mary, Clarence and George, heaven and earth, and God and humankind.

The joke on the Evil One is that in stealing the building and loan's eight thousand dollars, he forgets that eight is the number of new beginnings. In a way, Potter is also the Judas who betrays the Christ for the pieces of silver. While Potter's plans for a Pottersfield are paid for by the blood of the townsfolk, he doesn't realize that the blood of the sacrificial lamb will redeem the people from their plight. We might imagine Henry Potter later hanging himself and being buried alone in his own field. His last attempt at sabotaging Saint George ironically turns into a new beginning for the hero and his people.

INSIGNIFICANCE
THE DESTRUCTION OF
UNIVERSAL SIGNIFICANCE

Insignificance raises questions of philosophic and spiritual import, some of which we will wrestle with here. Based on a play by Terry Johnson produced at the Royal Court Theatre in London in 1982, Nicholas Roeg's 1985 film takes place mostly in a Manhattan hotel room that seems to be the center of the universe. Or at least it seems to symbolize the center of our human psyche wrestling with the universe. The story has four main unnamed principals—the professor (Michael Emil), the actress (Theresa Russell), the senator (Tony Curtis), and the ballplayer (Gary Busey). While these characters are not named, it is rather obvious whom they represent—Albert Einstein, Marilyn Monroe, Senator Joseph McCarthy, and Joe DiMaggio, respectively. The movement of the story itself is not significant. Without the dialogue that gives it its driving force, the plot would be a rather uninteresting, relatively actionless exercise in stage movement. But the significance is far deeper than the relatively insignificant movements. What is significant is what is said, and more importantly, what is not said but barely implied by what is said—essentially, what is provoked within the minds of the appreciative viewers of this excellent film.

THE STORY LINE

The plot is much more simple than the complex set of questions inspired by this thought-provoking piece of cinema-sophia. Einstein is spending the night in a luxury hotel room paid for by the American government because he has been subpoenaed by Senator Joseph McCarthy to appear before the House Committee on Un-American Activities the next morning. He refuses to go to this farcical meeting, but chooses rather to show up for a speaking engagement at a conference on world peace. At about three A.M. he is interrupted from his calculations by Marilyn Monroe, who has decided to demonstrate for him the specific theory of relativity. She also wants to make love with him, but she has a hard time persuading him. Once he is won over, the two are interrupted by her jealous husband, Joe DiMaggio, who angrily bangs on the door, demanding entrance. They reluctantly let him in. The married couple argues. Einstein leaves to get another room and has a philosophical discussion with a Cherokee elevator operator (Will Sampson). Senator McCarthy reenters the room at approximately eight A.M. and finds Marilyn in bed instead of the professor. He mistakes her for a whore who looks like Monroe and he socks her in the stomach, inducing a miscarriage. The senator and the ballplayer end up down on the street, while Einstein and Monroe end up in the room, continuing their dialogue about time, space, and relativity, and space-time.

THEMES

In addition to providing a fictional account of the meeting of four famous people, *Insignificance* frames several themes within the context of the dialogue. Most of these themes come in the form of contrasts:

EINSTEIN AND MONROE	MCCARTHY AND DIMAGGIO
intelligence	ignorance
potency	impotency
graciousness	exploitation
ascension	descension
reality	illusion
anonymity	fame
life	death
peace	war
unity	disunity
thinking	knowing
doing	thinking
rest	work
looseness	tightness
interior	exterior
timelessness	time
spacelessness	space
space-time	concreteness
Cherokee	American
significance	insignificance

These polarities provide the tension that puts the story in motion, and they provide the innate conflict that works toward a resolution of the open-ended, largely unanswered problems.

INTELLIGENCE VERSUS IGNORANCE

At the beginning of the film, while Marilyn is shooting the famous wind-in-the-skirt publicity shot for the film *The Seven Year Itch*, two technicians below the sidewalk grating are working the wind machine. While looking skyward, one of them speculates about the stars, while the other calls him a "philosophical fucking bastard," thus initiating a contrast of intelligences.

Einstein, of course, is considered one of the most intelligent men of his time. Contrasted with his brilliance in this film is just about

86

everybody else in the story. The senator tells him, "I'm not an educated man, but I'd sure like to know what you know." Monroe, after demonstrating the specific theory of relativity, admits that she does not fully comprehend it but somehow gets the essence of it. The ballplayer, after reconsidering his relationship with his wife, promises that he will read and get smarter for her. When he tells her that he has contracted a lawyer to talk about a divorce, she seems impressed that he has actually had a conversation with an educated man. The ballplayer tells Einstein, when talking about Marilyn, "She's smart enough with all that science and stuff. But that don't mean nothin' compared to feelings."

While the characters contrast intelligence with one another, there is another type of intelligence hinted at by the presence of the Cherokee elevator operator and alluded to by Einstein when he contrasts knowledge and truth. This other type of intelligence is far superior to what is normally considered intelligence.

POTENCY VERSUS IMPOTENCY

Both the senator and the ballplayer boast of their power and use it to their advantage. The senator tries railroading Einstein into testifying for him, and he socks Marilyn in the stomach. The ballplayer threatens to strong-arm both Einstein and the senator. DiMaggio brags about his baseball prowess, and McCarthy boasts of his position in the political arena. Yet both of these macho men are less than adequate sexually. The senator proves to be impotent, and Marilyn suggests that the ballplayer is a premature ejaculator. The low-angle shot centering on the bulge in Einstein's underwear, in contrast, is a cinematic sign of his inner potency.

Monroe and Einstein both recognize their weaknesses, and they show a history of being taken advantage of by the more outwardly potent—Einstein by political and military powers, and Monroe by her peers, her husband and the public. The irony here is that while Einstein is tossed around by the fraudulently powerful, it is his calculations, discovered in still, quiet moments, that have led toward the most powerful physical force developed by humankind. Even the senator tells him that he is known as the mommy and daddy of the H-bomb.

In Einstein's room are two books and some musical scores. The Dostoyevsky novel reminds us that authoritarian powers threw that author in prison for political reasons, yet his works have had a far more lasting influence than has the ruling regime of his time. Charlotte Brontë's *Jane Eyre* is a book about an intelligent woman used and persecuted by those more powerful than her. She overcomes her social obstacles to connect with a man of superior social standing. The sheet music is Mozart's, which reminds us that the archbishop of Salzburg selfishly used his power to try to dominate Mozart's life. Yet,

The professor, as Hermes, allows himself an attempted union with his admirer, Marilyn Monroe.

the power of Mozart's music has significantly triumphed over the power of the archbishop, who remains largely unremembered other than as an insignificant antagonist in the life of Mozart.

Besides the psychological signs of potency and impotency, there is also a more subtle sign of spiritual power. When the more skeptical of the wind machine technicians turns the switch to start the fan, a malfunction produces a large electrical spark, zapping the operator. A spark is a manifestation of spiritual as well as physical power. The alchemical scintilla and the cabalistic emantist are figures of sparks representing divine power emanating from an eternal force. This picture of the skeptical technician getting zapped sets the stage for a juxtaposition not only between belief and skepticism but also between physical and spiritual power and between outward and inward divinity.

GRACIOUSNESS VERSUS EXPLOITATION

Marilyn has been exploited all her life. The flashbacks of her youth reveal her submitting to a childhood peep show for some ogling boys. As a young, aspiring starlet she is nastily exploited on a casting call. Then, as a star, she tells the chauffeur that she plays not a who but a what, and she wishes they would turn off the neon sign exploiting her image.

Einstein feels manipulated by the powers of authority, no matter what form of government or what nation. That his calculations have led to nuclear destruction, and that the senator wants to use him to cause a further rift in the Cold War, makes him feel like a commodity caught in the bargaining haggles of the political marketplace.

While feeling selfishly used by others, both Monroe and Einstein exhibit an air of gracious generosity. Monroe wants to please Einstein through her somewhat naive but accurate demonstration of relativity. And Einstein prefers to speak to the conference on world peace rather than be used as a cog in the wheel of the American war machine.

ASCENSION VERSUS DESCENSION

Our story takes place largely in a high-rise hotel, or tower, a symbol of ascension and descension. This signifies, like the tower of Babel, an attempt to bridge the gap between heaven and earth. The ascensions and descensions taking place within this high-rise tower are signs of spiritual rising and lowering.

We have seen that the two characters exhibiting the most outward power flaunt the height of their status the most. The senator flaunts his lofty delusion that his concern is for the preservation of the free world. The ballplayer seems to be obsessed with the fact that he has rated in thirteen bubble gum series, including Hubbley Bubbley's and Chiggly Wiggly's. This unwarranted self-ascension implies an inevitable descent in more ways than one.

Compared to the two antagonists, Einstein and Monroe do not talk of their achievements. To the contrary, Monroe sees the sham of her star status. When the Cherokee elevator operator suggests to Einstein that the scientist is Cherokee, implying that he is at the center of the universe, Einstein humbly denies it, saying that he does not want to be "the center of anything, especially the [universe]."

Bare feet function as a sign of the transcendence of the two humble protagonists. After Einstein throws his papers out the window, and when the senator suggests that he is crazy for having lost his life's work, Einstein casually says, "And besides, I also seem to have lost my shoes." The camera pans from Einstein's bare feet to Monroe's uncovered tootsies. These shoeless feet suggest that while the senator and ballplayer need shoes for their worldly treks through life, Einstein and Monroe exist in a dimension where shoes are not required.

Both the ballplayer and the senator enter the story at ground level, and after having ascended and descended the tower at least a couple of times each, they exit the story again at ground level, never to rise again. During one of the many elevator rides, a group of Japanese businessmen ascend and exit. We never see them go back down. The irony lies in that, having dropped the bomb on Japan, America is now seeing the Japanese ascend in the business world, where they now surpass the Americans in some significant ways. Monroe enters the story at ground level and exits while still on the sixteenth floor. Einstein both enters and exits the story up on the sixteenth floor. We are reminded that "Whosoever exalteth himself shall be abased; and he that humbleth himself shall be exalted" (Luke 14:11).

The fifth central character, the Cherokee, goes up and down many times as an elevator operator, but when he gets a break from work, he goes all the way to the roof, above all the others, to participate in the Cherokee cosmos. He sings in Cherokee, looks up to the heavens in prayerful reverence, and laughs when he looks down at the street. Thus, his character hints at a resolution to the high-low polarity.

REALITY VERSUS ILLUSION
ANONYMITY VERSUS FAME

The two wind machine technicians typify the contrast between reality and illusion. The one who talks about the stars is quite the optimist, seeing glory in something that everybody else sees as merely commonplace. When he looks at the stars, he says, he feels that he can do anything. His partner, by comparison, is a pessimist, or perhaps a realist. When the optimist looks up under Marilyn's dress, he says he sees the face of God. Perhaps he intuits the spiritual interior of Marilyn's soul; on the other hand, his naiveté is pointing to the illusion of stardom. The difference between these two men points toward the contrasts between the main characters.

The ballplayer seems to be deluded by his outward success, as if his achievements were the basis of reality. His self-congratulatory stance is the epitome of illusion. Yet when speaking of his wife, he complains that his teammates treat her like a star, and he tells Einstein never to put a woman up on a pedestal. Similarly, the senator deceives himself into believing that he is somehow preserving the free world. In contrast, when the Cherokee compliments Einstein by suggesting that he is Cherokee, which implies being at the center of the

The Cherokee feels he has lost his faith. Einstein is more Cherokee than he realizes.

universe, Einstein humbly insists that he is not the center of anything. He also admits that with too much fame, he would not be able to survive the publicity, thus exhibiting an absence of self-aggrandized illusion.

Likewise, Marilyn knows the difference between reality and illusion. While the world sees her as a star, she knows better. When Einstein asks if her husband is famous, she facetiously says that he is God, giving comical license to star-studded illusion.

Several references to stars play a significant part in this film. Public media stars, of course, are carnal figures of radiant celestial stars, and this is where our illusory conceptions of media gods and goddesses take on astronomical shape. The glitzy kitsch of celebrity status and of schlockily glorious places like Hollywood, Las Vegas, Graceland, and Atlantic City testify to the illusions sustained by a star-hungry populace.

Metaphysically, a star is a symbol of the spirit, especially the five-pointed star drawn by Marilyn on her bathroom mirror. A star often stands for the forces of the spirit struggling against the forces of darkness. While Marilyn sees herself as a larger-than-life star, she is intimately familiar with the hypocrisy of it all, and thus she searches for an inner spark of illumination while looking up at the celestial stars.

LIFE VERSUS DEATH

While Monroe rides away from her publicity shot location, she converses with the chauffeur, who makes a significant Freudian slip. When she asks him to drive her to where she wants to go, he says, "I'm supposed to drive you to your death . . . destination," as if to indicate that her worldly sojourning is leading to an inevitable premature demise. In her life, her miscarriages produce death inside her, and her exterior life is dead, even by her own account. As opposed to the senator, though, her drive is toward at least a hope of life, however incorporeal.

Einstein flashes on pristine scenes of life, as seen in his visions of Japanese gardens and in his recollections of his fishing on a lake. With equal frequency he also presages images of death, in the pictures of corpses and in the destruction brought on by nuclear disaster.

A partner in an unfruitful marriage, the ballplayer looks longingly at Picasso's *Mother and Child*, while Marilyn holds a surrogate towel-baby in the bathroom. Though they both desire a child, the curse of death has greater sway over their relationship than the blessing of life.

The senator, while deceiving himself into thinking he is working toward life-giving freedom, is actually perpetuating death, through his drive to set up an opposition between the superpowers and in his socking Monroe in the stomach. This life-death polarity creates a dialectic pointing toward an eternal resolution.

PEACE VERSUS WAR
UNITY VERSUS DISUNITY

The ballplayer and the senator project attitudes of disunity, the ball-player through his argumentative nature and the senator through his perpetuation of the war mode. While the ballplayer plays a game of war on the ballfield, the senator is actually involved in the promulgation of real war. The senator remarks at one point that "some wise-ass senator wants to put a stop to the Nevada tests." The aggressiveness of each of these sexually inept warriors is the fuel that energizes the wars of the world, and it is this same warlike energy that feeds the film's conflict. While trying to persuade the professor to show up for the Senate hearing, the senator suggests that the professor will have to let the participants of the peace conference "slug it out for themselves." With a paranoid war mentality, he even insists that World War II was a Soviet plot.

In Einstein's flashbacks we see Nazi brownshirts ripping his boat sail, robbing him of his capacity to have peace on the lake.

Contrasted with these American and German warriors are the professor and the actress. While Einstein feels guilty that his peace-time creations have contributed to war, he does everything he can to work toward peace. He chooses to speak at the Conference on World Peace over the Senate hearing, and even his scientific work is symbolic of his mission of peace; as he says, "I'm trying to unify the fields." Marilyn is a victim of the warring elements at every turn, in her relations with men, and in her meeting with the warring senator.

While Einstein and Monroe hope for peace, Einstein feels guilty about burning children with nuclear detonation. Then he knows there is something even worse, to which Marilyn unwittingly testifies. She tells him, "They won't do it again. All the people with their fingers on the button are the ones who own everything—unless they figure out a way to blow up the people and leave the buildings standing." And, horror of horrors, Einstein visualizes her being blown up by a neutron bomb while the building is left intact.

THINKING VERSUS KNOWING

As opposed to the senator's desire to "know" what Einstein knows, Einstein puts the emphasis on something totally different when talking about knowledge. In his conversation with Monroe, he compares knowledge and thinking: "Knowledge isn't truth. It's just agreement. You can never understand anything by agreeing, by making definitions. Only turning over the possibilities—that's called thinking. If I say I know, I stop thinking. As long as I keep thinking, I come to understand. That way I might approach some truth."

This is true to the real-life Einstein's belief that imagination is far more important than knowledge. Here he hints at something far more important than mere data collection. The senator's mind is content to collect bits of information as grist for the mill of an unthinking mind. The information he gathers is not thought through or mixed with wisdom, but rather is merely used as fodder to further the causes of his preplanned, unthinking political designs.

DOING VERSUS THINKING

Having proved himself to be an apt thinker, Einstein thinks about his doing as well as his *thinking*. He wonders if his doing (done mainly through his thought) has caused the undoing of others. The senator suggests to him that there comes a point in a man's life when he has to decide what is more important, what he thinks or what he does. Immediately Einstein throws all his calculations out the window to show that his thought is more important. He says that he has thrown his work away four times before, and every time he remembers a little bit more, showing the value of thought over action.

Yet at another level, his actions are more important than his thoughts. His thinking *is* what he does, just as being a sex symbol is what Marilyn does. But what Einstein does with his thinking is used by others to kill. Therefore, by throwing his *doing* out the window, he is preserving his integrity by perhaps keeping his *doing* to himself. But other aspects of his doing are largely hidden from the general public: his reading literary classics, playing Mozart, giving speeches for the Mozart Appreciation Society, fishing, and thinking about God. For him, this part of his doing is just as important as his thinking-doing, yet these comparably mundane actions do not make him what he is as a public figure, it is precisely in these types of actions that he finds his center, the part of him that is preserved from war, exploitation, and delusion. In a sense, Einstein is seeing instead of thinking, much like the Cherokee, who sees Einstein's Cherokee spirit, and who prays at dawn in seeing his center.

REST VERSUS WORK

McCarthy and DiMaggio are the only two driven characters in the story. In fact, they are the only two we see sweating. By contrast, Monroe and Einstein are both much more relaxed and at peace. Einstein doesn't sweat even in his sweatshirt, though the dripping senator complains that it is a "dog of a night." Further removed, the Cherokee seems to be even more at peace, especially during his rooftop experience. This suggests that perhaps there is something peaceful inside toward which the film is pointing.

It seems that those seen working the hardest are the ones the furthest away from this place of rest. One of the curses of humankind is that we must work so hard in order to have periods of peaceful rest. The Book of Genesis tells us that God created the earth in six days, then rested on the seventh. And we, as recipients of this pattern, do as Paul suggests—we participate in the paradox of laboring to enter into rest (Hebrews 4:11). There is a rest appointed for the faithful (Hebrews 4:9–10) and no rest for the wicked (Isaiah 48:22). Whether we labor for the rest or not, the fact that we must work by the sweat of our brow (Genesis 3:19) gives us a feeling that there can be no ultimacy found in immediacy. But at least we can hope for that final resolution. The film points toward a restful place where work and sweat cease at the seat of ultimate peace and rest.

LOOSENESS VERSUS TIGHTNESS

Marilyn's insides, by her husband's description, are loose. Her every pregnancy ends in miscarriage. By contrast, DiMaggio says that he is tight, a sure sign to him of health and fortitude. But while Marilyn's physical insides seem to be falling apart, she is attempting to develop a healthy spiritual inside, through a greater intellectual awareness and through the participation of the wisdom of her newfound guru, the professor.

Her physical looseness bespeaks an ailment leading toward death. But this looseness on another level is positive in the sense that she is philosophically and spiritually loose—that is, more relaxed, closer to a sabbatical center state. While the ballplayer thinks his tightness is a good thing, he doesn't intuit that his tight mentality prevents him from seeing the greater truths of his insignificance.

INTERIOR VERSUS EXTERIOR

The loose-tight polarity is linked to an inside-outside contrast, the exterior and interior are further contrasted in the narrative. While McCarthy and DiMaggio both repeatedly emphasize the importance of exteriority, Monroe and Einstein are trying to draw toward interiority. DiMaggio says of his wife, "It's all bright lights on the outside, and the inside is all tore up." It is as if her body, her image, her fraudulent exploited idolized veneer, continues to run on the power of public plaudits, with no inner life. Yet in her quest, as seen in her dialogue with the professor, she is searching for the inner light. While Marilyn's exterior-interior split is mostly related to her own body and spirit, Einstein's polarity is drawn outward, as in his concern about the neutron bomb. It has the ability to destroy any living matter inside of buildings, but it leaves the exterior structures intact, which no doubt, in McCarthy's viewpoint, is better for real estate investment.

Einstein fears he is working toward destroying this inner center by working so much in the outer. He feels his knowledge is complicitous with the destruction of human beings, the execution of which testifies largely to the killing of the inner human spirit. But someplace in space-time there must be the quiet still point.

TIMELESSNESS VERSUS TIME

Whether with the Christian conception of linear time or the Greek idea of cyclical time, we all, like Augustine in his *Confessions* and *The City of God*, wrestle with the monstrous question of time. So do the characters in our film. Monroe does not have her own watch. It was taken away from her as a child, as is revealed through a flashback. In another flashback we see her given a watch by her husband, but she falls down drunk immediately after receiving it, as if to indicate the sudden limitation temporality places on her. The only time we see her actually use a watch is when, while showing Einstein the theory of relativity, she borrows the chauffeur's watch. When she asks the chauffeur if he has a watch, he begins to tell her the time; she interrupts him and says, "No, don't tell me the time. I just want to borrow it," indicating that her real home is apart from the confines of time. Even Marilyn's calendar picture is fragmented, indicating that her participation in time has torn her to pieces, an image more graphically completed by the ballplayer's tearing the fragmented picture into more fragments, and by the senator's inducing her miscarriage, literally tearing her into fragments.

Einstein has a watch, but it is stopped at 8:15, precisely the time his electromagnet terminated its time in his childhood, precisely the time during which the first atomic bomb was exploded, and precisely the time when the senator is demanding to meet him for the Senate hearing. This is an indication that Einstein too is out of time, or more appropriately, outside of time.

The ballplayer and the senator seem overly concerned with time and punctuality, much more so than are Monroe and Einstein. Even their respective actions reflect the rhythm of hurried time as each relates to it with his own franticness. The ballplayer tries to hurry his slow-moving wife out of the hotel room, while she lazily lingers until the leisure of the new morn allures more lollygagging. The senator speedily attempts a sexual union, while Einstein and Monroe's almost-union is captured in sacralized, salacious slow motion. The senator insists that Einstein will leave with him at 8:15 in the morning, while Einstein and Monroe casually dally in timeless, meaningful dialogue.

Einstein and Monroe even joke about time, as if they have a handle on eternity. Monroe asks Einstein, "Do you ever get a feeling it's later than you think?," indicating that their psycho-rhythms are out of sync with time-bound chronocrats. Their time is of a rhythm unconnected to the clockwork cudgels of Father Cronos. In slow motion, Monroe's shoulder moves in clockwise motion, meandering in momentous timelessness. But while trying to have union, Einstein and Monroe are blocked by the vicissitudes of voracious time. As people obliged to calendars, appointments, schedules, and timed commitments, their hoped-for union never comes. When she wants to make love with him and he says no, he adds, "But maybe you can visit me at my home." Fearing the long arm of time, she says, "You can never find the time for me." He reassures her, "I do have a great deal of time to offer there." But remembering her own obligation to time, she responds, "Oh. I'm sorry. I have none to offer you beyond tonight. I just thought we could come together somehow in the middle of all this—for an hour or so."

She tries persistently to break through the time barrier again. She asks Einstein, "You're calculating the shape of space, right?," to which he responds, "Yes."

"And when you finish, you will have expressed the precise nature of the physical universe."

"So?"

"So, so do it tomorrow. It will be here. I won't."

Finally, Einstein says to Monroe about one of her earlier concerns, "All who look up feel small and lonely. Does that make you feel better?"

"A little."

"Well, then?"

"Well, then what?"

"What the hell."

So they begin undressing in slow motion, in wonderful anticipation of the union, only to be interrupted by one of the aggressive time merchants, her husband. The contrast between the restless chronocrats and the timeless pilgrims is evident.

Not counting a weekly sabbath, the seventh day, the unrestful six work days in which the antagonists spend their time is the number of man, six, which is half the number of completeness, twelve, which is the number of hours on a clock and the number of hours in a day or a night. The six days of working time correspond to the six areas of space, and like space, time also has a seventh center point of perfection: the sabbath. In time there are past, present, and future, each of which, from a relative standpoint, has two directions, past and future—six altogether. In the center of all of these points is timelessness, where work and sweat cease, and where an eternal, timeless sabbath is found. This is the scintilla, the source of energy, the core of life and existence. It is this center point that is needed for ultimate union to take place. When two people are in sync with this center, they reside in the holy of holies where eternity rules the day and where time ceases to exist.

SPACELESSNESS VERSUS SPACE

Einstein is unsure of his conception of the shape of space or the universe, suggesting it is a "completely solid object being turned inside out indefinitely forever." The ballplayer, on the other hand, is very certain what the shape of the universe is like. Rather than showing a humble uncertainty, he adamantly insists that it is round, "like everything else in nature, like the flowers, the moon, and the sun. It's all based on a circle. Like the world. . . . Columbus and I think it's round. And it's a damn lucky thing for the United States too, 'cause if it wasn't for Columbus we'd all be Indians."

The ballplayer and the senator both show a remarkable affinity for space, like dogs marking their territory with tracks of urine, perhaps to bolster their sense of insecurity within space. Monroe and Einstein, however, know the limitations of space, in Einstein's theoretical formulation thereof, and in Monroe's all-too-personal realization of physical frailty. The latter two seem to be in a quest for a space without such limitations.

Like time, space also is divided into six points with a sabbatical center. In space we have height, width, and depth, each of which has either a fore and an aft, or a high and a low. And again, in the center of space is a still quiet place, an intermediate zone between cosmos and capacity. Like the center of time, the seventh, center point of space is also the place of eternal rest. But for those frantically working in the worldly rhythm of time and space, the center point is often never found.

SPACE-TIME VERSUS CONCRETENESS

While Einstein and Monroe veer toward transcendence, the senator ignorantly asserts, "I've come to the conclusion the shape of space-time is of no fucking importance," indicating his inability to see beyond his concrete limitations. Meanwhile, Einstein and Monroe continue to veer closer to the center of time and space.

While shampooing, Marilyn Monroe draws a star, which provokes a paradoxical question in her quest for space-time. On one hand, the star points to her star status, which is wholly dissatisfactory on a worldly plane. On the other hand, it points to a quest for spirituality, outside of time and space, since the star is a symbol of the spiritual quest.

Once the actress and the professor break through the barriers of space and time, they know the secrets of space-time, where relativity is most essentially realized. She shows him the theory of relativity and he shows her his legs in order to further demonstrate relativity and to further attempt a synchronization of their own constant nonrelative center points. They begin undressing, and Einstein asks her, "Is it late or early?," to which she responds, "It's relative." Unlike their sweating antagonists, these two have managed to some degree to experience mythic time and space. Beyond merely calculating space-time, they seem to participate in this mystical realm, this other-dimensional world on the other side of time and space. Without shoes, without the worldly concerns that so obsess their antagonists, and with a view to higher, inner things, they both are reaching for the beyond, in the middle. This center is the Zen still point. It is what the real-life Einstein calls the "cosmic religious feeling," and what Dante calls "the point whereto all times are present" (Paradiso, XVII, 17). It is the alchemists' scintilla, and Eliade's cosmogonic or "Great Time." The center is the space-time of Mahayana Buddhism, and Ezra Pound's "unwobbling pivot." It is Blake's timeless moment that he calls the "pulsation of an artery," and Keats's paradox of the Grecian urn. It is the ecstatic burning heart of Saint Theresa of Avila, the inner spark felt in the heart of Meister Eckhart, and the secret place of contemplation located by the mystics of both East and West. It is the way out of the Egyptian labyrinth. It is the central zone of the Hindu Wheel of Transformation. The center is Yahweh's still small voice. It is David's still waters, and Jesus' command to the sea: "Peace, be still." In essence, it is the *axis mundi* in the golden age of universal significance.

In addition to having almost consummated a relationship in the still point, both Einstein and Monroe represent spiritual figures reaching for the center. As a man of theory and mercurial dissociation from the things of this world, Einstein is a type of Mercury, a sky god who sometimes touches this time-and-space world, but mostly goes back and forth between the higher and lower planes. He is a unifier, a slippery god with silver wings on his feet instead of shoes. While the senator tries to hold him down to time commitments, he manages to glide past temporal restraints and throws his worldly work out the window, like an ethereal trickster god. Opposed to his adversaries, he's humble, giving grace to others lower than himself. He lives in a world of cosmos and space-time. While trying to unify the fields, he tries to bring time and space toward the center, which is sabbath, rest, or peace.

He is misunderstood and persecuted in time and space, but he's from outside time and space, something to be expected for somebody with his otherworldly stature. The Swiss authorities call him a Fascist. The Germans call him a Zionist conspirator. Others call him a Soviet communist, a warmonger, and a conscientious objector. But he knows better than the rest who he is.

As a woman of the flesh, Marilyn represents corporeality longing for spiritual liberty. While telling the chauffeur that she plays a what instead of a who, the film director juxtaposes her with a whore in the street. Her husband and the senator both insinuate that she is a prostitute, and flashbacks reveal her selling herself in order to get ahead. As a woman of the flesh, she is like the women hanging around Jesus, like Mary Magdalene. As a fallen woman, she wants to have union with the higher master, to meet together in the center. Abused and used as a whore, she wants to produce life but is prevented from it by selfish and brutal people like the senator. Feeling useless in a fraudulent world of celebrated glamour, she tries to use the tool with which she is most familiar to have union with the man she admires the most, her Mercurius-Christ.

CHEROKEE VERSUS AMERICAN

While Einstein and Monroe hint at a quest for the center, the Indian elevator operator laments that he has lost his, having participated for too long in the American life-style. When Einstein gets on his elevator, they talk about space-time centeredness:

103

PORTER: I know you. You're Cherokee.

EINSTEIN: I'm an old fool. You are Cherokee.

PORTER: No. I'm an elevator man. I get a paycheck. I eat a lot of hot dogs. I go up and down.

EINSTEIN: . . . a true Cherokee believes that wherever he is, he is at the center of the universe.

PORTER: But it's hard to believe in an elevator. You go up and down. I watch TV. I'm no longer a Cherokee. But I watch TV. And I see your face, and I hear your thoughts, and so I know, you are Cherokee.

EINSTEIN: No.

PORTER: But the thoughts in your head will lead you there.

Here the genetic Cherokee, whose belief it is to be at the center of the universe, has all but lost his faith. Too many American ascensions and descensions, too many hot dogs and too much television time have robbed him of his space-time, just as Marilyn has been robbed of her soul, and just as Einstein has been robbed of his thinking.

While going up and down all day long, the Cherokee's space is artificially exalted and lowered. But during his break in the morning, he gets a chance to steal away and renew his faith as much as possible in his centeredness.

Contrasted to this man of faith who humbly disqualifies himself as Cherokee are the two prime examples of Americanism, the senator and the ballplayer. Their religion is that of the great westward Columbian white hope, heirs of the conquerors of the Cherokee. Instead of being localized in a center, their religion is one of ever-expanding conquest. The American dream, manifest destiny, rugged individualism, Yankee ingenuity, and the spirit of the conquistador, the cowpuncher, the cavalry, and the commanders of the western frontiers who conquered the Cherokee are all parts of the spirit of these all-Americans. The juxtaposition between Americanism and Cherokee centeredness is illustrated with a picture of the American flag flying outside the hotel window. An eerie, electronically amplified voice forever repeats the patriotic lyrics of the hymn "America" as we feel the gnawing inner frustrations of our protagonists, almost as if they wished they were Cherokee.

Especially after reflecting on his conversations with both the Cherokee and the ballplayer, Einstein speculates on the contrast between the two. In his speculation, he also reflects on relativity and the quiet place:

> What I would like to do is to go to some quiet place and slip over the edge of the world the way Columbus never did, unfortunately. You know what your husband said? "If Columbus had done it, we'd all be Indians"—Cherokee. But instead, what are we? Americans, and look at us. He's the most knowledgeable; I'm this much knowledgeable. He's got the most power; I have very little power. She's this beautiful; I'm this beautiful. They will not take responsibility for their world. They want to put it on the shoulders of a few.

While the genetic Cherokee has lost some of his faith, true to his observation, Einstein is more Cherokee than he realizes. And Monroe is certainly trying to reach that inner peace as well.

When conveying their mythology, Native Americans speak of a perennial now. Their oral traditions are void of past or future tenses (Brown). A true Cherokee, therefore, is in the cosmic sabbath. This faith is removed from American star-status or self-aggrandizement; rather, it is a humble reverence for the things of true significance. And it includes taking responsibility for one's own thoughts and actions.

SIGNIFICANCE VERSUS INSIGNIFICANCE

The obvious illustrations of insignificance are seen in the ballplayer's baseball card series and in the senator's suggestion to the drunk in the bar that when one drinks a glass of water there is a good chance one might be drinking a piece of Napoleon's crap.

There are obviously various points of view expressed throughout the narrative, including one where Marilyn says of her wind machine experience, "This is delicious," whereupon the director on the set says, "That's an interesting point of view." The technician looks up at the stars and feels elated. The Indian looks down on the American street and laughs. The protagonists and antagonists seem to look at one another and laugh. But the look that is only hinted at is the inward one.

Einstein and Monroe realize that people look at their exteriors and make stars of them. Their interior is thought of as insignificant by the starmakers and the stargazers. What the star addicts don't realize, however, is that the external star is an illusion, a veneer of brilliance. What is not seen is the inner star, the hidden mystic spark. The seemingly insignificant inner spark, which the Cherokee sees in Einstein and which Einstein and Monroe see in each other, is actually the source of all life. This divine internal spark is being slowly destroyed in the American psyche as a result of the continued emphasis placed on the glorious external. The image of people being destroyed within buildings while the external structures remain is a fitting symbol of what is going on socio-psychically.

Einstein fears this ability to blow up the significant interior while leaving the insignificant exterior. For it is the internal center that is the constant in relation to the variables of external relativity. It is the significant interior that confers ultimate meaning rather than fraudulent stardom and death. Monroe and Einstein share their exteriors with one another, that is, they share what is variable and relative. What they do not share is what is not seen by either, what is not relative: their significant centers. Monroe's hidden interior is her torn-up inside, and more importantly, her quest for spirituality; Einstein's is his inner appreciation of literature and the arts, fishing, and God.

While Monroe and a neutron bomb detonation are analogies of one another, and both are analogies of insignificance, Einstein is a space-time mystic who sees beyond the illusion of physics. Monroe continues to operate almost like a building void of people, like a body with no spirit. Yet deep within her, in the midst of her internal physical sickness and in the midst of her star-sickness, her spirit has not completely died. It is her barely living centered spirit that is wise enough to attempt relative sharing with another kindred spirit. And it is Einstein's spirit that meets, in a relative sort of way, another spirit, with some cryptic and solemn words about the invariable center, to which all things are relative.

In the world of relativity, Einstein is the best thinker and Monroe is the best sex symbol. Yet he is not his thoughts, nor is she her sexuality. These externals are relative. What is not relative is their inner lives. What stays the same is not the clock but the focal point: who it is that *looks* at the clock. They are bigger than time and space. There *is* no time and space except as it relates to each of them as invariable internal constants around which their respective relative universes revolve. The point is to find that which remains in the midst of what is changing and relative. As Marilyn says, "I just thought we could come together somehow in the *middle* of all of this." The insignificance is everything that is relative—time, space, and how each person views the other, especially in our delusional conceptions of exteriors. What is significant is individuals living in a universe of insignificance. This is the inner significance that deals with the insignificant external world.

When one looks up at the stars, especially considering the relative insignificance our little planet has in relation to our galaxy, and further, how insignificant our little galaxy is in relation to the universe, it makes one feel small in relation to the vast cosmos. Pondering this causes one to question the significance of one's thoughts and actions. What effect do my relatively insignificant thoughts and actions have on a universe so vast? If I am that insignificant, like "all who look up," then what difference are my thoughts and actions going to make? Is my presence here merely an insignificant accident

107

of the cosmos, or do I have significance? If my thoughts and actions are mere quarks in a monstrous universe, then what impact will they have on my tiny corner of the cosmos? The senator might ask, "Furthermore, what's a mere nuclear explosion in relation to such a vast universe?"

A YEAR OF THE
QUIET SUN

AMAZING GRACE

W riter and director Krzysztof Zanussi based his 1985 film *A Year of the Quiet Sun* on the ancient folkloric sabbatical year known as the year of the quiet sun. The story takes place in postwar Poland, in 1946. An American military unit is sent to the site of a Nazi POW camp to investigate the whereabouts of American pilots missing in action.

THE CHARACTERS

Norman

One of the survivors of the camp, middle-aged Norman (Scott Wilson), volunteers for this mission and falls in love with a poor Polish widow, Emilia (Maja Komorowska). Though outward circumstances do not paint Emilia as a good catch, and though seemingly insurmountable obstacles would prevent their ultimate union, Norman persists in his unyielding love. He brings Emilia and her mother gifts, and he proposes marriage and happiness to Emilia, with a promise that her mother will be taken care of as well, with his love, and with provisions through his farming.

Emilia

We learn that Emilia was happy for a brief few months in her life, during her short marriage, which was broken by her husband's death. She is lovingly devoted to her aging and ailing mother. She is legally bound to stay in the now Communist state of Poland. It might take her a long time to get official verification of her husband's death before being legally free to marry again. Besides the outward circumstances that seem to keep her bound, she has trouble accepting inner freedom. Opposed to her judgmental mother, Emilia extends unconditional love toward others, while refusing it for herself.

The Mother

The mother (Hanna Skarzanka) is very gracious to her daughter and to Norman, but quite judgmental toward the prostitute across the hall and to Germans in general. From the beginning of the story and throughout, she expresses a desire to die, saying she has had enough of living in her state of sickness.

Stella

Across the hall from Emilia and her mother lives Stella (Ewa Dalkowska), a prostitute who apparently survived a concentration camp by providing sex to the SS men. She extends grace to the mother on her deathbed, and, opposed to Emilia, freely accepts grace.

THE MORALITY PLAY

The film opens with a train ride of postwar repatriated Poles coming back to their homeland. Emilia and her mother are on this crowded freight train, and we see Emilia dressing her mother's leg infection. Sitting by them are a nun, a child, and a man who we later find out is one of the local police officials in the women's town. Mother complains about being taken care of and would rather die. Emilia suggests that they should leave that decision to God. Her mother's response is, "But why? Christ died on the cross because he wanted to, not because he had to. So why can't we die when we want?" This opening conversation introduces an argument that runs in different forms throughout the narrative and that concerns choice, freedom, grace, and death. Eventually we discover the motivation of the mother's desire to die. It is an act of grace on her part, in order to set her daughter free.

Shortly thereafter we gain a new perspective of this gracious mother. While in their dilapidated apartment, the women disagree on a related issue. Talking about the prostitute living next door, the mother suggests that she should be shorn of her hair, the ancient religious treatment for prostitutes. In the same conversation, the mother heaps harsh judgment upon Germans. Emilia responds by saying, "They don't shave heads anymore. . . . Germans are human too." The mother rejoins with, "I know you're talking just to spite me. . . . You justify everything because you don't believe in justice." Emilia argues, "Better to justify than to judge." Immediately after this disagreement, the whore hollers over for a light, and Emilia graciously responds. In their theological split, the old mother represents the harshness of the Mosaic law, and the daughter represents the grace of a new covenant.

Norman first happens upon his love while she is painting in an abandoned car, an apt picture of beauty created out of ruin, or grace hiding in suffering. He finds out where she lives and shows up uninvited with a gift of paints for her. While he extends grace to her, she reluctantly accepts it, and only at her mother's urging. Here again their attitudes toward grace are juxtaposed, but now from the angle of receiving. The mother freely accepts grace in this case and encourages her daughter to do the same. The daughter, while adept at extending grace toward others, all but refuses it for herself. The soldier fixes their phonograph; the mother calls him a sweetheart and says, "If only I weren't so old," wishing she could receive the grace her daughter refuses.

They eat some sweet pork rations he has brought, and the women giggle as children over the meal. Perhaps there is a cultural explanation, hidden to most American viewers, of why they find sweet pork so funny. Whatever the reason, the pork reminds us of a biblical juxtaposition between law and grace. Pigs are forbidden meat under the Hebrew covenant. In the Christian dispensation however, along with other formerly forbidden foods, they are allowed. In the book of Acts the Apostle Peter has a dream wherein all manner of forbidden animals, including pigs, are let down from heaven on a large sheet, and he is commanded to eat of this new food, as an analogy of reaching out to the formerly forbidden Gentiles. Thus the laughter over the sweet pork symbolizes a breaking free from the law, into a dispensation of grace. What the mother and daughter can not laugh over in reality, they laugh over symbolically, and perhaps subconsciously. The mother, as an archetype of the law, judges the Germans, as the Gentiles are judged by the Mosaic covenant. The daughter, as an archetype of grace, accepts the Germans and the sinners, who are symbolized by swine.

The women's apartment is invaded by two groups of threes. First, three thugs rob their money, wreak havoc of their home, and rough them up. Then, after Norman arrives, three children enter their ransacked living room, singing a carol and carrying a homemade nativity scene. Here, with more biblical symbolism, we see a reversal of the gospel nativity. Instead of three kings bearing gifts of gold, franckincense, and myrrh, three authoritarian bandits rob what little gold the women possess. And instead of three adoring shepherds, three children also come to receive, but through grace instead of by force. The theological implications provided here are that power receives by force, and asking receives by grace. It is as if we are reading an epistle wherein Saint Paul, a former doctor of the law, likens the powerful law to that which takes away, as contrasted with the words of his master, who says, "Ask and ye shall receive."

Whether for profit or as a gift, we don't know, but Emilia takes some home-baked pastries to an unappreciative local police official who loudly complains to her, "Why so little? When will there be more?" She probably has not told him that a batch of her pastries and most of her ingredients were thrown on the floor by the abusive robbers. Contrasted with this complaining police official is Norman, who gladly partakes of Emilia's pastries, knowing very well how to receive. Of course bread is also highly symbolic of the sacrament of sacrificial giving, as the bread of life. Here, the policeman, a signifier of the law, ungraciously receives grace, in contrast with Norman, himself a representative of grace, who graciously receives the symbol of grace.

Since Norman and Emilia do not speak each other's language, and since Norman is so intent on communicating his deepest feelings to her, he finds an interpreter, who is apparently a junior member of the local postwar military regime. Unsympathetic, he jumbles their communication to ill effect, and the language-separate couple breaks out in laughter in front of him, while he fails to see the humor of it all. Norman later finds another potential translator, who happens to be German, one of the prostitute's boyfriends. But this time, because he still has residual anger toward his German captors, Norman himself fails to break through his own inner barrier. Through the local priest Emilia finds a translator in one of the local parish nuns. This kind sister also mistranslates, but for the good instead of for ill. This time, despite benevolent translation, and despite gracious offers by the good-hearted Norman, Emilia fails to break through her own inner barrier. Thus language is an analogy for division, as sharp as the barbed-wire fence of the POW camp, and as separate as the division between judgment and grace.

In the midst of this story of unbridged chasms and juxtaposed theologies, Emilia asks her priest in her confusion, "Father, I don't know what to hold on to anymore. . . . Does a human have a right to happiness?" She thus verbalizes her own paradox of being able to give freely but being unable to receive.

At one point we suspect that perhaps Emilia has learned to receive when she allows herself the luxury of making love with her suitor. This episode takes place in a dilapidated upper portion of her war-torn building, partly exposed to the elements, a picture symbolically

Stella the prostitute, as opposed to Emilia, freely gives and receives grace.

similar to her painting in the war-torn car. Despite her short consummation with grace, her heart remains unaccepting.

The obstacles preventing Norman and Emilia from uniting grow
greater toward the end of the film. The man who promises to sneak
mother and daughter across the border doubles the price, and mother
pays him all the money she has before she kills herself with a planned
exposure to cold and a refusal of much-needed penicillin. A dog barks
when Mother dies, reflecting the folkloric hour of the wolf. Emilia
finds the passage man, discovers there is fare paid for only one, and
gives the right of passage to Stella, the prostitute, since Stella was
robbed of her passage money by a customer while lovingly ministering to the dying, judgmental mother. Emilia tells Stella, "Mother made
me a present. But I don't want anything."

Rejecting grace, Emilia tells Norman that happiness can be found
"even in suffering," as opposed to Norman, who says he was an empty
man with no purpose until he met Emilia, a person to whom he can
give. Norman is transferred to Germany and tells Emilia, "Tell me
about it in Berlin."

Before Norman departs for the last time, the unlikely couple embrace in the side room of a dance hall. One of the local officials sneaks in on them and says to her in Polish, "I see you." "What do you see?" she asks. With the weight of the law behind him, he warns, "If you think you can leave with him without permission from the authorities . . ." "You have no authority over me," she says, "You only think you do." Here her suffering takes on scriptural significance, as she echoes the words of Jesus, who, when questioned by the secular authorities just before laying down his life for others, says, "You have no authority over me, except what has been given you from above. I lay my life down willingly." And here we are also reminded of Emilia's mother, who gives up her life for her daughter and who also echoes the gospel when she says that Christ died "because he wanted to, not because he had to."

Stella escapes across the border, and Norman waits for Emilia at the appointed time at the train station in Berlin. She doesn't get off the train. Norman sings "Amazing Grace" the entire time of his wait there, as if intuiting the fuller implications of the hymn's lyrics.

At the end of the film we see Emilia in 1964, in a church-run adult care center, as an aged, gray woman. The mother superior gets a phone call announcing that Emilia has been given a considerable sum of money from an unknown person in the states, and that she can receive part of the money immediately to go to America. A cab is called. She packs her bag; when it is time to go, she stumbles, and we are given a dreamy scene of a younger Emilia and Norman dancing in Monument Valley in Arizona. This recalls two previous scenes, one of them doing the same dance at the Polish dance hall, and another where Mother, in anticipation of Emilia's trip to America, reminisces on her deathbed to Norman of a scene she saw of Monument Valley in the film *Stagecoach*.

AMAZING GRACE

Although Zanussi leaves no overtly observable clue about the quiet sun in his tale, we do know about this principle, like other themes in his story, from the Jewish Bible. In essence, it is the thread of grace interwoven through the harshness of the law. Every seventh year, like every seventh day, is to be a year of rest. During the sabbatical year, there was to be no planting or reaping, which was designed to guarantee a perpetual replenishment of the land. Debts were to be forgiven and slaves were to be set free during this time (Exodus 21). After seven sabbaticals, there was a year of jubilee, which was cause for even greater grace and celebration, including the reversion of all property to its original owner.

Poland was invaded by the Germans in 1939. After seven years of occupation and war, we would assume 1946 (the year Norman meets Emilia) to be a year of the quiet sun, or a sabbatical year, when grace is extended and the captives are set free. Yet while Emilia is free to be

Everyone's offer of grace is accepted but Norman's.

liberated, she is also free to suffer for Stella's sake, just as her mother is free to suffer for Emilia's sake, and just as the American pilots were free to suffer for the women's sakes, and just as the women's spiritual liberator, Jesus, was free to suffer for their sakes.

Emilia receives her second chance of liberation in 1964, eighteen years after 1946 and thus not during a year of the quiet sun, not during a year of grace. When she makes an attempt to accept grace at this time, she stumbles.

So here we have several different ways of dealing with law and grace. Both Stella and Norman freely give and receive. Perhaps the victimization they endure inspires a release of grace in both directions. Mother gives conditionally, that is, only to those she deems worthy of grace. And she also receives conditionally, that is, if it doesn't prevent her from conditionally giving. Emilia has learned from her mother's example, but unlike her mother, she gives freely, even to those who don't deserve grace. And, more extreme than her mother, she does not receive at all, so that she may extend all the more grace to others.

The two different scenes of laughter, one over the sweet pork and the other over the mistranslation, speak of the renewal of grace after a period of bondage. Laughter, being a harbinger of newness, is a herald of the year of the quiet sun. Emilia can laugh only briefly, unable fully to participate in the complete cycle of renewal, feeling bound only to intermittent periods of grace.

We might look at this story as an unfortunate tragedy on the surface. Yet if it were not for Emilia's sacrificial giving, Stella would not have been saved from her potentially disastrous life in Poland, where the Communist officials despised her as a whore to the Nazis. We are not told who it was in the states that sent Emilia the money. It could have been Stella, a recipient of grace. When speaking of the Polish authority at the dance hall, Emilia tells Norman, "He doesn't understand anything"—much like many in our society who have forgotten the sabbatical year. In our selfish age of obsessive pain avoidance, this tale of grace is a welcome morality play. Emilia's suffering is her passion play, which extends compassion to others.

SHANE

THE AMBIVALENT, VIOLENT
PRINCE OF PEACE

As an archetypal American western, *Shane* inspired the naming of hundreds of American boys for a generation. Directed by George Stevens, with the title role played by Alan Ladd, this 1953 film ranks as a memorable classic. In the tradition of the lone western hero come to save a community of homesteaders, *Shane* is a paragon of the pattern. Shane, a cosmic drifter, has come from nowhere and is bound nowhere. In his words, he is headed "one place or another; someplace I never been." Similarly, the hero of the 1940 film *The Westerner*, Cole Hardin (Gary Cooper), says of his home, "My house is out there, with a sky for a roof." As to where Shane is headed, we only know it is "north." When he leaves little Joey (Brandon De Wilde) behind, he says, "I gotta be goin' on," leaving his immediate destination open-ended. But when the domestic Mariam (Jean Arthur) laments that they will never see him again, he says, "Never is a long time, Mariam," as if to hint that they will meet at the pass in the great western by and by.

The western hero rarely becomes domesticated. He lives between the sagebrush and civilization, between the desert and the den, belonging to neither world. He is like a lone, quiet god come from out of time as an answered prayer to those within time. We see this literally in Megan's prayer for a miracle in the 1985 Clint Eastwood film *Pale Rider*.

Shane lives between the sagebrush and civilization, between the desert and the den.

The subgenre of westerns of which *Shane* is a part can be called the range war western, the rancher-nester western, or the cattleherder-homesteader western, with the richer and more powerful beef contractors dominating and intimidating the poorer farmers. The dominant party in *Shane* is Ryker (Emile Meyer), a wealthy, land-hungry miser. In *The Westerner*, Judge Roy Bean (Walter Brennan), a pathetically corrupt lawman, sides with the rich cattle constituency. Judge Bean is law, judge, jury, executioner, *and* bar proprietor. In Michael Cimino's *Heaven's Gate* (1980), the evil force is concentrated in the Stock

Growers' Association, which is determined to exterminate the majority of the farmers. In *Pale Rider*, the split is found between the poor miners and the wealthy owner of a large mining company, appropriately named Le Hood.

The formula is a relatively simple one. The hardworking, beleaguered farmers are constantly harassed and intimidated by the wealthy community regime. The idea is to force the farmers to give up their claim so the cattle boss can have more land for open range. There is usually one individual or one family who encourages the discouraged settlers to rally together. At least one other family either leaves or attempts to leave and is talked into staying. Then there is one hotheaded individual within the group that fatally stands up to the beast through a combination of alcohol and naive bravado. This victim's death causes a greater split within the camp of the homesteaders, some vowing to leave in fear, and some angered into fighting.

At this point the ringleader of the oppressed is singled out by the ruling monarch as an unwanted obstacle in his path of total occupation. The principal farmer is offered a sizable buy-out. But conscience rules over avarice, and the offer is refused. Sometimes the quiet, new, and still largely unproven hero is also offered a large sum of money, which of course is also refused. Righteousness and loyalty prove to be stronger than blood money.

Sometimes even political corruption enters into the formula. The ruling elite sometimes has the law on its side, as in *Heaven's Gate* and *Pale Rider*. In *The Westerner* the ruling elite *is* the law. When all attempts at intimidation, financial offers, legal threats, and supposed negotiation fail, the selfish beast resorts to greater violence. This could include the burning or stampeding of the farmers' fields, the burning down of their houses, or ultimately, the contract killing of the principal farmer or the outside hero.

Of course the hero saves the day; otherwise he wouldn't be a hero. The preacher in *Pale Rider* guns down the crooked law officer and his gunslinging deputies. Gary Cooper in *The Westerner* wins a shootout with Judge Roy Bean. The cavalry comes to the rescue in the all-out range war of *Heaven's Gate*. And in the classic shootout in Grafton's saloon, Shane kills the hired gun, Jack Wilson (Jack Palance), boss Ryker, and, with the help of little Joey, Ryker's brother.

But much to the sadness of little Joey, Shane rides off into the night, probably never to be seen again. Joey's voice echoes off the mountains bordering the now peaceful valley, "Shane! Shane! Come back, Shane!" These words have echoed in the ears of an entire generation who saw this film as children.

MYTHICAL ELEMENTS

While *Shane* plays out a common western movie motif, it also carries more ancient mythical elements of a drama far older and more numinous than the inspiration of the filmic narrative. The domestic and generative family motif in *Shane*, as in the other films of its genre, is contrasted sharply with the money-grubbing bachelor king. The names of the central family in *Shane*, Joe and Mariam, like Jof and Mia of *The Seventh Seal* and like George and Mary of *It's a Wonderful Life*, echo the Holy Family and signify purity, faithfulness, hard work, domestic fruitfulness, and godliness. The family archetypally represents wholesomeness, tranquillity, peace, and prosperity through productivity. The enemy is usually without a family, indicating faithfulness to none other than himself, by whom any peace or prosperity comes through force or avarice. The threat to family life is a threat of the slaughter of innocents, which precipitates a night journey. In the Jewish Bible, it is the pharaonic command that all of the Hebrew newborn be slain, so they will not outnumber and eventually overpower the ruling Egyptians. In the Christian Bible, the Roman ruler makes a similar command in order to kill the rumored newborn king of Israel. But in *Shane* the night journey is circumvented by the arrival of the saving hero. The holy family is sheltered from the wrath of the evil monarch by the intervention of the Moses-Joshua—a divine deliverer and warrior who ensures the safety of the family, and thus of generativity.

When Ryker sends a message to Joe Starrett (Van Heflin) requesting his presence at the saloon, Starrett accepts the invitation and pulls out his six-gun for the first time in the story. At the time, Shane is sitting at the table with little Joey, showing him a false square knot, and telling him that it will not hold, symbolizing a grander, more ominous knot. Simultaneously, one of Ryker's men, Chris Calloway, has a conversion experience, and he rides over to tell Shane of the trap into which Starrett is headed: a meeting with the greatly feared Wilson (Jack Palance). This hired gun from Cheyenne drinks coffee instead of whiskey, no doubt to add to his evil sharpness. When he walks, even the dog gets up and moves away with his tail between his legs. We are reminded of the passage of the evil one in the book of Revelation: "And the beast gave him his power."

After wearing his farmer's work clothes throughout most of the narrative, Shane again dons his buckskin outfit and his six-shooter. He is determined to stop Starrett from sacrificing himself against a much faster draw. He stands in Joe's doorway, and the two of them engage in a vicious battle. Here we see Jacob (Starrett) wrestling with the angel of God. While determined to do his own bidding, Joe fights his toughest battle, this time with the good guy, and loses. Shane finally has to knock him out and set his horse free in order to fight his fight for him.

As Shane rides into town he passes three trees at the outskirts, indicating the three trees of sacrifice. Then he walks boldly into the bar and kills the three main bad guys, terminating the false square knot.

CAIN AND ABEL

While *Shane* is the story of a western range war, it is also an archetypal story of the hunter versus the gatherer, or the shepherd versus the planter. Played out repeatedly in history and in mythology, the story is as old as that of Cain and Abel. The opposing factions in *Shane* are separated into the following archetypal enmities.

CAIN	ABEL
gatherers	hunters
planters	shepherds
farmers	cattleherders
nesters	ranchers
vegetarians	meat eaters
meal culture	blood culture
villagers	barbarians
indentured servants	aristocracy
individual proletarians	corporate capitalists
partnership culture	dominator culture
matriarchal	patriarchal
ignorance/enlightenment economy	debt/payment economy
domesticators	warriors

The opening scene of *Shane* is of a docile deer drinking water and eating shrubbery on the Starrett farm. Little Joey pretends to shoot this herbivorous animal imitating the carnivorous side of the mythic split. Then Shane rides onto the farm—the man with one foot in both worlds. A gunfighter apparently looking for a life of peaceful domesticity, he is unable to leave completely the life of violence. His ambivalence is reflected in, on the one hand, his attraction to the Starrett family life, and on the other hand, his training little Joey how to draw a six-gun. After observing Joey watching him, Shane smiles and says, "I like a man who watches things around. Means he'll make his mark some day," as if to hint that perhaps Joey will be a shooter as well.

Shane's first experience in the local saloon as a gunless farmhand leaves him humiliated, due to his passive acceptance of violence directed at him. His last two experiences leave him the unanimous victor in the range war. At the end of the film, after killing the town badmen, his ambiguity comes out again as he tells Joey that he has to be goin' on: "A man has to be what he is, Joey. You can't break the mold. I tried it, and it didn't work for me, Joey. There's no living for the killing. There's no going back for more."

What does he mean by this? The first part is clear. He tried to break the mold of his gunfighter nature by attempting domesticity, but duty

123

Ryker the selfish cattleherder is a figure of Abel. Starrett the farmer is a figure of Cain.

bound him to further violence for a righteous cause. But then he says, "There's no living for the killing. There's no going back for more," implying that he can't go back to the gunfighter life-style either. Yet he can't break the mold of the gunfighter in him. Ever in a state of ambivalence, fighting the two worlds within his own soul, he exits the picture just as he entered it, with unanswered questions, as a timeless mystery man—a paradoxical man of violence who kills for peace. Shane the man of peace bears the double-edged philosophical sword that kills with one edge and heals with the other. Thus he carries within himself the eternal question of just war. Likewise, the Prince of Peace in the Christian Bible is painted as one with an awesome sense of peace and passive acceptance of violence on one hand, and as an angry vandalizer of the corrupt temple on the other—a man of ambiguity, recognizing the innate connection between violence and peace.

To further elucidate this internal conflict, let us first look at the progenitor of this conflict—a watershed of human violence—the story of Cain and Abel:

> And Adam knew Eve his wife; and she conceived, and bare Cain, and said, I have gotten a man from the Lord. And she again bare his brother Abel. And Abel was a keeper of sheep, but Cain was a tiller of the ground. And in process of time it came to pass, that Cain brought of the fruit of the ground an offering unto the Lord. And Abel, he also brought of the firstlings of his flock and of the fat thereof. And the Lord had respect unto Abel and to his offering; but unto Cain and to his offering he had not respect. And Cain was very angry, and his countenance fell. And the Lord said unto Cain, Why art thou angry? And why is thy countenance fallen? If thou doest well, shalt thou not be accepted? And if thou doest not well, sin lieth at the door. And unto thee shall be his desire, and thou shalt rule over him. And Cain talked with Abel his brother. And it came to pass, when they were in the field, that Cain rose up against Abel his brother, and slew him.
>
> And the Lord said unto Cain, Where is Abel thy brother? And he said, I know not; am I my brother's keeper? And he said, What hast thou done? the voice of thy brother's blood crieth unto me from the ground. And now art thou cursed from the earth, which hath opened her mouth to receive thy brother's blood from thy hand; When thou tillest the ground, it shall not henceforth yield unto thee its strength; a fugitive and a wanderer shalt thou be in the earth. And Cain said unto the Lord, My punishment is greater than I can bear. Behold, thou hast driven me out this day from the face of the earth; and from thy face shall I be hidden; and I shall be a fugitive and a wanderer in the earth; and it shall come to pass, that any one that findeth me shall slay me. And the Lord said unto him, Therefore whosoever slayeth Cain, vengeance shall be taken on him sevenfold. And the Lord set a mark upon Cain, lest any finding him should kill him.
>
> And Cain went out from the presence of the Lord, and dwelt in the land of Nod, on the east of Eden. (Genesis 4:1–16)

The first thing we notice about this story is that Cain is a tiller of the soil and his brother Abel is a shepherd. This watershed separation of cultures and philosophies marks a grand split between two entirely different ways of viewing human existence. More important, God looks favorably on the blood sacrifices of Abel, and he does not respect the fruit offering of the farmer Cain. Yahweh, the patriarchal deity that he is, is a jealous god, one that demands complete obedience, exclusive worship, and blood sacrifice. Because Cain's vegetable offering is not satisfactory, he sacrifices his own meaty brother.

Significantly, Abel's blood crys from the mouth of the earth, whom God calls "her" in some translations. While the patriarchate demands the blood of a meat offering on a phallic stone altar, the matriarchate demands blood in her vulvic, earthy mouth. But both demand blood. As René Girard writes, "violence is the heart and secret soul of the sacred" (Girard 1972, 31). When feeling unacceptable to the ruling order, Cain resorts to his own form of sacrifice—fratricide for the matriarchate, suggesting a possible shift of paradigm. In Shane's ambivalent sense of allegiance, he lusts for the smell of patriarchal gunsmoke on the one hand and spills the blood of his gunslinging brothers for the peace of the matriarchal valley on the other hand. Like Cain, he ends up a wanderer, in the land of Nod, east of Eden.

John Steinbeck's novel *East of Eden* is another story of the primeval brother conflict. Steinbeck's Cain, Cal (James Dean), in the film version also lacks a sufficient patriarchal offering; he reaches out to the absent mother as a way of attaining sacrificial sufficiency and peace.

In the Jewish Bible, the newcomer is usually favored over the older settler. Abel, the secondborn, the shepherd, is favored over Cain, the firstborn farmer. Elsewhere in scripture, Isaac is favored over his older brother, Ishmael. Jacob receives father Isaac's blessing intended for the older brother, Esau. And Joseph is favored over all his older brothers. This is all parallel to the larger story of the ancient Hebrews, a nomadic band of shepherds who invaded the land of Canaan, inhabited by the descendants of Cain, a domestic, agricultural people.

Joe Starrett, a spiritual Canaanite in *Shane*, reminds Ryker the cattleherder/invader that the cattle boss wasn't the first person in the territory. Trappers and Indian traders were there before him, and of course Indians were there before them. But Ryker, as a lord of the invading new horde, lays claim to the entire territory—even that of the planters, those derisively called sodbusters, squatters, and pig farmers by the ruling elite—where justice is meted out by "Judge Colt and his jury of six."

In mythology and in history, hunters are by and large warriors, as opposed to their more domesticated kin, the planters. Being nomadic and invading, their exclusive, masculine religion does not allow them to settle down into a restful life of domesticity. Being on the warpath allows no time to plant and wait for the natural fruit of the earth. Pillaging the spoils of those peoples who have labored in the earth is their forte.

One such blood deity that presides over one of these ancient cultures was Zagreus, known as the Great Hunter, who stood for an insatiable incontinence of desire, having previously been consumed himself by the Titans. The great Teutonic god Wotan, the commander of the Furious Host and the leader of the Wild Hunt, also is among the male deities who lust for blood and war.

The feminine counterpart of this ethos is settlement, agriculture, and participation in the natural cycles of Mother Earth, wherein the secrets of death and rebirth are revealed in the work of farming. The farmer, as a participant in these natural cycles, is a catalyst for the natural forces of regeneration. Farming gives rise to a belief in spiritual regeneration, since the primitive farmer sees a connection between the death and rebirth of seeds and that of human souls. While the feminine chthonic attitude would seem to be more peace-oriented, there are violent, bloodthirsty female deities as well as pillaging and murderous male ones. For the primitives devoted to some of these female deities, a male corn king is often demanded as fecundating blood sacrifice for the assurance of fertility. The folk song "John Barleycorn Must Die," still with us to this day, is a remnant of this ancient tradition of human fertility sacrifice.

While there are similarities between the hunters and planters, especially in terms of sacred sacrifice, one of their main differences lies in their respective views of time. The hunters and shepherds are more in tune with the cycle of the masculine sun, wherein very little variance rules their short daily cycle. The gatherers and planters, on the other hand, participate more with the feminine cycles of the moon and the earth. The rhythm of the masculine sun is short and repetitive compared to the longer, seasonal, changing rhythms of the feminine moon and earth.

A fixation on one cycle to the exclusion of the other produces a mythology that is unbalanced, like Ryker's. His solar "religion" dictates a quick and forceful attainment of goals, almost as if seasons and patience to wait for crops do not exist. A complete fixation in the feminine cycle, however, is not necessarily any better. Mariam Starrett's belief in a complete absence of violence is sometimes a naive hope in an unrealistic world. The middle alternative is the ambivalence of Shane—vacillating between peaceful, cyclical participation and righteous indignation, he brings about peace through violence.

TWINS, THE DOUBLE, AND THE MONSTER

The antagonists in *Shane* are separated by profession, attitude, and by a cyclical brand of religion. But at a deeper level, the antagonists of this range war, just as the antagonists of most wars, are more alike than they are different. The Western progenitors of war, Cain and Abel, were brothers. Elsewhere, brothers are at the fountainhead of cultural rifts worldwide. The Egyptian Osiris and Set, the Persian Ahuramazda and Angramainyu, the Greek Eteodes and Polyneices, the Roman Romulus and Remus, the Slav Bielbog and Chernobog, the English Richard the Lionhearted and John Lackland, the Iroquois Hawneyn and Hanegoasegeh, are all antagonistic brother pairs, progenitors of human conflict for their respective cultural heirs.

This split doppelgänger effect, while often pointing to the bifurcated human soul, shows up frequently in literature. Huck Finn and Tom Sawyer are like Esau and Jacob, the hairy man of the wilderness and the smooth man of civility. This internal conflict can also be seen in Shakespeare's *Comedy of Errors*, Thomas Mann's *Transposed Heads*, Graham Greene's *Ministry of Fear*, and Patrick White's *Solid Mandala*.

While it is human nature to make a foreign Satanic monster of the enemy, this demonizing of the foe is usually the projection of our own demons onto our brother. That's why it is so easy for civil wars to break out in countries that have not yet come to grips with their own internal darkness. Even after a civil war, not having learned their lessons, some nations still must project their demons onto foreign foes, never recognizing the fundamental truth that our enemy's aggression could very well stem from our own oppression. We overlook this because it is a rare person, including those in political leadership, who has reconciled the warring brothers within his own soul. If one has enough largeness to see one's own smallness, then one can employ the humility to act in a large way—in humble confidence.

When Shane walks into the saloon to face Ryker and Wilson, he first confronts Ryker and, acknowledging the shadowy violence within his own soul, says, "Your kinda days are numbered, Ryker." Ryker responds, "My days? What about yours, gunfighter?" Instead of denying the short cycle of his masculine solar religion, Shane humbly admits his participation in violent, numbered exclusivity. He answers, "The difference is, I know it." A man of ambivalence, he is comfortable in both spheres of existence. Unlike Ryker and Wilson, Shane recognizes that the monster is the brother, and more than that, that the monster-brother is the internal double—that eternal, internal struggle between those normally unrecognizable opposites within the individual and collective human soul.

WAR

We have seen the difference in attitude between the meat hunters and the seed planters. We recognize in them the poles of two seemingly different religions, internally related. When we ponder the contrast between Ryker's war of avaricious aggression and the settlers' love of domesticity, how is one in little Joey's position, to come to a healthy, balanced concept of division and of war? Certainly Ryker's oppressive aggression seems evil, but haven't millions of people throughout history, while considering themselves righteous people, managed to justify colonial imperialism as an inevitable and divinely inspired "manifest destiny," or as a "liberation" of indigenous peoples? On the other hand, complete pacifism like Mariam Starrett's, is still worthy of serious consideration. The philosophies and actions of Gandhi and Martin Luther King, Jr., both adopted largely from the teachings of Jesus, show the positive merits of passive resistance. Spike Lee's *Do the Right Thing* (1989) places the contrasting philosophies of Malcolm X and Martin Luther King, Jr., side by side, as if to say that both have equal value.

Since we are dealing here with religious attitudes in our mythic range war, we must ask: Does religion or religious literature encourage war or peace? Beginning with Western religious literature, we read repeatedly in the Jewish Bible of Yahweh's command for his people to commit genocide on nations worshiping foreign (mainly feminine) deities. The Hebrews are commanded in Deuteronomy, chapter 7 and elsewhere, to "utterly destroy" the tribes in the land of Canaan, and to show them "no mercy." A large part of the Bible is the history of a warring people, assigned to exterminate their older brothers.

The Koran commands followers of Islam to wage war against and to conquer all lands not in the "territory of Islam" (*dar al-Islam*). Such foreign lands are considered "the territory of war" (*dar al-harb*). The history of Islam, especially during its golden age, is largely the history of its warring and conquering spirit.

In the Christian Bible, which is generally recognized as a gospel of peace, in which Jesus commands his followers to love their enemies, we are struck with ambiguous statements such as Jesus' words, "Think not that I am come to send peace on earth; I came not to send peace, but a sword. For I am come to set a man at variance against his father, and the daughter against her mother, and the daughter in law against her mother in law" (Matthew 10:34–35). And while many ambassadors of peace have received their inspiration from the gospel of peace, there have also been many bloody warriors for the cross.

But the West is not the only region that fosters holy war. The *Mahabharata*, thought by many Westerners to be a book of peace, is a war manual also. In it we read, "Might is above right; right proceeds from might, right has its support in might, as living beings in the soil.

As smoke the wind, so right must follow might. Right in itself has no authority; it leans on might as the creeper on the tree" (Book XII).

Possibly as the scriptural text for the film *Heaven's Gate*, we read this in the *Bhagavad Gita*: "To a prince, nothing is better than a righteous war. Happy indeed is the prince to whom such a war comes unsought, offering itself, throwing open heaven's gate" (2:31–32).

From one of the great Eastern war books, the *Book of the Lord Shang*, we read the following Machiavellian passage, which prepares a state for war: "A country where the virtuous govern the wicked will suffer from disorder, so that it will be dismembered; but a country where the wicked govern the virtuous will be orderly, so that it will become strong" (1:12).

The 1960s witnessed thousands of Western youths flocking to the literature of the East, disillusioned with thousands of years of Western imperialism, two world wars, the Cold War, and Vietnam, a war literally between the East and the West. But what many of these eastward converts did not take into account is that the East also has had its history of wars and scriptural justifications for war. The World War II kamikaze pilots of Imperial Japan were convinced, as much as the crusaders of the Christian medieval age, that their sacrificial devotion to their religion, state Shintoism, would bring them glory in the afterlife. Not too long after, the West witnessed a resurgence of a seemingly long-dormant fundamentalism in Islam, bringing a fanatical revolution to the state of Iran, which caused some to question their conceptions of non-Judeo-Christian religions. Even in the 1991 Allied massacre of Iraq, soldiers on both sides of the conflict studied an ancient Eastern war text, *The Art of War* by Sun Tzu.

Can war, then, be justified? Is complete passivity justified? Little Joey, in *Shane*, is the student of both sides of the debate. After Shane shows Joey how to fast-draw, his mother says that "Guns aren't going to be a part of my son's life." Shane rejoins, "A gun is a tool, Mariam. No better or no worse than any other tool—an axe, a shovel, or anything. A gun is as good or as bad as the man using it. Remember that." But Mariam argues, "We'd all be better off if there wasn't a single gun left in this valley—including yours."

Shane was made only eight years after the first atomic bombs had exploded on civilian populations, wiping out two large cities and bringing temporary forced peace in a war-torn world. Mariam wants all the guns out of the valley. But is that possible?

RYKER'S RAIDERS

While we have looked at some justifications for war, we have only barely touched on some of the causes of war. No doubt Ryker and his men would say the cause for the division lies in the sodbusters' disrupting the cattlemen's right to a free range. The farmers would say that the cause lies solely in Ryker's unquenchable appetite for other people's land. As a bystanding audience we naturally side with the oppressed farmers because they are nice, hard-working people, while Ryker and his men are gun-toting, abusers of the wholesome god-fearers. But while we easily side with the good guys and while we can easily justify Shane's war against the monsters, we might overlook one of the other fundamental ingredients of the origin of war.

In Plato's *Republic* Socrates, as if discussing the philosophy of *Shane*, talks about vegetarianism, meat consumption, land, and war, with Glaucon: "And with such a [vegetarian] diet they may be expected to live in peace and health to a good old age, and bequeath a similar life to their children after them." In their conversation they conclude that people will not be satisfied with such a simple life, but rather, will want more, such as that provided by hunters and swineherds. The conversation continues:

SOCRATES: And there will be animals of many other kinds, if people eat them?

GLAUCON: Certainly.

SOCRATES: And living in this way we shall have much greater need of physicians than before.

GLAUCON: Much greater.

Though these words were spoken more than two thousand years ago, medical knowledge is only now catching up with this ancient wisdom, in understanding heart problems, cancer, and many other physical ailments associated with a high-fat, high-cholesterol, low-fiber, meat-eating diet. Socrates then goes on to tell of the economic and political ramifications of a complex societal appetite:

SOCRATES: And the country, which was enough to support the original inhabitants, will be too small now, and not enough?

GLAUCON: Quite true.

SOCRATES: Then a slice of our neighbors' land will be wanted by us for pasture and tillage, and they will want a slice of ours, if, like ourselves, they exceed the limit of necessity, and give themselves up to unlimited accumulation of wealth?

GLAUCON: That, Socrates, will be inevitable.

SOCRATES: And so we shall go to war, Glaucon. Shall we not?

GLAUCON: Most certainly. (*Republic* II: 372–73)

This prophetic observation of Socrates has unfortunately been overlooked by many economists, political leaders, and philosophers of war ever since it was inscribed in ancient Athens. Alexis de Tocqueville, an insightful visitor to the United States in the 1840s, observed, "In no country in the world is the love of property more active and more anxious than in the United States; nowhere does the majority display less inclination for those principles which threaten to alter, in whatever manner, the laws of property" (de Tocqueville, 2:256).

Ryker, as an immigrant cattleherder, as an heir of Abel, has a lust for more land, which is based on the market for more meat, which in turn is based on the consumer's appetite for more flesh. And the plight of the farmers in our narrative is the plight of the earth today, with a strange twist in carnivorous avarice.

Most of our current crop production is destined not for human consumption but for animal food, mostly cattle. Where free range ranching is still allowed, it destroys millions of acres of land, pollutes water sources, causes severe soil erosion, and upsets the natural eco-system by eating up the food of the natural wildlife and by shooting, trapping and poisoning predatory animals. Most livestock today is actually raised in inhumane, crowded conditions and given unthink-able amounts of hormones, antibiotics, and other harsh chemicals that seriously affect the health of the consumers as well as the animals.

The war over land that Plato wrote about long ago, like the conflict over land in *Shane*, is a direct result of a human appetite for flesh, a substance that has proven to be detrimental to human health in more than minimal consumption. What Socrates is saying is that a lust for flesh, besides causing health problems, will cause war, because of the amount of land needed to grow meat.

Consider these facts, gathered by John Robbins in his book *Diet for a New America* regarding land used to grow livestock feed:

- The livestock in the United States consumes enough grain and soybeans to feed more than five times the entire human popula-tion of the country.
- Livestock eats more than 80 percent of all of the corn grown in the United States, and more than 95 percent of all of the oats.
- To provide one person with a year's supply of meat requires three and a quarter acres of land. To supply one lacto-ovo vegetarian with food for a year requires a half acre. To supply one vegetarian requires only one-sixth of an acre.
- According to Department of Agriculture statistics, one acre of land can grow 20,000 pounds of potatoes. That same acre of land, if used to grow cattle feed, can produce less than 165 pounds of beef.

There would be no such thing as water shortages if there were a greater prevalence toward vegetarianism.

- Over half the total amount of water consumed in the United States goes to irrigate land growing feed and fodder for livestock.

- To produce a single pound of meat takes an average of 2,500 gallons of water—as much as a typical family uses for all its combined household purposes in a month.
- To produce a day's food for one meat eater takes over 4,000 gallons of water; for a lacto-ovo vegetarian, only 1,200 gallons; for a pure vegetarian, only 300 gallons.

Certainly there are many causes of war besides eating meat. But when one considers that the world's rain forests are being systematically slashed and burned at an alarming rate, primarily to feed the world's meat appetite; that the elimination of these desperately needed plants is significantly adding to our ozone depletion; that the world's starving could have enough food if we didn't have to feed the majority of our food to livestock; and that our water shortages are directly attributable to food grown for livestock production, one can not help but come to the conclusion that vested interests in the meat industry play a major role in geopolitical events, which have very much to do with war.

As modern participants in our geopolitical mythology, we must not forget the folkloric belief that we are what we eat. While decrying the abuses of Ryker and his raiders in our film mythology, we forget that he is the antagonist brother within our own soul. We must remind ourselves that the monster *without* is the double *within*. Ryker's rape of the land is our own voracious carnivorous appetite.

PEACE IN THE VALLEY

As Shane departs, he tells Joey to tell his mother, "There aren't any more guns in the valley," as if to say that violent sacrifice has brought peace. In the beginning and end of the film Shane wears his buckskin outfit and his gun. In the middle, as a domestic farmhand, he wears store-bought work clothes and no gun. The work clothes are made of cloth, from plant fibers—in essence, the duds of domesticity. By contrast, the buckskin outfit, an animal product, represents his nomadic, violent nature. But whether as a domesticated servant of the matriarchate, or as a nomadic warrior of the patriarchate, he desires peace. One way or the other, sacrifice must be made to insure that peace, for the deities demand the offering of blood for the sustenance of life.

So while Mariam can be assured (at least for a time) that there will be no guns in the valley, her aversion to guns has no doubt contributed to the good gunfighter's departure. But, like Shane, she is also ambivalent for she is attracted to the man with the righteous gun.

When we see Shane's vacillation between the worlds of the planter and the hunter, we are reminded that the Prince of Peace gave parables of both the farmer and the shepherd, both symbolic of himself as the planter-husbandman and the good shepherd, as well as the man with the righteous sword of truth. On one hand, Shane the planter is a priest of the eternal return as revealed in the secret of seeds. On the other hand, he is a priest of blood sacrifice, as revealed in the secret of death. But whether through planting or hunting, the eternal return brings the participant into the cosmogonic cycle of death and life. The Prince of Peace is connected to both.

Whether from the fast-draw or from the lover of the peace in the valley, Joey will learn about the philosophies of conflict and peace. But however he learns it, he is sure to learn that the combination of masculine aggression and feminine passivity leads to consummation, which produces life. It is incumbent upon the recipients of this life, however, to work out a solution for peace.

BABETTE'S FEAST
and
THE COOK, THE THIEF,
HIS WIFE AND
HER LOVER

TWO STORIES OF REDEMPTIVE
RITUAL SACRIFICE

Two sumptuous films about eating seem to be the antithesis of each other, but when seen in a religious light, both reveal themselves as being more alike than some of us would care to admit. *Babette's Feast* (1987) appears as a soft, sweet, idyllic story of love expressed in a classic French feast. *The Cook, the Thief, His Wife, and Her Lover* (1990), by contrast, is a film of gross vulgarity, gluttonous piggishness, murder, and forced cannibalism. Though no two films would seem to be more dissimilar, both are linked by a common theme of sacrifice.

Winning the American Academy Award for best foreign-language film for 1987, *Babette's Feast*, based on a short story by Isak Dinesen, is a seemingly simple story about a woman cooking a meal. But the simplicity stops at the dinner table. Under this culinary offering of French cuisine is a veritable treasure of primordial symbolism. By contrast, *The Cook, the Thief, His Wife and Her Lover* was rated X by the MPAA. Its naked honesty, and its raw expulsion of gastronomic bile, was too much for the rating system's capacity to digest in one sitting.

Let us have a brief overview of these stories before analyzing them together.

BABETTE'S FEAST

Babette's Feast centers around the home of Martine and Philippa, two never-married daughters of a Norwegian Lutheran minister. Having never experienced the pleasures of the secular world, they both have devoted their lives to serving the people of their little community. Years after their father's death, a small, loyal following still gathers occasionally at the two sisters' humble home.

When the two women were much younger and prettier, many young men had fallen in love with them. The story portrays the attraction of two of these men in those early years. One is a young Norwegian army officer, Lorens Loewenhielm, whose aunt lives not too far from the sisters. In love with Martine, he does not have the nerve to tell her so. He also fears believing his family's myth that one of his ancestors married a female mountain spirit and that, periodically, one of the family members is blessed with second sight from that union. So instead of pursuing the earthy angel, Martine, and the possibility of second sight, he has a vision of a successful military career, which he diligently follows.

A famous Parisian singer, Achille Papin, falls in love with Philippa. With her father's permission, he gives her voice lessons after he has heard her angelic voice in church. Unable to withhold his true feelings, he kisses her hand and is informed by her father that she has decided to terminate the lessons. Brokenhearted, like Colonel

Loewenhielm, Achille Papin also goes off to pursue his career without his lost beauty.

Years later, in their middle years, the sisters answer a knock at the door to find a Frenchwoman carrying a letter of introduction from Achille Papin. Fleeing her country's civil war, in which her husband and son were executed, and narrowly escaping the bloodied hands of a General Galliffet, Babette Hersant pleads with the two sisters to allow her to cook for them and take care of their house. They reluctantly agree, and she faithfully works for them for twelve years, at which point we arrive at the centerpiece of the story, her feast. Having won ten thousand francs in the French lottery, she begs the sisters to allow her to cook a real French meal for the hundredth anniversary of their late father's birth.

By this time, the brothers and sisters of the minister's little sect have fallen out of grace with one another. Babette sends to France for the ingredients of the special meal. At the last minute, it is announced that Lorens Loewenhielm, now a general, will be dining with the group, with his aging aunt. Then the wonderful meal begins.

The general, being the only man of the world present, is the only one sophisticated enough to recognize and appreciate the fineness of the delicacies. The finest amontillado, turtle soup, blinis Demidoff, Veuve Cliquot 1860, and the main dish, *cailles en sarcophage*, make the appreciative general proclaim the event and the offerings a miracle. The only place where he has seen such fine cuisine was at the Café Anglais in Paris, years earlier. At that restaurant he was being honored by a Colonel Galliffet, who having fought a duel over a woman, proclaimed that the restaurant's female chef was the only woman he would be willing to spill his blood for again. Galliffet also told Loewenhielm that this woman had the capability to turn a meal into a love affair, where one is unable to distinguish between physical and spiritual appetites.

Well, the wonderful feast does just that. Inspired by the meal and its spiritual seduction of the general, the old sectarians reconcile their differences. The next day, Martine and Philippa discover to their horror that Babette has spent her entire fortune on this one meal.

Having learned the secrets of sacrifice, Babette spends her fortune on the redemptive meal.

When they empathize with her probably remaining poor for the rest of her life, she says that as an artist she could never be poor. She learned from Achille Papin that true wealth for an artist is to be released to do one's very best, which of course she has done.

THE COOK, THE THIEF, HIS WIFE AND HER LOVER

This dark intestinal twisting of human interaction, *The Cook, the Thief, His Wife, and Her Lover*, also centers around eating, but instead of around one meal, around seven meals, one each evening of the week at the Café Hollandais, dominated by a disgusting diner, Albert Spica. This pig of a man rules a crew of crude henchmen who extort protection money from restaurateurs, apparently with threats of food poisoning and rats.

The cook is a fine French chef, Richard, who barely tolerates the offensive antics of the barbarous thief. Richard is a master of the high art of French cuisine. His kitchen staff is abused by Albert, including one young choirboy, who ends up in the hospital after having a gun shoved in his mouth, being force-fed his own buttons, and suffering a beating by Albert's band of gluttonous abusers. The chef, Richard, charges the most for black food, because, as he says, people have a need to eat death. Eventually, it is Richard who cooks the murdered Michael, Albert's wife's lover, who is served to Albert.

The thief's wife, Georgina, is very quiet during most of her dining with her barbarous husband. Finding a relationship with him impossible, she opts for a covert affair with a patron of the restaurant, right under her husband's scandalous nose. Whether in the water closet, the bakery pantry, or the meat refrigerator, Georgina and her lover, Michael, enjoy the intimacies denied her in her abusive marriage.

Michael is an intellectual, voraciously devouring books during his every meal. The proprietor of a book depository and a cataloger of the French Revolution, he and Georgina must hide out at his book depository after Albert learns of their illicit affair.

After the choirboy is sent to the hospital, Georgian goes to visit him, while Albert and his men find Michael at the book depository. They shove pages of his books down his mouth and viciously kill him. Georgina finds the gruesomely abused body and talks Richard into cooking Michael for Albert's last supper.

DIFFERENCES

Before we can see how much alike these two films are, we must first see how unalike they are. The following partial list shows these obvious differences:

BABETTE'S FEAST	THE COOK, THE THIEF
giving	taking
Babette, a lover	Albert, a killer

Babette, an artist	Albert, a pseudo-artist
peace	violence
Babette acts alone	Albert acts in concert
food brings reconciliation	food brings hatred
food brings contentment	food brings vomiting
good people are bad	bad people are bad
rejection of sexual union	lust for sexual union
meal becomes a love affair	meal causes a love affair
sacrifice through will	sacrifice through irony

Where one film expresses compassion, the other exudes hatred; where one reflects beneficent eating, the other exposes maleficent gorging; where one inspires feelings of quiet repose, the other forces anguish and disgust.

Now let us look at some of the obvious similarities between these two outwardly disparate films.

SIMILARITIES

While thinking of the stark opposition between these films, we may forget that they have more in common than their general cinematic forms. This is what they largely have in common:

class struggle

French chef, French cuisine

artists and intellectuals

eating

religious sacrifice

sexuality

second sight

These major themes are the ingredients with which the mythic fare is cooked in these filmic feasts. Let us eat our way through each of these offerings.

CLASS STRUGGLE

Besides being good ground for religious interpretation, both of these films also yield fruitful content for an economic study of social classes. In both films there is a backdrop of class struggle between the ruling elite on one side and the proletariat, artists, and intelligentsia on the other.

In *Babette's Feast* we are told that the French aristocracy violently suppressed human rights. Babette, casting her lot with the Communards, along with her family, has fought against an unfair system of human exploitation and had to flee for her life when the opposition was crushed. General Galliffet, who, as a younger colonel said he would be willing to die for this culinary genius, decides to kill her when he discovers her in opposition to his oppressive side of the class struggle.

In *The Cook, the Thief*, Albert Spica represents the oppressive upper class, even though his accent and mannerisms reflect the worst of the British lower class. He represents the decadence of the ruling elite. His wife, by contrast, and her lover, Michael, exhibit accents of a higher class while identifying with and defending the rights of the oppressed. They fraternize with the kitchen help, Georgina visits the abused choirboy in the hospital, and Michael has apparently devoted his career to cataloging the French Revolution, a grand historical theater of class struggle, where the ostentatious monarchy was dethroned by the violent anger of the people.

The nouveau riche Albert is the epitome of the proletariat's worst fear. With the outward trappings of elegant style, his crudeness speaks of lower-class betrayal and polished barbarism. Having risen to a higher state of wealth through his thievery, and having developed a certain obligatory sense of upper-class connoiseurship, his baseness still belies his fraudulent status. Those under his ruthless power become victims of his unchecked oppression, much like the story of aristocratic or bourgeois exploitation of familiar history.

Oppression by the aristocracy is the seed of revolution.

FRENCH CUISINE

The French cuisine in both films is an appropriate theme to contrast the class struggle in each. It is royalty, the aristocracy, and the bourgeoisie that actually enjoy the fine art of French cuisine and have made it what it is, probably the highest form of European culinary expression. But it is also these same landed elite that oppress the people whose art it is they patronize. General Galliffet severely reversed his praise of Babette when he learned she was a member of the ranks fighting against his class. His radical switch from the highest praise to a lethal condemnation of her is symptomatic of a kind of class loyalty that can be far stronger than personal affection.

Albert, having raised himself up from the lower classes through his criminality, considers himself a bulwark of quality, having developed the tastes of the upper class. His love affair with the finest of French cuisine is supposed to be a sign of class attainment, but it is actually a gross display of vulgarity, in his perennial abuse of his power over others. He even verbally abuses and humiliates the chef who gives him his sense of class.

The upper class in our stories exalt the fine artists of French cookery because it gives them their own sense of exaltation, then they just as readily debase the same artists if it will maintain their own sense of exaltation. It is like a wealthy patron commissioning an artist to sculpt a grand work of art, then kicking the scaffolding out from under the artist because he blocks the view of the high art.

ARTISTS AND INTELLECTUALS

Both films contrast those with the second or higher sight found specifically in the artist and the intellectual, with those of limited immediate vision, such as is found in the selfish powers that are. As a young officer, General Loewenhielm rejected his family myth of second sight in exchange for the glory of his military career. While acting on higher sight of self-sacrifice and genuine altruism, Martine and Philippa measure well in this area of second sight until we see them contrasted to the deeper sight exemplified in Babette's life. Of course the aristocracy of Babette's past was extremely limited in its sense of spiritual vision, having proven themselves selfish by their oppression of those of lesser status. Babette, having been influenced by the artist Achille Papin, authentically lives the philosophy in which she so ardently believes. Rejecting the glory of being the best culinary genius of the age, she humbly devotes herself to the pursuit of the highest art, that of "turning a meal into a love affair, where one cannot distinguish between physical and spiritual appetites." With all of her earthly resources, she sacrificially gives of her artistic self and miraculous changes take place among the naïve recipients of her sumptuous fare.

Albert, a murderous sociopath, is the antithesis of one with second sight, in spite of the fact that he insists that he is an artist. The proof of his artistic classification, he insists, is the way he combines his business (extorting money from restaurateurs) and pleasure (dining on the finest of French food). Like Babette's noxious General Galliffet, Albert has only his immediate and personal status in mind in all social interactions. Those with second sight in *The Cook, the Thief* are Michael (the intellectual), Georgina (Albert's wife), Richard (the chef), and the abused choirboy, among others. Michael, having made a lengthy study of French history, knows too intimately the lessons of the past. After his death, Georgina pulls out of his lifeless mouth the title page of his favorite book, *The French Revolution*, with which he was suffocated. As an astute intellectual, he sees the reality of what Albert and his ilk are incapable of seeing, the destructive nature of and the inevitable demise of unchecked political appetites. Georgina, the lover of the intellectual and sympathizer to the artists, also possesses second sight. In fact, it is she who comes up with the idea of cooking Michael for Albert's last meal. The choirboy sees the need to support the intellectual and his lover by supplying them with French cooked food. And Richard the chef intuitively sees the spiritual truth behind the price of black food and the cooking of Michael (which we will more fully explore later).

EATING, IN ECONOMIC TERMS

The obvious motif in which our dinner spread is served is in the act of eating itself. While all of the major characters spend much of their time nourishing themselves on the sustenance so delicately prepared for them, there are deeper implications to this mere ingestion of foodstuffs. When we look at all of this mastication from a socio-economic vantage, we can see a clear linkage between eating and class difference. On the surface, of course, the rich and poor eat in different ways, and from a different menu. What the rich may forget however, especially the selfish rich, is that their hubristically consumed meals are symbolically linked to their own potential consumption. Shakespeare has aptly illustrated this, and, by virtue of his writing, also illustrates the second-sighted artist. We find this allegory of food in *Hamlet* (Act IV; Scene III):

> KING: Now, Hamlet, where's Polonius?
>
> HAMLET: At supper.
>
> KING: At supper! Where?
>
> HAMLET: Not where he eats, but where he is eaten. A certain convocation of politic worms are e'en at him. Your worm is your only emperor for diet. We fat all creatures else to fat us, and we fat ourselves for maggots. Your fat King and your lean beggar is but variable service, two dishes, but to one table; that's the end.
>
> KING: Alas, alas!
>
> HAMLET: A man may fish with the worm that hath eat of a king, and eat of the fish that hath fed of that worm.
>
> KING: What dost thou mean by this?
>
> HAMLET: Nothing but to show you how a King may go a progress through the guts of a beggar.

Here we see the true status of the wealthy, in the food chain common to all flesh. When viewed economically, food is essentially the basis of any economy. No matter how sophisticated the economy or how removed a culture might be from the growing of food and the exchanging of agricultural commodities, food is still the base and common denominator of all wealth. Since all flesh is inextricably tied to the perennial food-quest in order to sustain life, there is no escaping the most basic and primordial economy of food supply. Food is the raw material of labor, commerce, and the social system itself, no matter how complex or wealthy a civilization might be.

When the aristocracy of Babette's story despise the artist who prepares its fine edible art, she moves on to feed the souls of others, who, lacking elegance of taste, possess a greater richness, albeit of an invisible variety.

When Albert and his men are at the book depository killing

Michael, he asks, "What is the use of all of these books? You can't eat them." His lack of second sight blinds him to the value of eating words, and especially blinds him to his own prophetic words, in that he promises to eat Michael after he kills him.

EATING, IN ARCHETYPAL TERMS

Now that we see food in a socioeconomic light, let us turn our attention to the psychological and spiritual significance of food. Our two movies are more than invitations to cinematic banquets. Focusing on eating and the human interaction connected with this eating, our stories reveal eating as something more than a mere ingestion of living substance. A parallel symbolism found in both films is the connection of death with food. Babette's entrée is *cailles en sarcophage* (quails in a sarcophagus). Related to this is Richard's emphasis on the higher prices of black foods because, as he says, they make people think they are eating death. What we have here is a reminder of the basic truth of food. Essentially, the eating of food at all levels of the food chain, as Hamlet has illustrated for us, is the consumption of life forms by other life forms. There must be death and devouring of life in order to sustain life.

Seen at the level of mere physical eating, this is obviously what happens—one form of life, either vegetal or animal, is sacrificed so that other life may live. Seen at the socioeconomic level, this is essentially what the aristocrats and bourgeois do in our stories in order to sustain their sociopolitical status. General Galliffet killed Babette's husband and son in order to maintain his own position. Seen from an interpersonal emotional perspective, this is certainly what Albert does to all of the people in his life. He verbally and physically abuses all others, psychologically killing and devouring them in order to live on a higher plane of existence in his mind.

Animals use the same instrument, the mouth, for kissing, killing, and eating their victims. Humans certainly do the same, though in a more sophisticatedly symbolic manner. Albert Spica devours his many victims with his acerbic verbal attacks. He even goes so far as to promise that he will eat Michael after killing him.

With the mouth we kiss people as a sign of our affection. When we love others a great deal we even say that we feel like eating them up. With the very same instrument with which we love people and feel like eating them we also hate them and feel like eating them. With the mouth we will either love and devour or we will hate and devour. But one way or another, we cannot escape the masticating nature of our mouth.

As infants, the very first sign of love we are given is through feeding at mother's breast. From that point on, we gather together with those we love, to dine together. Thus we learn that food is a symbol of love.

Even the three major types of eating disorders are intimately connected with love. The anorectic is symbolically pushing love away in the act of rejecting food. The bulimic has a love-hate relationship with love. The compulsive overeater wants to gobble up all the love she or he can consume. The main reason women develop eating disorders more often than men is that, psychosexually speaking, woman is the receptive feminine mouth in the symbolic interaction of the sexes, opposed to the masculine seed or food that goes into the vulvic mouth.

Simultaneous to our connection of love with food, we learn that people say cruel things to one another with devastating consequences. Thus we learn that the mouth is an instrument of cruelty. We either dine together in love or we make war with one another with our mouths. Babette prepares the best possible food at great expense for those she loves. Albert force-feeds dog feces to one of his enemies, then he luxuriates in the finest of culinary offerings. Babette is concerned with the physical and spiritual welfare of those whom she serves. Albert stabs a fork into the face of a bearer of bad news, then sits down to eat.

149

RELIGIOUS SACRIFICE

If we take our food symbolism a step further, we can see that those who are devoured take on a sacrificial character. The priests of the Mosaic covenant eat the sacrificial meat offered to God as surrogate consumers of the divine meal. Primitives often thank the animal they kill and eat as an acknowledgment of its sacrificial death. General Galliffet and his aristocratic colleagues had to sacrifice those who stood in the way of the status quo in their digestion of the uprising. The recipients of Albert's consuming nature are sacrificial victims to his voracious appetite. If Babette had not come so close to the jaws of sacrificial death herself, she might not have had as much of a sense of the sacredness of self-sacrifice. As it is, her feeding of the others symbolizes her own inner awareness that she is in essence offering herself as a sacred morsel in order to give life to the recipients of the divine shewbread. By contrast, Albert sacrifices everybody but himself, indicating that he views himself as a deity worthy of meat offerings, rather than as one who can give life to others. He is like Erysichthon, the abusive man cursed with insatiable hunger because of his murderous nature. This mythic figure actually devours all his wealth in order to satisfy his hunger, and he eventually loses his life devouring his own flesh.

As we have seen, the entire food chain is a repetition of one form of life giving of itself in sacrificial surrender in order that other life may survive. The sacrificial meal gives life to the recipient of the nurturing manna. On a grander scale, the earth itself, while giving life, is also a consuming maw that is perennially hungry for more sustenance. The trek from the womb to the tomb is merely a temporary granting of life between eternal periods of consumptive death. Man plants his seed into the hungry vulva of woman and the death of the buried seed produces life. This life is given temporary tenancy in the world of dining and devouring. This human life, outside of the orifice of the grave, either becomes life or death to others. Then, about the time that one seems to begin learning the lessons of the life outside the cave, the body is turned into fertilizer, to give life to other life forms. Thus, the cycle continues indefinitely, switching death into life which becomes death which is turned back into life again, ad infinitum throughout the cycle of the eternal return.

Now the violence of all of this mastication and digestion of life is the heart and soul of the sacred. For it is in the participation in sacrificial ritual that the meaning of life is found. Sacrifice is at the center of human society, because we all eat food. The perfection of the high art of French cuisine is symbolic of making an art of sacrifice. René Girard, in his book *Violence and the Sacred*, tells us that violence and the sacred are inseparable and that only sacrificial violence can put an end to violence. Thus, when violent consumption is ritualized or made sacred in a unanimous participation by the sacred society, it serves to quell uncontrolled violence. So, ritualized sacrifices maintain life in the same way that eating maintains life. The eucharistic words "As often as you eat this bread, do this in remembrance of Me" are no mere formalized words of meaningless ritual, but are rather tied to a primordial and universal order of life, yielding the temporary tenancy of life in order that other life may temporarily shine in the glory of the sun. All creatures have their day in the sun, but eventually they must become food for the sustenance of other life. Since life centers around the necessity of killing life to create other life, religion itself is based on the violent mastication of sacrifice—the ritual of the violent unanimous devouring of the victim. The secret of life is in the pudding, or, as it is commonly said about authenticity of character, the proof of the pudding is in the eating.

Babette's main course of quail in a sarcophagus and Richard's emphasis on the mortificational aspect of black food signify this religious element of eating. General Galliffet's killing of Babette's husband and son represents to her the sacrificial slaying of two quails who give up their lives for the freedom and for the quality of the life of others. This sacrificial martyrdom no doubt nurtures more spiritual life within her, which in turn gives more life to others. As she and her menfolk fought as communards against an unjust oppression by the privileged, their deaths were seeds buried in the ground of a life-yielding harvest of spiritual food.

Like Babette's General Galliffet, fat Albert does not realize the significance of his sacrifice of Michael. While he questions the value of inedible books and feeds the pages of *The French Revolution* to Michael, he is completely ignorant of the life-giving element in this death. While he stuffs his own face with the basis of physical life, his spiritual death blinds him to the life he creates by the consumptive murder of his sacrificial victim. Had he known the inner truths of the French Revolution or of eating he could have lengthened his temporary tenancy in the sun to a somewhat longer duration.

As it is, Michael's death unifies Albert's yet living victims to enact the most significant and meaningful ritual of the story. With necessary unanimity, Georgina, Richard, the choirboy, and a host of other victims elegantly, ceremoniously, and religiously serve a French-baked Michael to the voracious glutton of the Café Hollandais. Here Richard the chef, as a Prometheus, steals the culinary fire from the angry god for the benefit of humankind. And suddenly, for the first time in the story, the king of fine cuisine loses his appetite. He exclaims in ironic horror, "My God! Jesus!" and he is reminded by Georgina that the holy feast is not God, but "Michael, my lover." (Ironically, the name Michael means "who is like God.") Here, in his final blasphemy, at his last supper, the irony of his sacrificial meal comes full circle. His having symbolically devoured others has come back to haunt him in a religious pageant as dramatic and as ironic as the French Revolution. The regent of culinary elegance vomits. Georgina points a gun at his head with the benediction "Bon appetit (That's French)." He ingests a portion of the transubstantial communion, then Georgina calls him a cannibal and shoots him. Thus, true to the nature of sacrificial societies, it is best to have the culprit be responsible for his own violent death, lest violence to the violent spread his contagious disease. Here also, according to the tradition of primitive kings, the royal pain in the ass takes on the role of the victim himself—although in Albert's case, it is by his own ironic doing, and it is for real.

The cure of the sacred community is to sacrifice the sole malignant victim after feeding him his own benign victim.

A Hindu proverb says, "Man becomes the food of the divinity he worships," which, in Albert's case, has ironically baked true. For by severely despising others one is actually worshipping them, which makes one susceptible to being devoured by them. Such hatred/worship can be seen in the world of anthropological study, as recorded by Margaret Mead: "When the Mundugumor captured an enemy they ate him, and laughed as they told of it afterwards. When a Mundugumor became so angry that his anger turned even against himself, he got into a canoe and drifted down the river to be eaten by the next tribe" (Mead, 70). Thus, Albert's self-propelled murder is actually his being devoured by those he has worshipped with his hatred.

To show another similarity between our two cinemyths, we also find reference to cannibalism in Isak Dinesen's original version of Babette's Feast:

The brutish pig of the Café Hollandais is the legitimate ritual sacrifice.

Martine remembered a tale told by a friend of her father's who had been a missionary in Africa. He had saved the life of an old chief's favorite wife, and to show his gratitude, the chief had treated him to a rich meal. Only long afterwards the missionary learned from his own black servant that what he had partaken of was a small fat grandchild of the chief's, cooked in honor of the great Christian medicine man. She shuddered.

Alas, we might assume that such cannibalism is found only in fiction or in stone age tribes, but as recently as 1991, victims of the toppled Haitian Duvalier regime publically ate some of their former oppressors (Stumbo).

Both chefs in our stories, being the masters of the furnace and hearth, are like Hephaestus and Hestia. As deities of creative fire, Babette and Richard have both altered the course of the draconian status quo. In both stories, the truth of creativity and food is profound.

SEXUALITY

Now let us tie in another very crucial theme found in our cinematic sacrificial rituals. The sexual elements in both films are also closely related to this theme of ritual sacrifice. We first recall that Martine and Philippa, the two puritan minister's daughters, are apparently sexually chaste all of their lives, and that Georgina and Michael sneak an affair behind her husband's back. At the beginning of her story we watch Georgina sensually munching on a piece of asparagus. As opposed to her, we are told that Albert is really not interested in sex, at least not in the normal consummational variety. He has instruments of oral hygiene and culinary arts that he employs for sexual pleasure. We also know that this mismatched couple does not have any children. This absence of normal sexuality points toward the ultimate consummation—sacrificial death.

Albert mentions in one of his vulgar diatribes that since the anus and the vagina are so closely situated, "It goes to show how eating and

154

sex are related." Actually there is more truth to his statement than he is capable of realizing. It was illustrated earlier how the sexual union of man and woman and the union of the diner and the dinner are similar. Eating and sex are both analogies of one another, and they are also both analogies for death, just as death is symbolic of the eternal spiritual cycle. If we can see the integral connection between these seemingly disparate categories of life—eating, sex and death—it will be easier to discern the meaning of our cinematic feasts and of the grand banquet of life.

In our cinematic stories, the interplay of sexuality and the absence of it both complement our menu of ritual sacrifice. The complete absence of sexual union (with the young suitors) in *Babette's Feast* first leads to a certain disunion. The young men go on to their respective careers apart from the women they love. Then, ironically, both men, being separated from their heart-flames, are instruments in bringing union to the separated souls of the sectarians—Achille Papin, through sending Babette to the two sisters and General Loewenhielm, through his own union of physical and spiritual appetites. Through inflicted violence in Babette's life, as is generally true with sacrificial victimization, union is brought to the sect, indirectly, by the inner union of General Loewenhielm. Redemptive victimization works toward the reconciliation of the communion eaters, as they verify, it is "just like the supper at Cana," a wedding (union) feast.

Similarly, an ironic exchanging of opposites in *The Cook, the Thief* also works toward an ultimate end of ritual redemption. The absence of sexual union between Albert and Georgina leads to a union between Georgina and Michael, which leads toward ultimate disunion (the sacrificial violence inflicted on Michael and the choirboy), which in turn leads to an ironic union of Albert and Michael (the cannibalism), which works toward an ultimate union and redemption of the living victims.

The song of redemption at the Café Hollandais is sung by the choirboy with the lyrics signifying the ironic truth of the horrific tragedy:

Wash me and cleanse me.
Wash me thoroughly from all my iniquities
and cleanse me from my sins.

Georges Bataille insists that the genesis of war, sacrifice, and orgy are identical (Bataille, 116). Indeed, in our stories, as in life, they have their origin in the food chain and in our religious way of dealing with it.

SECOND SIGHT

When young Colonel Loewenhielm rejects second sight for his military career, like many military men today, he gives up a tremendous mythic boon. While this blessing still quietly resides in his heart to a small degree, ironically, it is an experience he has as a soldier (his dinner at the Café Anglais) that gives rise to the orgasmic spiritual blessing at the end of the story. So whether he wants the mythic second sight or not, it is his infection with this heavenly disease that spreads the angelic contagion to the appropriate contractees of redemption. And while Loewenhielm, first as a young colonel and later as an older general, might have missed the fuller blessings of second sight, Babette, the one who receives the severest impact of short-sighted violence, possesses second sight to the most profound degree. At the end of the story, when she tells the sisters that she, as an artist, could never be poor, the truth of second sight erupts into a little orgy of inner wisdom. She says that she heard from the lips of the great artist Achille Papin that "Throughout the world sounds one long cry from the heart of the artist: Give me the chance to do my very best!"

It is only through her own personal tragedy of living through the act of sacrificial ritual that she is able to do her best. For in her feeding of the self-complimenting aristocracy at the Café Anglais, she might be considered the greatest culinary genius of the age, but she does not do her best until she feeds the ten-thousand-franc birds in a coffin to the class of people she fought for in the civil war. We are reminded that

The general recognizes the meal to be a love affair, in which one is unable to distinguish between physical and spiritual appetites.

Babette served the sisters for twelve years before serving her feast to twelve people, indicating the cosmic order of the feast. As the Lutheran patriarch would have said, "Mercy and truth have met one another, righteousness and bliss shall kiss one another." Her second sight, no doubt given to her in the all-too-personal witness of sacrificial victimization, gives her the wisdom to understand that it is in consumption that one dies, and it is in death that resurrection is accomplished.

In *The Cook, the Thief*, again, it is the artists and intellectuals who possess second sight. The one who brags the most about being an artist is the most fraudulent in his sight, and his lack of sight blinds him to his own sacrifice. The ones with the most second sight talk about it the least, and they unite the most in the elimination of the blind king.

After Georgina spends the night with the corpse of Michael, the morning sun slowly rises to illumine her analysis, indicating that Michael's death will yield a life in the sun for another life released from the dark maw of the earth.

So both films, while cooked with completely different recipes, contain the same seed of sacrificial redemption. The brothers and sisters of *Babette's Feast* are redeemed through Babette's surrogate self-sacrifice; the members of the sacred society of *The Cook, the Thief* are redeemed through their sacrifice of the legitimate victim.

An Eskimo shaman has said that the greatest danger lies in the fact that humans' food consists entirely of souls. According to premodern thought found all over the world, all food is possessed of certain spirits. The danger to modern consumers of food is that, while we no longer believe in such primitive thinking, we consume one another with our techno-secular appetites. Thomas Moffett wrote in 1600, "Men dig their graves with their own teeth and die more by those fated instruments than the weapons of their enimies" (Moffett).

Hoggishness is the curse of human society. Like Albert, we sometimes forget that food the material is food the immaterial. And we forget that a corn of wheat must be buried in the ground and die, before it can bring forth fruit, because he that eats of this bread shall live forever.

PART 3

FEMININE MONSTERS

In this section, feminine monsters rule the day (or the night, in most cases). The theme of the feminine monster has shown up many times in literature, as in Shelley's *Medusa*, in Oscar Wilde's *Salome*, in Keats's "La Belle Dame Sans Merci," and in many other forms.

Viewed cursorily, since the monsters are overtly feminine, such depictions of feminine dragons might be considered antifeminist by some. Granting that most of our Western myths have been largely invented by ruling patriarchy, nonetheless, enough of the feminine truth still prevails. While these cinemyths serve as prophetic warnings to patriarchy, they also show that ultra-matriarchy can be just as destructive. There are redemptive elements in each film that guide the mythic pilgrim away from extremities.

LITTLE SHOP OF HORRORS

THE BATTLE BETWEEN HEAVEN
AND EARTH

The Little Shop of Horrors, a dark farcical comedy of a man-eating plant with an unquenchable appetite, was almost forgotten after its original low-budget 1960 production. Then, about twenty years later, the story was revived as an off-Broadway musical play which ran for about five years. The 1986 film version of the play brought even greater popularity to the story. Although there is more depth in the original 1960 film than in the later versions, the play and the 1986 film (directed by Frank Oz) have the attractive additions of musical, technical, and dramatic sophistication, which make the symbolic saga accessible to a wider audience.

The mythic structure of *Little Shop* has considerable relevance for our present societal questioning of patriarchy. The narrative draws together several disparate strands of myth which synthesize into one larger, multi-encompassing myth. The principal tribal story tellers of *Little Shop* are Roger Corman, the producer and director of the original 1960 film, and especially the screenwriter of the original story, Charles B. Griffith. Corman, having cult status for his numerous B-grade horror films, shot the entire project in two days and one evening, on a budget it might seem, with digits not many more than the days spent filming (actually, less than thirty thousand dollars). Rumor has it that Corman was challenged with the idea of making a film centering around a studio storefront set that was soon scheduled for demolition. So he quickly solicited the screenwriting talent of Griffith, who churned out the script of the now cult classic in a week's time. Perhaps if more time and deliberation had been given to the making of the film, the subconscious numinosity of it might not have been as rich.

The two had previously collaborated on Corman's 1959 *A Bucket of Blood*, from which *Little Shop* heavily borrows. In *A Bucket of Blood*, a waiter in a Beat café accidentally stumbles across a plan for making sculptures out of the people he kills, which brings him an addictive degree of recognition. Another source of its theme is apparently a short story by the playfully macabre British writer John Collier. Collier's "Green Thoughts" involves a man-eating plant and contains elements similar to the later *Little Shop*. There are also echoes of Tennessee Williams's 1958 play *Suddenly Last Summer*.

The collaborators, working against time, selected the major themes of *Little Shop* from previous works, and in a more subtle and subconscious way, its mythical content was appropriated from a variety of sources.

THE PROBLEM

Like most good stories, *Little Shop* presents a problem to be solved: there are difficulties involved with living and working on "Skid Row," where "the tragedies are deeper, the ecstasies are wilder, and the crime rate is consistently higher than anywhere else." In this rundown area, business is bad, relationships are lousy, and there is a gnawing communication breakdown which bespeaks a Beckett-like alienation between the characters. This breakdown of relationships is comically signified in the language of the 1960 version, which pushes the characters into Yiddish theatre mispronunciation of words and phrases: "Cesarean Salad," "I could eat a hearse," "flower saloon," "a finger of speech," "Beverly Ills," "Eat something; it will calm your aggramation," and "I want to talk on you." From the unlucky shop at 1313 Skid Row, the characters in the later two versions sing for a way out. Audrey, the impoverished floral designer, dreams of "Better Homes and Gardens," with Tupperware parties and TV dinners.

THE ILLUSIONS OF SOLUTIONS

Audrey doesn't see much hope, so she settles for masochism. Her boyfriend in the last two versions is Orin Scrivello, a dentist who deals with his unresolved issues through sadism. But the character that promises an actual way out of Skid Row is the plant, Audrey, Jr. or Audrey II (the plant's name in the later two versions) christened and nurtured by Seymour Krellborn, the nerdish would-be horticulturist working for Gravis Mushnick (1960 spelling), the florist. The day after the plant receives her first drops of human blood, she grows and draws immediate business to Mushnick's florist shop. With an insatiable hunger for human flesh, Audrey Jr. brings success to Mushnick and "Son" (Seymour). The more people she eats, the more success she promises, and the bigger and more powerful she becomes. And as Mr. Mushnick says, she has a scientific name, "but who can denounce it?"

Two girls from Cucamonga High School (1960 version) have been assigned to buy two thousand dollars' worth of flowers for their float in the Rose Bowl Parade. A naive pair, like Seymour and Audrey, they want their float to feature Audrey, Jr. with their queen sitting inside of her, with crown and scepter. Once the faces of the digested victims bloom on the plant, the girls exclaim, "Now the float will be perfect!" The difference between these girls and Audrey and Seymour, is that the latter set manage to turn their naïveté into a nativity, as will be shown. But first we have to look more closely at Audrey, Jr.

THE BATTLE

This "strange and interesting plant" suddenly appears in an Oriental garden shop during a total eclipse of the sun. Seymour Krellborn buys the plant for $1.95 and things are never the same again. It may seem that the eclipse is just a campy sci-fi way of introducing the vegetable. But, as often, there is significance to this detail, which is actually our first indication that something archetypal is askew. Symbolically, the moon's overshadowing of the sun suggests one of the major themes of the story: feminine elements upstaging the masculine. And thus, throughout the chronicle, the eternal war between masculine and feminine is fought on the battlefield of Mushnick's flower shop. Mushnick's first name, *Gravis*, speaks prophetically of the carnage and seriousness of this battle.

It is significant that most of the victims eaten by the plant in the three versions are overmasculinized characters employing phallic objects to selfishly procure advantage over the more passive characters in their lives. The sadistic dentist who painfully inserts penetrating tools into patients' vulvic mouths is eaten by the plant in all three versions. The burglar in the 1960 version who brandishes a gun to achieve his phallic goals, becomes another victim. And Mushnick, who catches the disease of uncontrolled machismo in the later two versions, is also swallowed by the plant. In the 1986 movie, he calls Seymour a "schmuck" and waves a threatening gun before being eaten.

Although she possesses a male voice, the plant seems obsessed with vortically swallowing the clobbering patriarchal principle, wherever it appears in her environment. This devouring motif draws upon a celebrated tradition of subconscious symbolism. In primitive folklore, there is found the widespread motif of the greatly feared *vagina dentata*, the vagina with teeth. The people-eating plant in our story is most apparently a modern equivalent. The engulfing, vulvic lips of Audrey, Jr., the dominating women of the story, and their battering phallocentric polar opposites are signifiers of the global, primordial, perennial war between the sexes, which is a metaphoric extension of the separation between the sky god and *Terra Mater*, Mother Earth.

Both Audrey and Seymour, being naïve, underdeveloped, and adolescent in their orientation are psychological victims of this perennial battle. In their passivity, they are respectively pommeled and devoured by the older and more selfishly seasoned participants of the war.

All that's needed for a little excitement is a mythic adventure.

Audrey is literally beaten by her dentist boyfriend. When Audrey goes on a date with him, the plant wilts in sympathy. Seymour, similarly, is psychologically eaten by his mother, Mrs. Winifred Krellborn, in the 1960 version.

THE COMBATANTS OF THE WAR

Mrs. Krellborn and Mrs. Shiva

The hypochondriacal Mrs. Krellborn, obsessed with life and health, is ironically a devourer of life who lives parasitically off her son Seymour's energy. She insists that Seymour not get married until he buys her an iron lung. She aptly calls herself "a complete sea hag," testifying to her mythical role as a devouring sea monster bent on drowning her wayfaring son into the sea of motherly dominance. Yet she has another, less obvious role as a personage pointing up her son's need for a spiritual rebirth.

Mrs. Krellborn's first name, Winifred, was borne by the seventh century Saint Winifred, or Saint Gwenfrewi. The legend surrounding

165

her life is that she is beheaded by a rejected suitor, whereupon the earth opens up and swallows him. Her head is miraculously restored to her, and where her head falls, there suddenly arises a spring, which later produces healing. Mrs. Krellborn personifies a perverted version of Saint Winifred. She swallows Seymour as the earth swallows Saint Winifred's rejected suitor. Her obsessive search for medication and health elixirs is a reversal of her namesake's production of the miraculous spring. She jealously warns her son about Audrey: "Never trust a woman who is too healthy." And she goes to a Dr. Mallard for medical care.

Mrs. S. Shiva is a philosophical cousin of Mrs. Krellborn's. Her name is sometimes pronounced "Shiver," and she is an obsessive buyer of funeral flowers for her constantly dying relatives. This pathetic mourner announces another death of a relative every time she walks into the florist shop (1960 version). In addition to its resemblance to the name of the Hindu god of death and destruction, her name in Hebrew speaks of "sitting in mourning for seven days." The plant droops when Mrs. Shiva so much as walks into the room. An addition to her Jewish irony is that her initials are S.S., the acronym of the Nazi death squad.

These two doom merchants are the Scylla and Charybdis of this story. They are all-consuming female vortices, like Homer's female sea monsters in the *Odyssey*, ready to devour any male challengers.

The Dentist

On the masculine side of the war we find the sadistic dentist (Dr. Farb in the 1960 version, or Dr. Orin Scrivello in the later two versions). The name Scrivello is derived from the Latin *scrivener*, or *scribe*, in Greek *keirein*, to cut, befitting his piercing personality. His first name is more significant. Eugene O'Neill used the name Orin in his play *Mourning Becomes Electra*, as a modern equivalent for Agamemnon's son Orestes, who revenged the murder of his father by killing his mother, Clytemnestra and her lover, Aegisthus. To punish this violent revenge the Furies visited Orestes with madness. And thus, we can see within

Orin Scrivello a madness connected with his matricidal sadism. In the 1986 movie, Orin is depicted reverencing an enshrined icon of his deceased mother in between abusive sessions with his patients. The dentist extends his love-hate relationship with his mother to passive people in his life. He sings: "Open wide. Here I come. I get off on the pain I inflict!" The orgasmic lyrics testify to his bludgeoning phallic nature.

The Patient

The perfect antithesis of this penile hammer is the masochistic patient "getting off" on the inflicted pain. This overly-feminized character is played with remarkable skill by Jack Nicholson in 1960 (one of his first screen roles), and by Bill Murray in 1986. Their patient's solution to the problem of pain is to make love to it.

In the 1960 version, the patient, Wilbur Force, is appropriately enough an undertaker who does funeral business for Mrs. Shiva. (She recommends him to the abusive dentist). The name *Wilbur* means "wild boar," which certainly does not fit his effeminate personality, unless one assumes the passive violence of death, through whose force all must meet the undertaker sooner or later. In this capacity, Wilbur Force is a signifier of Hades, the god of the underworld, the jailor of the dead. In his business relationship with Mrs. Shiva, Wilbur Force, as Hades, takes possession of those that Shiva, the destroyer, kills. He is her "wild boar," an agent of her ruthlessness.

In Rome, Hades (as Pluto) was thought to help crops grow and to produce wealth. In this function, he is also an associate of the killer plant. The more the plant grows (by sending people to the house of Hades), the more financial success is promised to any avaricious believers of the proposition.

In the 1986 version, the masochistic patient is named Arthur Denton, who pleads lustily for "a long, slow, root canal." The etymology of this name provides a mythical cross-signification to his character. The Celtic origin of Arthur means "bear," similar to the wild boar connotations of Wilbur. The Teutonic origin of Arthur means "eagle of Thor," the Scandinavian god who is associated most often with his malevolent, skull-cracking hammer. Arthur's last name is Denton, which refers to tooth. But whether as Arthur or Wilbur, the patient is in love with the painful end of the dentist's phallic hammer. It would seem that the joke here would be that the patient has a "dent-on" for the damaging dentist; the passive and more than receptive patient concavely unites with the convex "hard-on" of dentistry.

Dentist and Patient as Poseidon and Hades

Just as the dental patient is a representative of Hades, the god of the underworld, the dentist is representative of Poseidon, the trident-bearing god of the sea. (These two gods are inferior brothers to Zeus, the lord of the gods). Poseidon is known for his viciousness and uncontrolled wrath, Hades, for his passive reception of the dead. They go together like a spade and a grave. One kills and digs; the other opens wide and receives. The dentist's addiction to his nitrous oxide gas mask makes him look like a scuba diver under water receiving air from above, as befits his underwater role as Poseidon. The sense of Skid Row as the house of Hades is well brought out in the original black-and-white film, where shadows are very prominent in Corman's visual telling of the story, indicating a land of shades needing redemption. (Unfortunately, there has been a colorized video of the 1960 film released.)

Audrey

Audrey says she met the abusive dentist at a club where she moonlights, called "The Gutter." To make money there, she puts on "cheap and tasteless clothing . . . not nice clothes like these." With her "low and nasty apparel," she attracts the hoodlum dentist, and he becomes her downfall. Here too is concealed an elaborated version of an earlier myth.

In the seventh century, there lived Saint Etheldreda, whose name

168

evolved into Saint Audrey. She died of a throat tumour, which she regarded as a punishment for her early love of necklaces. At Saint Audrey's Fair, held in her honor, it was the custom to sell cheap necklaces; the word *tawdry* originally described these necklaces sold in her honor. Later the word tawdry came to mean what it does today: cheap and garish goods, like the clothes Audrey wears to "The Gutter." The parallel extends further: Audrey, Jr.'s naivete in taste and circumstances becomes a curse to her as well. In the first two versions of *Little Shop*, Seymour crawls into the plant with a large knife, as if to perform radical and fatal surgery on a throat tumour. The implication of the parallel between Audrey, Saint Audrey, and Audrey, Jr., is that cheap "tastes" are detrimental to the health of the feminine.

Leonora Clyde

Speaking of cheap tastes, there is an interesting prostitute named Leonora Clyde in the 1960 version. Seymour happens upon this seductress after being hypnotized by the plant and instructed by it to bring more food. Leonora tries to snare him with her beauty several times and fails. She finally succeeds at stopping him with the old slip-on-the-banana-peel trick. Her name, Leonora, is a derivative of Eleanore, which is derived from Helen. Leonora is the farce's Helen of Troy. Like Helen, whose sexual license touches off the Trojan War, Leonora uses sexuality for selfish purposes and becomes, like her phallic-sadistic counterparts, a victim of the plant.

The Detectives

Helen's brothers in mythology are Castor and Polydeuces, two perpetual search-and-rescue heroes constantly on expeditions to right wrongs. In our story, the detectives, Sergeant Joe Fink and Officer Frank Stooley, are like these mythical twin sons of Zeus, here engaged in a "Dragnet"-style "just the facts" investigation of the murders.

Byrson Fouch

Found only in the 1960 film, is one character who is symbolic of the sky god, Zeus himself. He is named Byrson Fouch and is called by Mushnick, "Mr. Yellow Vest." Antithetical to the man-eating plant, Mr. Yellow Vest eats flowers in Mushnick's shop. Just as the sun is symbolically connected to the supreme male god, so the sun color of Byrson's vest is symbolic of his role as Zeus. As a confidently wise flower-eater, Byrson Fouch receives invincibility by eating plants, and like Zeus, he gains power from the plant in his war with Mother Earth. Seemingly above most of the pettiness of the embattled participants, he seems to disapprove of the selfish beating and eating in the shop.

In classical mythology, there is a war known as the Gigantomachy between Zeus and Gaia, the goddess of the earth. Being allied with a band of giants, Gaia employs a plant, the juice of which would make her giants invincible and immortal. But Zeus, in a show of his typical insight and strategy, hides the plant from his foes and eats it himself. In the 1960 *Little Shop*, Mrs. Shiva and Mrs. Krellborn are allied with Gaia, the feminine earth deity, and we might say that Audrey, Jr. is an embodiment of Gaia. When Mrs. Krellborn boasts, "They're presenting my son with a trophy!," Mr. Fouch responds, "What'd he do, run away from home?" While death and destruction happen all around him and hysteria progressively abounds, Byrson Fouch stands proud and poised, knowing in his Olympian way that he will not be consumed by the burgeoning sexist war. It is actually he that encourages Mr. Mushnick to put the plant on display in the first place, as if he knows something of which the rest of the characters are unaware.

In mythology, Zeus is quite unlike his two inferior brothers, Poseidon and Hades. Poseidon unjustly vents his wrath on unsuspecting mortals, and Hades receives in his underworld the unfortunate victims of his brother's wrath. Zeus, on the other hand, apart from his occasional vents of rage, is a protector, seeking to preserve life, and is often seen intervening in the affairs of victims. Unlike Dr. Farb, or Orin Scrivello, D.D.S., the Poseidon figure, whose "temperament is wrong for the priesthood," Byrson Fouch (as Zeus) projects mostly benign spiritual values. While the combatants of the war consistently cudgel and digest one another, Byrson stands alone, like Zeus, watching, yet lending encouragement to Seymour, the chief victim of both sides of the conflict.

MAGICAL CURES

There is a remarkable obsession with health and the possibility of imminent death in the story. Mrs. Krellborn obsesses over her health, yet exudes an air of death. Mrs. Shiva despairs over her dying relatives, and emanates a cloud of doom. Mrs. Krellborn is fanatically consuming substances such as Dr. Slurp's tonic, cod liver oil, sulphur powder, achromycin, and Epsom salts. If we were to analyze her in relation to the ancient myth of the Gigantomachy, it is as though she is forever feverishly seeking the promised vitality of Gaia's magical plant, from which she is cut off.

In the stage version, Audrey herself shows a touch of this obsessive neurosis when she creates a "floral" arrangement of Bromo Seltzer, Bayer aspirin, Preparation H, and other over-the-counter medications. Mr. Mushnick, ever the Jewish straight man, speaks of Beverly *Ills*. Mrs. Krellborn listens to KSIK radio. There are arguments during every meal scene. And the doctor and patient are both sick in mind.

Why all of this deluge with intake and headache? According to the myth of the battle between Father Heaven and Mother Earth, Zeus stops the light of the sun, the moon, and the stars, so that his enemies can not find the magical plant. He himself, however, finds the plant in the dark, eats of it, and receives power over his foes. In *Little Shop*, Byrson Fouch eats the only vegetation that carries any possibility of renewal, leaving the other characters helplessly lacking the source of power and life.

The other participants are repulsed by Mr. Yellow Vest's eating flowers. In their "clear-sightedness," they partake of all that seems to promise health, giving the sky god exclusive access to the true spiritual and symbolic *elixir vitae*. His act suggests an integration of the feminine, and a healthy acceptance of the transitoriness of life, since flowers speak of short life, and eating speaks of the grave.

Interestingly, of all of the characters in the story, Byrson Fouch is the only one who we know as married. Mrs. Krellborn apparently chased her husband off with her cooking. Mrs. Shiva's husband has surely died, along with her other relatives. The dentist and the patient don't need marriage partners; they have each other. Mr. Mushnick never mentions a wife; he takes Audrey out to dinner and offers her a cigar. And Seymour and Audrey only dream of marrying (except in the 1986 version, where at the end of the film they marry). Byrson Fouch is the only character in this farcical gender war who has managed, at least to some degree, to blend the opposing forces of the anima and animus together.

The other characters form battle lines which ironically reverse their chosen positions in the sex war. The dentist, Mushnick, and the burglar, are ultramasculine in their fight, but paradoxically become rather feminine because of their emotional indulgence in the battle. The ultrafeminine fighters, Mrs. Krellborn, Mrs. Shiva, and Leonora, become rather masculine in their aggressive attempt to vaunt their femininity. In this polarized atmosphere, Byrson alone exhibits a balanced grace throughout the narrative.

Seymour and Audrey receive subconscious guidance from this mysterious Mr. Yellow Vest. Receiving verbal emotional support from Mr. Fouch, Seymour is seen on more than one occasion looking admiringly at him. In contrast to Seymour's opinion of the other adults in the narrative, he says of Mr. Fouch, "He's a nice man!" Eventually, following his example rather than opting for the habits of flogging and engulfing one another as the rest of their would-be single mentors do, Seymour and Audrey decide to unite for the common good of producing and preserving life.

SOME IMPLEMENTS OF WAR

The implements of the sexual conflict are guns, dentist's drills, all-consuming lips, biting words, and provocative sexuality. Alongside these obvious emblems of gender war, there is a more subtle spiritual-sexual subtext to the story. The first victim to fall prey to the never-satisfied plant (in the 1960 version) is a railroad dick. He is unintentionally hit on the head with a rock by Seymour, then he is run over by a train. The two police detectives begin their probing into the cavernous mystery which only deepens with each successive death. Later in the story, Leonora Clyde slips Seymour a banana peel and is also unintentionally hit on the head with a rock, which results in her being eaten by the plant. The narrator, Detective Joe Fink, says toward the end of the story, that "the mystery is drawing to its climax."

All of this narrative about dicks, rocks, and banana peels has spiritual significance beyond the obvious coarse comedy. Colloquially, a dick is a detective, one who investigatively penetrates hidden mysterious areas. And in the vernacular, a dick, of course is also a penis. A rock (*petra*, in Greek) recalls peter, both the phallus and, according to Roman Catholic theology, the rock on which Christ built his church. A rock also has primitive religious significance because it is often the dwelling place of a god.

Seymour unwittingly kills two people with rocks. The first one, the railroad dick, has drawn Seymour deeper into the impending mysterious crisis and begun his temptation to gain through others' losses. The second, the prostitute, is ironically caught in her own snare. Like a devouring vagina, she uses a banana peel (the covering of a masculine symbol) to entrap Seymour and is done in by a masculine symbol, a rock. Her plight is similar to that of the dentist, who, as a bashing erection or possibly as a *penis dentifrangibulum*, takes advantage of feminine creatures, and is in turn eaten by his counterpart, the *vagina dentata*. In the logic of the comedy, it seems that we are overcome by and therefore *become*, part of that which we fear the most.

When Seymour flips the rock like a coin (for "your place or mine"), he asks Leonora if she chooses wet or dry. To her detriment and death, she chooses wet, after Seymour spits on one side. What she does not realize is that wetness is symbolically positive in the feminine natural realm but negative in the masculine spiritual realm. Dryness and heat are related to the predominance of fire, the active and masculine

element, whereas wetness corresponds to water, a feminine and passive element. Because she offers her femininity to the masculine as
employment, she is swallowed. Like the dentist, she selfishly tampers
with the spiritual dimension of life to her own demise.

We are also reminded here that the monster Scylla is eventually
turned into a rock. And when Cronos (Time) eats his children, he eats
all but Zeus. Rhea gives him a rock swaddled as a baby to eat instead.
And thus, Zeus is saved from time, for eternity. A scripture verse also
comes to mind: "Fall on the rock, or the rock will fall on you."

SEYMOUR AS ODYSSEUS

There are several allusions to generations within the narrative. There
is Audrey and Audrey, Jr.; Mushnick and Son (Seymour); Mrs. Krellborn and Son; Mrs. Scrivello and Son; and Mrs. Shiva and her nephew,
Officer Frank Stooley. But probably the most significant generational
relationship in the story is an invisible one—that of Byrson Fouch and
Seymour. As was mentioned earlier, Mr. Yellow Vest, the embodiment
of Zeus, is no doubt a mentor—in effect, an adoptive father to
Seymour. In this respect, there are several mythical parallels between
Seymour and Odysseus, the heroic figure of Homer's *Odyssey*.

On his long and arduous journey home from the Trojan War, Odysseus has several encounters which parallel Seymour's adventures in our
comedy. He is guided consistently by Athena, the daughter of Zeus, the
patron goddess of war. He and his men are imprisoned by the cyclops,
Polyphemus, who eats two of his men every night until he and his
remaining men escape by burning out the eye of the cyclops. For this
act of violence to a son of Poseidon, Odysseus incurs the wrath of the
sea god. Later, Odysseus comes to the land of the Laestrygonians, a
group of savage man-eating giants. He passes also the island of the
Sirens, keeping his men's ears plugged with wax. And he has himself
tied to the mast so that he can hear the Sirens' beautiful singing without
being wrecked on their rocky coast. He then passes the female sea
monsters Scylla and Charybdis, while losing more of his men and

eventually his ship. He finally reaches his homeland where he kills the suitors of his wife, Penelope, and reconciles with this faithful woman.

In Seymour's odyssey, his guide, instead of Athena, is none other than her father, Zeus himself, in this case, Byrson Fouch. Seymour's imprisonment by the cyclops is living with his mother and working for Mushnick. His Poseidon is of course the wrathful dentist. The element of the man-eating Laestrygonians is found in the plant. The Sirens appear as several characters in the three versions of the story, all of whom tempt him to keep feeding Audrey Jr., which means profiting from the sexual war.

One of these Sirens is Hortense Fishtwanger, literally, a gardener who "twangs" fishes. Her role is to give Seymour a trophy for nurturing a strange and interesting plant, but she is actually abusing him in his fish role as Odysseus-Christ, the journeying redeemer (signified, for example, when she reprimands him about the pronunciation of her name). Of course the fish is symbolic of the Christ.

The sea monsters, Scylla and Charybdis, are found, as we have seen, in Mrs. Shiva and Mrs. Krellborn. Penelope's suitors are the dentist and the plant. And Penelope herself is Seymour's beloved Audrey, who forever remains true to Seymour.

Just as Penelope tries drowning herself in the sea when hearing a false rumour that Odysseus was slain, Audrey allows herself, in the stage version, to be eaten by the plant with the hope of resurrection with Seymour, like Romeo and Juliet. And this is where the unfolding story "draws to a climax."

HAPPILY EVER AFTER?

There are actually four different endings to the story, including a five million dollar one that was scrapped from the 1986 movie. In the 1960 film, Seymour climbs into the plant with a knife, intending to kill the plant. The plant blooms to reveal Seymour's face with the other victims, and then dramatically and pathetically droops, indicating its death.

In the stage production, Audrey is almost eaten by the plant, but is rescued by Seymour. While dying in his arms, she says, "Give me to the plant, so it can give you the things you need, so we'll always be together." After she dies, he honors her request. Later, Seymour goes into the plant with a knife to kill it, but is killed and eaten himself. The plant lives on in this version, with plans of devouring Cleveland, Des Moines, Peoria, New York, and beyond.

In the 1986 movie, Audrey is almost eaten, but is rescued by Seymour, who battles and kills the plant. Seymour and Audrey then get married and move into their suburban home, "somewhere that's green." After they cross their threshold however, a small, new plant of the same variety appears in their flower bed, indicating that the sexual war will start anew.

The ending that was cut from the 1986 film is different still. Audrey and Seymour are both eaten, Audrey II breaks free from the pot, and cuttings of the plant are sold in supermarkets all over America. And to the tune of "Don't Feed the Plants," Audrey II bounces from the Brooklyn Bridge, eats a subway train, and destroys the Roxy Theatre where *Jason and the Argonauts* is playing.

As a result of an unfavorable reaction with a test audience, this original ending was dropped from the 1986 version. But despite our current addictions to happy endings, the ending of the 1960 version, plus maybe a part of the stage ending which permits the deaths of both Seymour and Audrey, is the most satisfactory, philosophically speaking. The mythic parallel in this case is the story of Romeo and Juliet, drawn from the myth of Pyramus and Thisbe, victims, and yet conquerors of the eternal struggle between the sexes. Seymour and Audrey ultimately gain the victory over the shadow side of love.

PIETÀ COMPLEX

Seymour Krellborn's longing to identify with Fouch as a father figure, coupled with the element of his smothering mother, suggest a complex inevitably predisposing him toward his tragic death. We can call this phenomenon a pietà complex. Like other sensitive, creative male children raised by enmeshed mothers, Seymour takes on messianic traits associated with the Christ Child, just as several cult figures of the 1960's did—the Beat poet Jack Kerouac, the Jewish comedian Lenny Bruce, and the Japanese novelist Yukio Mishima. While Jesus' spiritual father progressively replaces his earthly father throughout his life, his mother seems to be constantly at his side, even, tearfully, to his dying breath. Likewise, Seymour's natural inheritance forlornly destines him to this same strange phenomenon of being led to his own messianic maternal grave.

The name Seymour is derived from Saint Maur, or Saint Maurus, a Christian Moorish saint with messianic attributes. The name Krell, in German, means quick-tempered, irritable, or cross. Seymour Krellborn, like many artists from motherly-enmeshed backgrounds, seems born into adversity, just as the name Odysseus means a "victim of enmity." He is like a matriarchal vegetation god, a John Barleycorn, destined to be swallowed up by the great *Terra Mater*.

There are at least six times that Seymour literally kicks a bucket in the original comedy. It is as if in the midst of all of the tragicomic blunderings around them, Seymour and Audrey intuitively see the kernel of truth in the inevitable, that Seymour is destined to be sacrificed. Perhaps they intuit from Mr. Yellow Vest secrets of the cycles of nature. Exposed to the sun god, they become illuminated and learn the cycles of seeds and orbs. Just as the moon is hidden in darkness for three days before being resurrected, and just as the sun disappears each night before returning to day, and just as seeds die before giving life, so must Seymour "kick the bucket" in order to accomplish his orbic mission. As a signifier of the marriage of matriarchy and patriarchy, he can truly "see more."

In the stage play, while pondering his woeful dilemma, Seymour stays up all night in anguish, depicting a Garden of Gethsamene experience. In the 1960 film, Audrey quips about Seymour, "Give him a chance to resurrect himself." And if there is a resurrection doxology in the musical, certainly the song "Suddenly Seymour" lends itself to this theme.

LESSONS FROM THE SEMINARY

Now, looking at the whole drama from a broad mythic perspective, we seem to be looking at a particular cultural problem, captured in fantasy, in the significant year of 1960. Its background is the perennial war between the anima and the animus, which has by this time produced a breakdown of communication. Constant bloodshed has become the name of the game. The phallic elements bludgeon the vaginal; the vaginal elements envelop the phallic. A mysterious sun god, the chief of the gods, enters this bleak picture without really doing anything to stop all of the bloodletting except infusing his spirit into the soul of a sheepish person who is consistently scourged and consumed. Here the disparate myths blend into one bigger myth.

The *sponsus* and *sponsa* unite for a life in the Elysian Fields—someplace green.

This sun deity, the chief of the gods, is hated by Mother Earth (Gaia). She would gladly eat him if she had a chance. Her plan is to empower and immortalize her allies through the magical elixir of the plant. To escape detection, the sun god, Father Heaven, easily turns off his light, so his foes cannot find the secret *solution*. But in the dark, he finds it and drinks it himself.

Suddenly, we see his son in the dark, in the middle of the night, talking to his sky father about his decision to drink from a poisoned cup. "Father, if there is any other way to solve the problem besides me drinking this, then let this cup pass from me." But rosy-fingered Dawn comes, and the son drinks the cup. Without deserving the bitter potion, he lays his life down in order to restore communication. He hopes to instill reconciliation where there was war. Mother Earth's response to this son of the sky deity is to gobble him up. The sky deity's response to her devouring of his son is to just let it happen. The swallowing of the son of the sun into the womb of the earth reminds us of Jesus' saying, "A seed must go into the ground and die before it can bring forth fruit."

At the "climax of the mystery," as the sun god's seed is planted in the womb of Mother Earth, the camera (1960) focuses lingeringly on a billboard that reads, "Skid Row Seminary." Here the religious thrust of the farce becomes explicit. A seminary, of course, is a school of theology, an institution where one studies about God and spiritual issues. The word comes from the Latin for seed plot, or garden, from which we get the words *seed, semen,* and *seminal.* With the billboard now in plain view, the whole story now makes perfect sense.

It seems that Audrey and Seymour have found a way out of their Skid Row after all. Like Romeo and Juliet, and like Pyramus and Thisbe, adolescent in their personalities and having a childlike faith, they surpass the warring elements of the modern adult world around them, and meet as one "on the other side," in the Elysian Fields, "somewhere that's green."

The green land that Audrey sings of is analogous of the *chymical* wedding between two once separate entities: heaven and earth. The sun god plants his seed in Mother Earth and together, they produce and nurture life. The interchanging union of earthy elements combined with sky-rain and sunshine produce photosynthesis, manifested mainly in the color green, a color of life. (Coincidentally, Ellene *Greene*, played the role of Audrey in the 1986 film, and Vincent *Gardenia*, played Gravis Mushnik.)

Our cinematic seminarians, Corman and Griffith, seem to have told us at the beginning of the decade of the gender revolution that there are metaphors associated with our sexual differences that have a significance broader than the microcosm of the sex-war narrative and broader than the macrocosm of our modern demythologized age. The indicators of the mystery, at this juncture of needed cultural transformation, seem to point toward the sky god's seed being inevitably broken and buried in Mother Earth, after which there may finally be resurrection, life, and reconciliation.

THE TRIP TO
BOUNTIFUL
PARADISE REGAINED

Horton Foote's screenplay *The Trip to Bountiful*, based on his stage play, was made into a subtle, sweet, and quietly touching film with small but moving human drama. What this 1986 film lacks in Hollywood pyrotechnics it makes up for in the still, small fire of the heart. In our analysis of *The Trip to Bountiful* we will first review the story as if divided into three main chapters:

1. Paradise Lost: The Barren City
2. The Pilgrimage: The Hope, the Obstacles
3. Paradise Regained: The Arrival in Bountiful

PARADISE LOST

The movie, directed by Peter Masterson, opens with a flashback of a young mother playfully chasing her young son through a colorful field of flowers—an idyllic, "once upon a time" remembrance of a better life. Then we cut to the protagonist, an old woman (Carrie Watts, played by Geraldine Page) quietly singing, "Jesus is tenderly calling

thee home," as if the magic of the lyrics will transport her to her
paradise of dream time. As the scene unfolds we learn that it is in the
middle of the night. She can't sleep during a full moon, and apparently
her son, Ludie (John Heard) with whom she is living, can't either.
They have a conversation about former times in the small town of
Bountiful, times of his childhood, times of her prime, times before
their present state of frustration, which includes her increasing forgetfulness and heart problems (she calls them sinking spells), but mostly,
the problems of having to live with Ludie's nagging wife.

Ludie sleeps in a separate bed from his wife of fifteen years, Jessie
Mae (Carlin Glynn). He's planning on asking his boss for a raise in the
morning, since he feels that he is not making enough money for the
hard work he does. Ludie's fellow worker Billy Davis, while owning his
own home and car, is about to have his fourth child. With slightly less
income, and with no children, Ludie lives in a two-room duplex with
his perennially complaining wife and his physically frail, devoted
mother. He tolerates his wife, intercedes in the arguments between the
two women, and bemoans his financial hardship.

His sweet mother is encouraging. She feels trapped in their small
apartment, where she sleeps in the living room, does most of the
housework, is ordered around by her impossible daughter-in-law, to
whom she is is obligated to turn over her pension check and is bound
by Jessie Mae's strict rules.

We get hints that Jessie Mae might spend a lot of Ludie's hard-
earned money and Mama's pension check on Coca-Colas, clothes,
furniture, hairdos, and movies. She is narcissistic, rude, inconsiderate,
grossly immature, and a constant thorn in the side of her poor mother-
in-law.

Jessie Mae wakes up and starts arguing with Mrs. Watts. The rules
are always an issue: no hymn singing, no pouting, no hiding your
pension check, no running, no going off to Bountiful, no noise. The
rule-making Jessie Mae chain-smokes, yells, nags, and projects her
abundant faults onto others.

In the first section of the film, we find our three main characters
living in Houston, because that is where Ludie can make a living, and

that is where Jessie Mae is the least upset. But the price to be paid is taxing on all three of them. There are several indications that this bountiful city life yields a wasteland at the psychosocial and spiritual level. The indicators of the wasteland are several: boredom as expressed in Jessie Mae's demand to go out more often, in Ludie's financial frustration, in Mrs. Watts's seeming imprisonment by Jessie Mae, in her craving to go back to her youth, in the apparent sexual absence between Ludie and Jessie Mae, in the barrenness of Jessie Mae's friend Rosella, and in the communication breakdown between Mrs. Watts and Jessie Mae.

To ease the pressure of this wasteland, Ludie tries to keep peace in the home while seeking a raise. Jessie Mae's solution to this barrenness is to spend more time and money outside of the home. But Mrs. Watts wants out altogether. Bountiful is where her heart belongs. So she hides her coveted pension check from her money-consuming daughter-in-law and plans a quick getaway to the land of her dreams.

THE PILGRIMAGE

The risks of her trip are several. She has heart problems with accompanying fainting spells. Being that Jessie Mae and Ludie know of her hoped-for trip, she could be found out. And there is no guarantee of friendship or support once she gets to Bountiful. But despairing of her present circumstances, she undauntingly sets out on her journey. Not having been to the small town of Bountiful in twenty years, she sallies forth with whetted anticipation. With hymn lyrics promising heaven, Mrs. Watts can not be stopped in her personal mission. Several lyrics beckon her to her promised land: "Jesus is tenderly calling thee home," "We shall gather at the river," and "Blessed assurance, Jesus is mine! Oh, what a foretaste of glory divine!" Her hymns seem to be her guide and armor, strengthening her resolve for her lone pilgrimage.

Determined as she is, Mrs. Watts asks for a ticket to Bountiful at the train station only to be told that trains don't stop there. So she goes to the bus station. But the buses, she is told, don't stop in Bountiful either.

It looks as though the town closed up long ago. The closest bus stop is Harrison, to which she buys a $3.50 ticket. At the bus station she meets a traveling companion, Thelma (Rebecca deMornay), a pretty young woman going home to stay with her parents while her husband is overseas. Mrs. Watts complains to Thelma that nobody has heard of small-town Bountiful, a telling symbol of modern city life.

She narrowly escapes Ludie and Jessie Mae at the bus station, and happily begins her trek to her old hometown, on the bus at last. She comforts her worried traveling companion with the Ninety-first Psalm, and she learns that the translation of Corpus Christi is the body of Christ. When she arrives at Harrison late at night, she realizes she has left her purse on the bus and has to sleep overnight at the bus station. In spite of outward obstacles, she maintains a blind faith toward her destination, telling Thelma how "everything is working out," and "The Lord must be with me." Her only potential contact in Bountiful, Callie Davis, her girlhood friend, was found dead "just day before yesterday," but go on she must.

While only twelve miles away from her final destination, she wakes up at the Harrison bus station only to find out that she is to be held there against her will by the bus agent and the local sheriff, with news that her son is on the way to pick her up. She protests, "No sheriff, or king or president is going to keep me from going to Bountiful." Another fainting spell and several protests pass before the sheriff volunteers to drive her out to her old home.

PARADISE REGAINED

Sitting in front of her childhood home, Mrs. Watts continues to reminisce about the place she has been talking about her entire trip. Her father would never allow anybody to shoot birds there, and she speculates that the birds therefore felt freer on his land than elsewhere. She and the sheriff happily recognize bird types. While walking through her dilapidated, abandoned, childhood home, her trip takes on meaning and purpose. She seems to have found herself here.

The monster, Jessie Mae, in her relentless pursuit of the escaped pilgrim.

Ludie arrives, taking the place of the sheriff. But according to Ludie, "It doesn't do any good remembering." His life is in the city. Mama remarks how blue the sky is. Ludie looks like his mother's father (a good-looking man) according to her. While at Bountiful, Ludie is reminded of his own present situation, never having had children of his own.

Jessie Mae, angry at Mother Watts, and uninterested in the history or significance of Bountiful, waits in the car until her patience is spent. Then she comes hollering about rules, worrying about Ludie losing his job over this venture, and complaining about ruining her good shoes in "this swamp." But Mama feels so revived and inspired by her trip to Bountiful, she kisses a surprised Jessie Mae on the cheek. In spite of Jessie Mae's continual haranguing, Mama exults, "I had my trip, and it's enough to keep me happy the rest of my life." Before she leaves, Mrs. Carrie Watts slowly sits down on the ground and reverently picks up some dirt in her hands.

185

THE TRIP TO BOUNTIFUL

Oppositions

Our narrative is an amalgam of oppositions. We see a division between Ludie and Jessie Mae (possibly no sex life), a constant rift between Mama and Jessie Mae, and several other oppositions, as shown in the following diagram:

WASTELAND	BOUNTIFUL
bound in the city	free in the country
barrenness of Ludie and Jessie Mae	fruitfulness of Billy Davis and his wife
financial stress of Ludie	prosperity of Billy Davis
arguing in cramped apartment	peace in Bountiful
infirmity of old age	health of youth
boredom of Jessie Mae	excitement of Jessie Mae
worry of Thelma	peace of Mama's biblical promises
loneliness of Thelma	reuniting with Thelma's parents
present barrenness of Bountiful	former prosperity of Bountiful
impatience of Jessie Mae	patience of black lady at bus station

With so many elements opposed to one another, it is no wonder that everybody is reaching out to something beyond them for peace, reconciliation, or hope. Thus, *The Trip to Bountiful* is the quest for heaven. It is the natural human tendency to reach out of time into eternity. It is the spiritual journey, the religious pilgrimage, the hope of a better world, the reach for beyond, a step into the other side. Heaven promises peace and a reconciliation of these uncomfortable opposites.

Time and Eternity

Considering all of these oppositions there is one that stands as the overarching division, that is the separation of time and eternity. The atmosphere inside the tiny Houston duplex apartment speaks loudly of temporal time. Space limitations, rules of conduct, disagreement, and the cares of this world are all the concerns of the day, the hassles of the present, with little hope for a brighter future. Mama's desire for Bountiful is her thrusting herself out of this time and space dimension and out into *in illo tempore*, or sacred time. It is her attempt to regain paradise. What she has to put up with in the Houston apartment is certainly not what she had looked forward to for her old age. Naturally she would hearken back to a more pleasant time and place. To her, her Bountiful is in mythical time, where all is prosperous and peaceful, and where even the birds feel a certain specialness.

Mama Watts can't sleep during a full moon, which indicates that her clock is wound more to the cycle of the moon than to that of the sun. She has her heart set more toward eternity than in time, which is more common for old people than for the young. She has lived her life, and now she has her mind set toward the other side. As opposed to the linear time by which Ludie and Jessie Mae are bound, Mama Watts is seeking the eternal return, longing for the mythic time of the cosmic cycle. She says she hasn't had her hands in the dirt for twenty years. If she could only go back to Bountiful and put her hands in the soil, she would experience the richness of the cycle of nature and escape, even momentarily, to the land of bounty, where time stands still but where eternity goes on in its ever peaceful fashion.

In temporal time we have only three times: past, present, and future. The captivity Mama feels in Houston is an ever-present reminder of the limitations of the present. At her age, with nothing more to look forward to, she has only the past as an escape. Thelma, Ludie, and Jessie Mae, all being younger, are looking toward the future, to brighter days. But Mama already did that when she was younger. Being that she doesn't have much time left, her present is actually her grim future in temporal time. By looking to the past, she imagines a mythical future. These three time zones in our narrative can be diagrammed as follows:

PAST	PRESENT	FUTURE
youth	middle age	old age
Thelma	Ludie and Jessie Mae	Mama Watts

potentiality	barrenness	captivity
loneliness	sexual absence	depression
home to parents	boredom	regression
good health	good health	heart problems and forgetfulness
attention getting	material distractions	attention getting
worry about hubby	worry about money	worry about life

Caught in a time and space continuum, these three time zones are one's only options. But an eternal frame of reference gives one another option, which is what Mama Watts is striving for. By determining to go to Bountiful, even though that is in her past, she paradoxically catapults herself off into the eternal future, into *in illo tempore*. With this choice, her time diagram changes from a limited, linear, three-zone existence into a cyclical diagram. We could put the three existing time zones into three quarters of a cycle as follows:

youth
Thelma
summer

middle age
Ludie and Jessie Mae
autumn

old age
Mama Watts
winter

The only problem with this cycle is that there is a corner missing. Obviously what is missing is birth/rebirth, or spring, the first quarter of the eternal return. The number four represents completion. And this is the glory of eternal time as opposed to temporality. It completes the circle.

At the top of our circle we have Thelma, Mama's young traveling companion, who still has most of her life to look forward to. Like Mama, she is also headed back home, but for a different reason. Her homeward journey is a temporary trek back to her loving parents, to stave off her loneliness while her husband is overseas. In the large cycle of eternity, her regression in time is only temporary, as is common for people of her age, fresh away from home. She is just making a pit stop for emotional refueling for her longer cycle of life, most of which is still ahead of her.

At the autumn stage where Ludie and Jessie Mae find themselves, there is no turning back. They are almost at middle age, and there is nothing for them in the past. Ludie's past is living with him in the form of his aging mother.

Jessie Mae's past is still hauntingly controlling her life in the form of her adolescent personality, which fits her age about as well as bobby socks on a matron. While she carries her childhood personality into

The pilgrim, Mrs. Carrie Watts, finds a friend in Thelma, a fellow traveler.

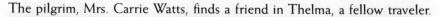

her present, she is neurotically locked into a dead and dying existence, even infecting others with her malady of negativity. Usually it is people with a childlike personality who revive others around them. But with Jessie Mae, it is the opposite. Instead of gracing others with childlike humor, she infects others with childish gall. As a near middle-aged adult, while traversing toward the future, she is actually a malignity of childhood. While her body and time are heading speedily toward their final destination of advancing age, her personality has never made it past the developmental lessons of childhood. While being caught in a time warp of a childish temperament, the good side of childhood (playfulness, and joy,) is menacingly absent. And of course, this is what is so glaringly absent in our cycle of time. The wonder, naïveté, hope, and song of Mama Watts is pathologically missing in Jessie Mae, and thus infectiously missing in Ludie, by exposure to the disease. As he says to Mama at Bountiful, "There's no use in remembering."

Mother Watts fits into the last section of our quaternity, at old age, near death, in the winter of life. By hearkening back to time past, in her present quarter of the cycle, she is actually trying to complete the circle. What would be thought of as her regression in linear time is actually a progression in cyclical time. In her reviving of her childhood, she is trying to fill in the missing quarter of the quaternity. In her quest for Bountiful past she seeks heaven future. She proclaims her wish to die in Bountiful, and she digs her hands into the earth there, where two of her babies are buried, signifying an urge for the completion of the natural cycle of life. Her Eden past is a figure of her paradise future.

But to participate in that cycle, to be reborn in mythical time, to enter heaven, an act of childlike faith is required, such as that which she carries on her pilgrimage to Bountiful. This is where choices are made between oppositions, and where cyclical participation reconciles polarized opposites.

Choices

Mama Watts's first act of faith is that of choosing Bountiful over her miserable existence with Jessie Mae. She decries fifteen years with Jessie Mae as being too much. A choice is therefore inevitable.

During her pilgrimage she reminisces to Thelma about the bad choice she made in marrying her husband, knowing that she didn't love him. Surveying her present state of affairs, she asks Thelma if she thinks God punishes us for "the things we do wrong," like marrying a man she didn't love and not marrying the man she did love. She reveals that she was prevented by familial circumstances from marrying the man she truly loved, Ray John Murray. We could speculate that her life would have been much different had she followed her heart in her youth, instead of marrying somebody she didn't love. As even temporal time has cycles of good and bad, her son Ludie has apparently repeated her pattern and also married somebody he didn't love, the repercussion of which has come around to perpetually haunt her. She couldn't marry the man she loved because their fathers were not speaking to one another. We are reminded that Jessie Mae had a quarrel with her girlfriend, with whom she did not speak for a period of time. Here, the classic theme of Pyramus and Thisbe expresses itself. But unlike the classic myth, Carrie Watts chose to obey her father and suffer the postsequences. Pyramus and Thisbe, like Romeo and Juliet, disobey the dictates of their home rules and die in their youth in order to meet on the other side. Carrie Watts chose to follow the rules given to her, and she has lived with the negative consequences ever since. Now that she is close to death, she finally gets the courage to break the rules.

A repeating theme of doubles and choices drives this idea in our narrative. While at the train station ticket window, we see two identical-looking nuns standing behind her, waiting patiently. Contrasted to this pair is a set of twin men standing behind her at the bus station ticket window, waiting quite impatiently. While talking to the bus agent in Harrison, the topic of drinking comes up, with the agent mentioning a merchant whose son made the wrong choice of drinking away his inheritance. The agent then mentions his own two sons: "One drinks, the other doesn't."

Then there is talk of Mrs. Watts's girlhood friend, Callie Davis, being compared to the irresponsible former inhabitants of Bountiful. She is described as a woman who loved to farm and garden, a real earth mother. Unlike all of the other former inhabitants of Bountiful, Callie Davis, the very last resident, knew how to preserve her land so it would continue to produce throughout her lifetime. She was even seen driving a tractor the day before they found her dead.

This contrast of doubles forces the opposition of morals, like the good and evil angels of Marlowe's *Doctor Faustus*, like the polarized doubles of Poe's "William Wilson" story, and like Stevenson's *Doctor Jekyll and Mister Hyde*.

These double oppositions also force individual choices. Callie Davis, a woman with her hands in the dirt, made right choices and reaped the bounty thereof, as opposed to the former farmers of Bountiful who turned Eden into a wasteland. Related, at least philosophically, is another Davis, Billy Davis, a man who apparently has made some right choices. He is blessed with his own house, a wife, and four industrious children, as opposed to Ludie Watts, who, despite a comparable income (plus mother's pension check) is unable to move out of a cramped duplex apartment and remains frustratedly childless after fifteen years of marriage.

Participating at least spiritually with the cycle of nature, Mrs. Carrie Watts speculates on the future of Bountiful, according to choices. She sees what was once a prosperous and thriving cotton growing community. But it is all woods now because of improper farming techniques. As the sheriff testifies, "The land just played out." She guesses that some day people might come back to Bountiful, cut down the trees, plant cotton again, then wear out the land again, whose children will sell the land again and move into the city, like their predecessors of old. Then the trees will grow up again, repeating the cycle of nature, which will always revolve in its natural orbic mission, despite the choices humans make along the way.

According to the inner lessons of the film, we can have a full quaternity and reap the blessings thereof by making the right choices, thus blessing not only ourselves, but our posterity. Or we can make the wrong choices and reap the whirlwind thereof. The bounty of Bountiful has been turned into a wasteland by poor choices. So people then choose to move off to the city, where life is promised to be more bountiful. But because they bring poor choices with them, the bounty of the city is soon turned into a wasteland as well. We hear a paraphrased version of the bus agent's cry echoing in our ears at this point: "There were two people, one chose for the good, the other didn't."

By taking her trip to Bountiful, Carrie Watts completes her circle. She is supplying the missing quarter of her quaternity, by going through an inner rebirthing experience. By putting her hands into the earth of her homeland, she is symbolically reviving the quarter of birth/rebirth/comedy/spring. Ironically, one of the few places in the film where anybody laughs is on the way to Bountiful at a changeover stop. A man mentions that the name of the city of Corpus Christi means "the body of Christ" in Spanish. When he wants verification from a Mexican man at the bus stop, the Mexican doesn't understand because he doesn't speak English. The Anglo man laughs. And here we have an ironic joke. The missing ingredient of the cycle is actually the seed that is buried in the earth and is reborn as a fruit-bearing plant of springtime. Thus, the missing verification is the *corpus christi*, the body of the dying god who is reborn as a child of springtime humour. Mrs. Carrie Watts renews her faith in this missing ingredient and completes the circle. As the circle unites the opposites, so too do choices complete the circle.

THE GRADUATE

THE TERRIBLE MOTHER FROM THE
BLACK LAGOON

For months after it was released in 1967, *The Graduate* was an extremely popular film, especially with high school and college-aged audiences. One writer recalls seeing youths lined up around the block every night for months at his Manhattan neighborhood theatre. The drawing power, at least on the surface, was related to the major theme of the generational gap within the film, which was of course a major *leitmotif* in Western culture at the time. Besides the cultural gaps evident within the film (of young and old, rich and poor, and linguistic differences) the other major themes are morality, communication, entrapment, sexual differences, sex role reversals, sexual symbolism, and of course, the mythic element.

CULTURAL GAPS

When *The Graduate* was released, the generations of America had probably never been at more alienated positions. The college students of the day were the first wave of post–World War II baby boomers. The Vietnam War was in full swing, and so was the antiwar movement. Most prewar parents grew up during the Great Depression and were now living in a healthy and prosperous postwar economy. The children of the bomb, the first rock 'n' roll generation, had developed a completely different set of morals, ethics, and philosophies from that of their parents.

The film's protagonist, Benjamin Braddock (Dustin Hoffman), sums up this feeling when hiding in his room, away from the guests at his graduation party. When his father asks him what he is worried about, Benjamin mentions his future. He hopes that his future will be "different," no doubt implying different than that of his vapid parents and their friends. Benjamin is the only person his age at the party given in his honor. He is treated like a child, and in fact it is more like a birthday party for a small child where there are more adults present than children. The clincher of the evening arrives when a family friend, Mr. McGuire, calls Ben aside and gives him a word of advice: "Plastics. . . . There's a great future in plastics." The youthful audience laughed heartily at this symbol of the older generation's plastic society. What the younger set viewed as their parents' obsession with material comforts seemed merely phony, vacuous, and smug.

While some of the older generation, such as Mr. and Mrs. Robinson, sleep in different beds but have secret affairs, many of the younger generation sleep openly with strangers, even without beds. But not Benjamin. He has been enculturated into the mindset of the older generation, still dressing conservatively and exhibiting the most appropriate manners. Even after being corrupted, and while in bed with the older Mrs. Robinson (Anne Bancroft), he courteously calls her Mrs. Robinson. But while all outward appearances show Ben to be a product of the old guard, he has some serious inner doubts about the efficacy of that worldview.

At the Taft Hotel, the place of Ben's affair with Mrs. Robinson, while Ben holds the door open, many old people walk out and some young people walk in, signifying that unless things change the young people will merely continue more of the same patterns of their parents. Some young people are destined to repeat the pattern, like Carl Smith, the medical student with whom Mrs. Robinson's daughter Elaine (Katherine Ross) exchanges marital vows. Besides being accepted by both sets of parents as a perpetuator of their system, Carl proposes that he and Elaine would make a "great team," using the lingo of the status quo, as if spoken by a corporate executive or sports aficionado of a macho culture.

MORALITY GAP

One critic of *The Graduate* complained that the film's ending suggests that the morality of the hero and heroine would turn out to be more conventional than that of their parents. I wouldn't agree at all. It seems that there is a clear distinction between the worldviews and morality of the established familial system and that of our young protagonists. Both sets of parents, as well as all of their friends, live in a figurative and literal world of black and white. In fact, all of the clothes, furnishings, houses, cars, and accessories owned by both sets of parents are shown in literal black and white design. Even the hotel rooms in which Ben and Mrs. Robinson meet are decorated in black and white. At one point Ben's mother wears a black-and-white op-art dress, fraudulently aping a design of the hip subculture of the time. Mrs. Robinson's underwear is black and sometimes white. Her house is white, with a black door. Even the patio awnings at both houses are striped black and white. All of this signifies a black and white fundamentalist mentality. Elaine's room, no doubt furnished by her parents, is all white, with the exception of Elaine's portrait. Grey issues are not allowed in a world of striking contrasts and forced polarities. Of course a black and white world is also devoid of color and *joi de vivre*.

Mr. and Mrs. Robinson, we are told, had to get married because of a pregnancy. But they now sleep in separate rooms. Thus, we learn that their traditional morality forces them into reluctant situations in spite of the fact that they might be unhappy in their moral decisions, thus forcing a life of dishonesty and inauthenticity. Throughout most of the film, in their conditioned responses, both Benjamin and Elaine, the offspring of the polarized generation, buy into the old mentality. It is only later, and at different times, that each of them finally chooses the life of personal authenticity.

COMMUNICATIONAL BARRIER

Along with a significant cultural and generational gap we find a communicational barrier between the young and old in this film. Although the Simon and Garfunkel songs in the sound track were written before the film, they all are very appropriately fitted to this story. The alienation, communicational breakdown, materialistic religion, grass roots prophecy, and disconnected frustration depicted in the songs, particularly in "The Sounds of Silence," are all evident throughout the narrative.

At both the evening graduation party and the birthday pool party at Ben's house, the communicational style of the older generation is hyperbolically inane, insipid, phoney, one-sided, comically bourgeois, dehumanizing, mannerdly vulgar, and highly reflective of their world-views, which are crassly materialistic and conventional.

Any direct communication between Ben and any member of the older generation is very awkward and forced. One classic example is Ben's short talk with Mr. McGuire, the prophet of the plastics industry:

"Ben."

"Mr. McGuire."

"Ben."

"Mr. McGuire."

Ben's father, Mr. Braddock, and his partner, Mr. Robinson, are both attorneys—professionals who one would think should have a knack for communiction. But they and their families and friends all seem to be plagued with a degenerative inability to communicate. Benjamin, on the other hand, was the head of the debating team in college, the assistant editor of the college newspaper in his junior year, and the managing editor in his senior year—good background for one concerned with interlocution. Certainly, at least in his formal training, he knows the rules of formal logic, correct grammar, and proper human interaction. But when he gets around the people who supported him in his studies, he seems to catch their invisible communicational disease.

When Ben moans to be different, one thing is sure: he doesn't want to speak the language of his inherited culture.

When Ben dons the scuba gear, on which his father so proudly boasts spending two-hundred dollars, in essence, he is reluctantly wearing the burdensome language of his parents' generation. His lack of hearing while wearing the gear symbolizes the style of communication into which he was born. He longs secretly for a new language "for those who have ears to hear." The words of the older prophets are written in the language of profits. But as the song goes, the words of the younger prophets "are written on the subway walls."

Even when Ben takes Elaine out on their first date, he is forced to communicate to her with rudeness and total disrespect, being caught in a double bind, while under the seductive influence of Mrs. Robinson. After Ben's apology to Elaine, he explains to her that, "Ever since I graduated, I have had a compulsion to be rude all of the time." If this is true, it is no doubt an honest rebellion against the outward manners, yet hidden and subtle rudeness of his parents, and an honest admission of his true feelings. After Ben and Elaine really begin communicating, it seems that nothing will stop them. In fact, while eating at the drive-in hamburger joint, they even have to roll up their windows to block out the noise of their own age-peers.

Even the conversation between Mrs. Robinson and Ben during their affair is just about nonexistent, mostly at Mrs. Robinson's insistence. Ben pathetically asks Mrs. Robinson while in bed, "Mrs. Robinson, do you think we could say a few words together first this time?," only to be rebuffed by her "I don't think we have much to say to one another."

In the beginning of the affair, it is Ben who turns off the lights, in apparent embarrassment, while Mrs. Robinson turns them on, in apparent unashamedness. As the affair progresses, the light switching reverses. He turns the lights on to talk; she turns them off, to have sex.

Since Elaine's liberation from this world of communicational disaster is much later than Ben's, she operates at length with the infected residue of the disease. At Ben's apartment in Berkeley, when he tries to tell her the truth, she plugs her ears and screams. Later, when she leaves Ben a Dear John note, it is delivered impersonally by her roommate instead of herself. It speaks of her confused and inherited ambivalence: "I love you. But I don't think it will work out." Even Ben has a couple of relapses of faith. In the hotel room with Mrs. Robinson, in his frustrating attempt at conversation about Elaine, he despairs with "Let's not talk about it. Let's not talk at all."

ENTRAPMENT

When the older people speak to Ben, unlike most Americans, they close in on him, presenting a feeling of confinement and space limitation. This is only a small symbol of a greater entrapment, the visual signifier of which is glass. There are scenes of the bored and worried Benjamin looking forlornly into his fish aquarium, as if to identify with aquatic boredom and captivity. To make the connection more complete, we see Ben himself entrapped in his own metaphorical aquarium. At the pool party, wearing his scuba gear under water with a look of depressed surrender, Ben reminds us of the fish in the tank. He is somebody that is owned, fed, and held captive.

When Ben looks out of his bedroom window at the people at poolside, we again get the feeling of his captivity. Also in the telephone booth at the Taft Hotel Ben even expresses sounds of suffocation in his confined space behind glass.

During Mrs. Robinson's attempt at seduction, Ben cries, "Oh God, let me out!," revealing his deeper incarceration.

The last scene of confinement is at the wedding, in church. But this time it is not Ben who is in the confining aquarium. It is Elaine and all of the wedding guests. Ben is again looking through glass, but this time he is looking from the outside in, heralding a freedom call to Elaine.

SEXUALITY

Mrs. Robinson's seduction of and affair with Benjamin is the obvious sexual theme in the narrative. The affair is an acute symptomatic

The submersion of Benjamin's keys in the fish tank prefigures his own submersion into the motherly sea of *massa confusa*.

eruption of a more complex systemic problem. While Mrs. Robinson finds a sexual outlet through her illicit affair, Mr. Robinson finds himself engrossed in the sexual conversation of the bland newlywed television program. Cinematic signs of displaced or sublimated sexuality reveal this gnawing problem in our black-and-white culture, as if the cinematic mythmakers want to remind us of missing love. The signs abound, from the phallic lamps on the strip joint tables to the phallic shadows cast by the chandelier in the hotel room. And while at Berkeley, Ben catches his first glimpse of Elaine through a vulvic statue opening. Throughout the film there are many conversations and words spoken in doorways, also symbolizing this yearning for vestibular intercourse. We see Mrs. Robinson calling out to Ben while standing on her open and inviting threshold. There are red-jacket porters walking through promiscuous doorways at the Taft Hotel, calling Ben Mr. Gladstone. And there are several frustrated conversations in the lonely doorway of Ben's Berkeley apartment.

To offset the fraudulent sexuality of the older generation with the honest sexuality of the younger set, we are given juxtaposing signs of impotency and potency. When Ben announces to his parents that he will be marrying Elaine, his father exults in happy pride and picks up the phone receiver to call the Robinsons with the good news. Mrs. Braddock shrieks in an almost orgasmic frenzy. But when they find out that Elaine does not yet know of the marriage plans, the erect phone receiver in Mr. Braddock's hand slowly limps flaccid.

As a symbol of compensation, Mr. Robinson smokes a cigar at two significant times during his talks with Benjamin. The first time, at the Robinson household, in typical macho bravado, he encourages Benjamin to "sow some wild oats," and to "have a few flings" during his summer vacation. In the same breath, he suggests that Ben take out his pristine daughter, Elaine. The second time we see Mr. Robinson smoking his phallic cigar is at Ben's Berkeley apartment. Here Mr. Robinson verbally threatens Ben with legal action but cowardly runs away when he feels physically threatened.

As a subtext to the sexual elements, there are traditional sex role reversals. The successful attorneys might be tyrants at the office, but they come across as weak and submissive men at home. In her dominating nature, Mrs. Robinson has abandoned the traditional passive feminine role. We have also alluded to Ben wanting to talk in bed, a clear reversal of the traditional male stereotype. Of course this film was also created at a time when the concept of *unisex* was gaining ever increasing popularity among the youth culture of the 1960s.

Benjamin is the most androgynous of all of the characters in the story. While exhibiting strong masculine drive in his pursuit of Elaine, he also shows sincere feminine sensitivity in his need for communication and in his nurturance of Elaine, signs of his ability to reconcile polarized opposites.

But before Ben ever asserts himself, we see him as a lured and imprisoned passive male stud, as if owned and exploited by an Amazon woman. At Ben's graduation party, when Mrs. Robinson talks him into driving her home, she throws his car keys at him, and they land in the fish tank. This highly symbolic sign is our first clue to the deeper nature of the developing story. A key, of course being a masculine device, is submerged into the feminine element of the microcosmic sea.

There is a glimpse of sexual contrasts in the cars driven. The Robinsons' car is a large black wombish Lincoln Continental. Ben's car, by comparison, is a red convertible sports car, an explicit symbol of hot masculine sexuality in his society. In his high speed pursuit of Elaine, his car glides him ever closer to his ultimate consummation, signified by his sensual drive through a tunnel.

MYTHIC ELEMENTS

The numinous elements of the film are numerous. The obvious mythic archetypes are the hero, the beast, and the maiden in distress. Ben's wielding the cross to fend off his enemies at the church is also overtly recognizable.

Mrs. Robinson

We are never given Mrs. Robinson's first name, but we don't need it. She reveals herself as the Terrible Mother of mythology. Being that there are traditionally two aspects of the Great Mother, a good and a bad aspect, we are shown in her the evil side of the great goddess. With Mrs. Robinson's aggressively persistent and manipulative personality, we are reminded of the all-consuming negative side of the Great Mother. Subtle but sure revenge is Mrs. Robinson's ploy, fitting her role as the terrific queen of the terrestrial world. The Terrible Mother is the maw of the earth, the beginning and end of human existence. She manifests herself as the Good Mother if she is treated fairly, but as the destructive mother if she is crossed. Certainly Mrs. Robinson feels betrayed. Whether as Kali, Hecate, Ishtar, or one of the Gorgons, she presents many webs and snares for those victims of her insatiable tomb.

While she wears black throughout the entire film, to indicate which side of the polarized mother she represents, there are only a few exceptions to Mrs. Robinson's color code. One of them is a piece of her underwear which at one time is white (but it does fit her black-and-white mentality). During her first encounter with Ben at the hotel she has a leopard coat, and at the wedding service she sports a leopard collar. Even one of her black dresses and a piece of her dark underwear reveal cat patterns, indicating her identification with predatory creatures. This reminds us of The Lady of the Beasts, a variation of the earth goddess, who is personified in myth as the goddess of the hunt, or the goddess of animals, often pictured with wild beasts, signifying her ferocious nature.

Mrs. Robinson is the queen of Benjamin's materialistic world. While the rest of the middle-aged drones seem to play peripheral roles, Mrs. Robinson's cunning and seemingly omnioptic eyes engage the others

With the exception of a few animal prints, the Lady of the Beasts habitually wears black.

in her hungry royal designs. Besides seducing Benjamin into a pro-
longed affair, like a vengeful goddess, she claims rape after her act is
exposed.

As was alluded to earlier, the sinking of Ben's keys in the tank is his
submersion into the Great Mother of the deep. Originating from
ancient mythology of the Water Lady, several languages still maintain
a word for ocean or sea which is linguistically connected to mother, as
in the German *Meer* (ocean), and *Mutter* (mother); and the French *mer*
(sea), and *mère* (mother).

Benjamin Braddock

Ben's metaphoric drowning into this maternal ocean is reemphasized
by his father's pushing him down to the bottom of the pool. In spite of
the fact that he doesn't want to participate in his parents' silly games,
wishes, and parties, he feels overwhelmed and outnumbered, so he
reluctantly dons the scuba gear and surrenders himself to his seemingly inevitable bondage to the queen of the deep.

The system into which Ben was born might be patriarchal and male-
dominated outside of the home, but the religion of matriarchy reigns
strongly within. The men are allowed to congratulate themselves on
their financial prowess as suppliers of upper-middle-class trappings,
but they deceive themselves into thinking that they sit on a throne at
home. This is no "Father Knows Best." The men in this subculture are
virile and potent on the surface, but impotent in communication or
emotional expression.

Feeling helpless against this unchangeable system, Ben acquiesces
and sinks to the bottom of the pool, just like the key in the fish tank.
He stands there holding his Neptunish spear as if guarding an underwater castle, but we intuitively know that his stance is mere perfunc-
tory protocol. There is a greater authority over this mock Poseidon,
being the great goddess of the earth and sea. As we gaze at this sad
image of Ben at the bottom of the pool, we hear a voiceover of Ben
phoning Mrs. Robinson, to accept her ensnaring affair. Despite Ben's

questioning his future, he gives in to the system. He humbles himself before the royal matriarch and does her bidding.

Elaine Robinson

Elaine makes the perfect maiden in distress. She's young, pretty, influenceable, and easily confused by the prevailing winds of change. When her Moses is present she gladly follows his lead. When he is temporarily removed, she is quick to bow down to the golden calf, that of Carl Smith, the promising young medical student.

MYTHIC DRAMA

Underwater Submersion

After being confused, worried, and bored with his life, with no hope of a "different" future, Benjamin hopelessly dives into the underworld of the queen mother. In their bedchamber, as soon as Ben closes the door of their first hotel encounter, the lyrics "hello darkness my old friend" reflect the depth of his submersion. It is as if he is regressing, not merely back to childhood, as he is treated at his parties, but here he goes even further, to the eternal womb/tomb.

Although Mrs. Robinson is not Ben's actual mother, her relation to him has maternal overtones. She does happen to be his father's partner's wife, a close friend of the family all of Ben's life, and the one who inflicts the taboo against seeing Elaine, as if Elaine were his sister. We are reminded here of the mother-son cults of religious lore, such as that of Ishtar and Tammuz. After being rejected by Ben, Mrs. Robinson's lust, like Ishtar's love spurned by Gilgamesh, turns to hate.

While Ben is threatened with the queen's jealous vengeance with the demand not to see Elaine, he is placed in a double bind by his complicitous mother. Mrs. Braddock threatens to have all of the Robinsons over if Ben refuses to date Elaine. Here, lying on the pool

raft, floating over his watery subconscious and over the sea of matriarchal omnipresence, Ben submerges again under water, and is reluctantly rebaptized into what he fears is his inevitable destiny.

Ben's Conversion

So without an obvious way out of his double bind, Ben decides to take
Elaine out, but he purposefully treats her rudely with the familiar
systemic lack of communication. To get out of the bind he even
employs a frontal assault by taking sweet and innocent Elaine to a strip
joint. What is designed by Ben to halfway please the goddess and her
co-conspirators, while getting him off the hook, actually works against
the system and infects Ben with a love for Elaine. True to the spiritual
principle of extremities, the more he tries to offend her to be set free
from her, the more he is drawn toward her. The ironic act that causes
the graduate's conversion experience is the stripper's twirling of her
nipple (graduation) tassels over Elaine's innocent head. When Elaine
breaks down and cries, the submerged and passive Benjamin suddenly
ascends from his fish tank and stands up to defend his own oceanic
victim. And thus, his conversion becomes the hinge upon which the
second half of our heroic story swings.

Obstacles toward the Rescue

The next day, when Ben drives over to pick up Elaine for a second date,
he is confronted outside by the wicked witch of the San Fernando
Valley. She threatens to tell Elaine of the affair, so Ben makes a mad
dash in the rain to Elaine's house to beat her to it. Dripping wet with
their sin, both Benjamin and Mrs. Robinson appear to Elaine like two
creatures that just crawled up from the black lagoon of the queen's
watery abyss. Yet while he has finally escaped from the lair of the
dragon lady, our hero has yet to rescue the maiden. Shocked by the
news of the affair, Elaine shrieks and pulls away from her would-be

hero/lover. At this point, she herself is sucked into the vortex of the system, casting her allegiance with her fraudulent family.

So begins the heroic mission. Now that he has liberated himself from the underworld system, our knight errant is obsessed with rescuing his fair damsel from the goddess's influence. And just as all heroes worthy of the title must face a horde of foes, so does our Benjamin confront the obstacles in the way of the mythic boon.

Now avoiding Ben, Elaine retreats to Berkeley, and Ben follows with heroic intent. He catches up with her on a bus, and it briefly appears as though he has pulled her up from the underworld of familial binding. But there is the obstacle of the tall, handsome, blond medical student that Elaine has been dating. This Carl Smith is approved by her family. He has all the right credentials, and he has been talking of marriage.

At the very beginning of the film, while Ben descends into Los Angeles on the airplane, he wears black and white. Then throughout the entire film both Benjamin and Elaine wear colors (besides black and white), signifying their subconscious identification apart from their families' morality. But toward the end of the film, Ben again wears black and white, then while at Elaine's gym class, we see them both in black and white. And throughout the rest of the film they both ironically wear black and white, reminding us of *enantiodromia*, the cataclysmic reversal of opposites, an indication that there is hope ahead.

Hints of the Trickster God

And here we have our first in a series of cosmic bookends. An ironic joke is found here with the black and white clothes of our young couple, coupled with a painting at the beginning of the film. Outside of Ben's bedroom the camera lingers on a black-and-white painting of a clown. Of course, a black-and-white clown is as ironic as a multicolored pall-bearer. Either would secretly remind us that the trickster god is not far away, planning a sudden reversal of opposites, while it might be least expected by the evil conspirators.

More Plots and Obstacles

But with or without a trickster god helping him, there are still more plots against our hero. There is Ben's suspicious Berkeley landlord, who seems to haunt him regularly to add to his potential discouragement.

Ben walks into his apartment one day to be surprised by the presence of Mr. Robinson, who presents a legal threat. We are reminded of Heracles who is appointed to rescue Persephone from the underworld, only to be confronted by Cerberus, the watchdog of the deep.

Driving madly from Berkeley back to Los Angeles, Ben stands up against The Lady of the Beasts who announces the imminent wedding, to which of course he is not invited. So the hero drives all the way back up to the San Francisco Bay area to find out from Carl Smith's fraternity brothers where the wedding is to be held, only to hear sexual jokes about his loved one, with a general hint that it might be in Santa Barbara.

Lest we think that Ben is losing the game, we see him driving across the San Francisco-Oakland Bay Bridge, signifying his mission to bridge the gaps—in communication, between the sexes, and within his own soul. So, while discouraged, he doesn't give up, but rather makes a mad dash back south several hundred more miles to Santa Barbara. After hundreds of miles of driving, it is appropriate that Benjamin finally runs out of gas a few blocks from the church. For up to that point he has been driving a car that, no doubt like the gas, was purchased for him by his father. Besides, he was also the captain of the cross-country team. His last few blocks to the church are, appropriately, on his own foot power.

The Passion Play

When he finally reaches the church, of course the door is locked, in keeping with the ancient tradition of keeping out any former suitors. But persistent to the end, Ben goes upstairs just in time to see the groom kiss the bride. Upon seeing this tragic scene from outside the glass barrier, Ben looks heavenward and begs "Oh Jesus God!," as if to echo the messianic passion cry, *"Eloi! Eloi! Lama sabachthani!* (My God! My God! Why hast thou forsaken me?)" (Matthew 27:46). And, as if to make his final rebellion against the beastly system, Ben yells out at full volume, "Elaine! Elaine! Elaine!" Coming from a culture of meaningless and absent words, Ben's passionate words remind us that Jesus is called the *logos* (word), that reconciles once separate entities.

From the nave below, Ben's image outside the glass upstairs presents him as an icon of the crucified Christ, with outstretched arms, as if he were a stained glass figure of the gospel passion. At both sides of this dying savior we see the shape of crosses made by the support bars of the windows, as if to represent the two criminals who died on each side of Jesus.

Redemption Story

Now the story comes full circle as we witness the conversion and salvation of the maiden. At the beginning of the film, in conjunction with the song "The Sounds of Silence," we see people through Ben's scuba mask talking, but we can't hear what they say. Now at the end, during Elaine's conversion scene, she looks at Ben's passion and is visibly moved. Then she looks at her parents and her newly married husband, all cursing at Ben, but we do not hear their words. This second cosmic, cinematic bookend confirms her allegiance to the crucified outsider.

Now the lyrics of the song make more sense to us: "And the people bowed and prayed to a neon god they made . . . but the words of the prophets are written on the subway walls." Here we have a striking juxtaposition of two different religions, one that glorifies the conventional, the powerful, and the materialistic, and the other that humbly and singularly calls out communicative words of simpleness, authenticity, and truth; it is the religion of wealthy papal Rome contrasted with that of the authentic Saint Francis of Assisi.

An appropriate ironic joke in the church scene is the near-blind organist in a black-and-white floral print dress, playing wedding music

The hero and heroine emerge from the cavern of the Terrible Mother.

that sounds more like a funeral dirge. Here we find another bookend, as we are reminded once again of the black-and-white clown in the beginning of the story. At this fraudulent wedding, a wedding is used to block a wedding. A blind and death-sounding musician reveals the ironic truth of the dirgeful ceremony. Even the church is white with black trimming, and the wedding guests wear mostly black, as if at a funeral.

When Elaine heeds the call of the redeemer, she walks back down the aisle, reversing the steps with which she so recently committed herself. As if released from Plato's cave, she finally sees in full color, rather than in the mere black and white of the shadowy cave wall. Our hero fights off the groom and Mr. Robinson. The Terrible Mother, as an insatiable cave, tells Elaine, before slapping her, "It's too late!" Elaine retorts, "Not for me!" Ben then fights off the crowd of black and white confederates with a cross, the symbol of his passion. Successful in his mission, he then locks the systemic morlocks into their wombish cavern of materialistic religion. It is as if we are reading the book of Revelation where the beast and demons will be locked into the bottomless pit for a thousand years. Benjamin symbolically kills the Dragon Lady, just as Perseus kills the Gorgon Medusa, before uniting with Andromeda.

Another bookend cinches up our story at this point. In the beginning of the film, Ben holds open the door at the Taft Hotel for old people to walk out and for young people to walk in. Now, at the end, he locks a door to shut old people in, with only two young people walking (actually running) out.

After leaving the confines of their past, the victorious royal couple then board a public transit bus, her in her wedding gown, and he in his tattered battle attire. And here, yet another bookend taking us back to the very beginning of the film. Earlier we see Ben in a jet airplane with a crowd of bored and lifeless upper-middle-class long-distance travelers as we follow Ben toward his hopeless roots. Now we see Ben and his newly redeemed bride on a plebeian bus with a crowd of surprised and curious proletarians as we follow Ben and his loved one away from their roots. Thus, the cosmic bookends remind us of the eternal return, but this time the clown of the new birth has color in his face. The comic picture of a *hieros gamos* shows us a royal smiling couple, speaking loudly, but not saying a word.

BLUE VELVET

EMBRACING THE SHADOW

Like some of David Lynch's other works, such as *Eraserhead* and "Twin Peaks," the power of *Blue Velvet* is found more in the extranarrative than in the narrative itself. In other words, unlike many thrillers or mysteries where the enigma is found only in the plot, *Blue Velvet*'s mysterious power is found more outside of the plot, in odd clues like the black hardware clerk, who seems to see with blind eyes, or the odd residents of Pussy Heaven, or the romantic Ben (Dean Stockwell) lip-synching "The Candy Colored Clown" into a mechanic's lamp, or the sleazy woman dancing on the car. Such clues have no overt logical connection to the narrative itself, but they point to a greater mystery, outside of the narrative, beyond the film, to the human soul. This means that you and I are included in the mysterious plot.

Like a good suspense thriller, such as Hitchcock's *Rear Window*, *Blue Velvet* does not leave us with the traditional "whodunit" question mark. We already know who did it, what was done, and to whom it was done. What is so mysterious is not the interesting plot, but you and I, the voyeuristic viewers of the plot, like Jimmy Stewart watching the murderer from his Hitchcockian rear window. *Blue Velvet* doesn't so much lead us on an investigatory search for hidden murderous elements in the story, like a mystery does. Rather, it leads us on an examination of our own mysterious human nature. It challenges us to question our own motivations and it implicates us in our own extranarrative shadowy intrigue. The question is not with Frank Booth and his merry band of underworld strangers. The real mystery is in our own hearts. This is the power and success of *Blue Velvet*.

Listening to the reactions of viewers after seeing *Blue Velvet* reveals part of the mystery to this extranarrative arcanum. Some people, of course, are horrified and sickened over watching the film. Others have a need to see it again, and wonder for weeks over the unconnected clues that have no apparent logical connection to one another. For the latter viewer, this "senseless" film makes sense in a mysterious sort of way, provoking questions not only about the film, but also about people's reactions to the film, inspiring in the true philosophic tradition, thinking about thinking, questioning about questioning, and questioning about our own mystery. In this regard, the film is a tremendous success. Some get it. Others don't. Even the fact that many do not get it attests to its success, because that strengthens the labyrinthine quality of the film, in its extranarrative aspect.

James Wall, the editor of *The Christian Century*, cites *Blue Velvet* as the best film of 1986, the year of its release. And we can certainly understand why, when we uncover it as a highly religious film. To understand more of this extranarrative mythic film, let us look closer at some of the elements therein.

LUMBERTON

The film opens with a pristine, white-picket-fence image of Everytown, U.S.A. (actually Lumberton, a logging town). Flowers, nice pretty houses all in a clean row, and a smiling fireman waving from a fire truck are all obvious pictures of normality, conventionality, and tranquillity. But not for long. Mr. Beaumont apparently has a stroke while watering his lawn, then the camera goes underground for a grotesque scene of what appears to be bugs noisily eating one another. This is our first clue that what is on the surface is not to be trusted, nor is it even as important as what is underneath. There is a dark world of *terra incognita* hiding just beneath a manicured suburbia.

On his way back from visiting his father in the hospital, Jeffrey

Beaumont (Kyle MacLachlan), our main protagonist, finds a human ear in a field just behind Vista, just behind "where we live." While we already have seen our first clue of the extranarrative in the underground bugs, now we see our first clue to the intranarrative, in the ear. Being the circumspect citizen that he is, Jeffrey Beaumont takes the ear to Detective John Williams, a friend of his father's. Later that night, after being ominously asked at home, "Jeffrey, you're not going down by Lincoln [street] are you?," and with his curiosity getting the best of him, Jeffrey goes over to Mr. Williams's house (near Lincoln), only to be instructed not to tell anybody about his find, and not to ask any more questions about it—a guaranteed push into Jeffrey's further investigation.

At this point, Detective Williams's daughter, Sandra (Laura Dern), has her curiosity pricked, and becomes Jeffrey's accomplice in his detective work. She tells him that she knows that a nightclub singer,

While wrestling with his own shadow, Jeffrey has an ambivalent relationship with light and dark.

Dorothy Vallens (Isabella Rosselini), is somehow involved in the mystery. So Jeffrey disguises himself as a pesticide man and steals a spare key out of this Dorothy's apartment.

With her key, Jeffrey sneaks into her apartment to continue his investigation. She catches him and mysteriously exhibits some sado-masochistic tendencies toward him. Then, while hiding in a closet, Jeffrey witnesses Frank Booth (Dennis Hopper), who, having entered Dorothy's apartment, verbally and sexually abuses her. Jeffrey comes back later and begins an affair with Dorothy, while discovering clues about Frank along the way, such as his having kidnaped Dorothy's husband and son. Also involved with Frank in a grander scheme of some kind is Detective Williams's partner, Detective Thomas Gordon, whom Jeffrey calls "yellow man." Drugs are involved. A drug dealer is killed. A woman has her legs broken. Dorothy's son is hidden at a place called Pussy Heaven. And there is a well-dressed man carrying an alligator briefcase involved with Detective Gordon. Not much more of the narrative puzzle is revealed beyond this. Eventually Detective Gordon and Frank Booth get killed and Dorothy is reunited with her son. But there are many more strange things that take place beyond this intranarrative intrigue that force us to look deeper into our extranarrative quest.

All of this strangeness takes place in a seemingly peaceful, normal American community, where all is well on the surface. But, again, the revealed is not the real intrigue. In fact, much of the intranarrative mystery is never revealed (such as who shoots Detective Gordon and Dorothy's husband, or why they are shot, or why Donnie, Jr. is housed at Ben's Pussy Heaven, or why Ben gives Frank drugs *and* money). Following Lynch's lead, we must join the bugs and go beneath ground level in Lumberton, to the deeper labyrinth of this participatory secret.

REVEALED AND CONCEALED

From beginning to end we are confronted with a contrast between that which is revealed, benign, and on the surface, and that which is concealed, malignant, and below the surface. It is this contrasting element of the film upon which the extranarrative intrigue is based. A list of such contrasts runs as follows:

REVEALED AND BENIGN	CONCEALED AND MALIGNANT
manicured law	carnivorous bugs underneath
Mother and Barbara watching TV	picture of gun on TV
peacefully watering lawn	stroke while watering lawn
peaceful walk through field	finding a human ear in field
Vista, where we live	found ear behind where we live
detective work is great	detective work is horrible
Dorothy lives on Lincoln Street	Booth shot Lincoln
Detective Gordon as a good cop	Detective Gordon as a criminal
well dressed man	Frank Booth in disguise
Booth as a sentimental baby	Booth as a murderous maniac
sexual pleasure	sexual pain
church and organ music	talk of a strange world
productive factory	lab of death
love letter	bullet
robins as love	robins as devourers of bugs
Lumberton normal citizens	Frank and his friends
Jeffrey as himself	Jeffrey in disguise as bugman
Dorothy as a loving mother	Dorothy as a sadomasochist
Jeffrey as a lover of Sandy	Jeffrey as a lover of Dorothy
Barbara cannot eat a bug	Barbara eats something gross

That which is revealed and seemingly innocuous is belied by its hidden and shadowy counterpart. The narrative's master of contrasting shadows, Frank Booth, seems to live in the hidden side. Dorothy Vallens turns off the lights for him and he says, "Now it's dark," both before and after his sexual abuse. He also obsessively commands her not to look at him. At Ben's, when the light is turned off, he again says, "Now it's dark. Let's fuck!," feeling more at home in his morlockian cave.

There are some dark images that, besides not seeming to fit the narrative, don't even seem to fit an extranarrative construction, put there God knows why. For example, there are three fat men standing

216

still on three separate occasions, for no apparent reason. One is standing in front of a store, twirling something in his hand, first clockwise, then counterclockwise. Then, when Jeffrey is heading toward the Williams' house, there is a fat man wearing sunglasses at night, standing still in the street with a small dog on a leash, for some unknown reason. Lastly, fat Detective Gordon, toward the end of the film, is standing in Dorothy's apartment as if shot and in a state of shock, or in a drug-induced trance, apparently half dead, but standing still in the oddest of ways, with no clues given to the oddity.

Whether we know the meaning of these strange images or not, is not as important as the fact that they inspire meaningful questions for our exploration. Of course, some of these images are no doubt trademarks of Lynch's sense of humour, and they certainly add to the interest level of the film, even if they have no conscious or subconscious meaning. For the shadows that do make sense, they illumine our dark story of contrasts. For those that don't, we are grateful for not having all of the answers, in keeping with the tradition of mythical quests. For as with secrets, if all is revealed, mystery would cease to exist.

BLUE VELVET

One of the images that can be somewhat revealed is blue velvet, the title of the film. The theme song, "Blue Velvet" is sung by Dorothy Vallens, called the Blue Lady by the M.C. at the Slow Club. She wears a blue velvet robe at her apartment. Frank Booth carries a piece of this robe around with him for sentimental and apparently erotic reasons, at one point fondling it as he watches her perform, at another point, using it to wipe off the lipstick he has kissed onto Jeffrey's face. We also know that Frank's beer of choice is Pabst Blue Ribbon.

What is the connection of blue and blue velvet to the intranarrative plot? Possibly not a great deal, unless we acknowledge the obvious connection to Dorothy's blue sadness, and the correlation of the story with the song lyrics. But we are not so much concerned with narrative mystery. After all, we are not mystery buffs or suspense addicts, but religious pilgrims.

When the camera takes us underground in the film's opening scene, we must follow the director's lead in his underworld venture. From that point on, a world of depth and darkness is the real esotericism, more than that which is on the surface.

The color blue naturally is most often associated with the heavens, but also, since the sky is above, for verticality. Blue therefore signifies not only the height of the blue sky above, but also the depth of the blue sea below, which reflects the blue sky. Blue is darkness made visible. When Hades kidnaps Persephone, his chariot is drawn by dark blue steeds. Keep this in mind as more of the extranarrative arcanum is revealed.

CHARACTERS

Detective Thomas Gordon

This corrupt police investigator, known to Jeffrey as "the yellow man" plays two roles: that of the upright and moral cop, and that of the corrupt and criminal cop, befitting his name Thomas, which means "twin," and befitting the contrasting elements of our story. In his good cop role, his color yellow would signify his illuminating sunlike virtues. His bad cop role changes his radiant image to that of a tarnished sun spot.

Sandra Williams

Sandra, Jeffrey's investigative partner, bears the name of a mythic prophetess, Cassandra. She is introduced to us by her slowly stepping out of the dark, into the light, as she reveals to Jeffrey a major clue to the intranarrative mystery. It is she who tells Jeffrey about Dorothy Vallens, and it is she whose prophetic dream comes true, in keeping with her namesake.

Dorothy Vallens

Dorothy Ellen Vallens is married to a Donald James Watts. Her husband and her son, Donnie, Jr., have been kidnapped by Frank Booth and his evil band of ruffians. The name Dorothy means "gift of God"; as such, she has been stolen and owned by an underworld boss. In the same way that Hades, the god of the underworld, captures sweet Persephone, and holds her in his underworld prison, so too has Frank Booth taken possession of the blue lady, the lady of the deep, the gift of God. She lives on the seventh floor, room 710, of the Deep River Apartments, signifying both the height and depth of her blueness.

Jeffrey Beaumont

Our hero is Jeffrey Beaumont, whose given name means "peace of God," or "peace of the land." Beaumont means "beautiful mount," signifying the dwelling place of gods and heroes. It is through him that peace is restored. In keeping with the tradition of heroes, Jeffrey acts alone, unlike Frank and his evil crew, who always seem to be in concert. Early on, Jeffrey says to Sandy, "I'm seeing something that was always hidden," true to the nature of the traditional seer, hero, and peacemaker. As a seer, he must reveal his vision. As a hero, he must suffer the pain of his mission. As a peacemaker, he must make war. Like Heracles and Orpheus, he gains entrance into the house of Hades, and escapes alive. Like Hermes, the trickster god, he gains access to Dorothy's apartment disguised as a bugman, an exterminator of underworld pests. In fulfilling his mission, the beast is slain, Dorothy, the gift of God, is redeemed, and the peace of God is restored to the land.

Frank Booth

The wicked antagonist of our film is Frank Booth, a man of disguise, sentimentality, gross vulgarity, sexual peculiarity, frustrated creativity, and murderous intent. His name, Frank, is derived from an ancient word, *franca*, the javelin used by the Franks that invaded Gaul in the sixth century. It was from this javelin that the Franks actually derived their name. Of course Frank's personality, like his name, is overtly phallic—in his language, in his treatment of others, in his sexual obsessions, and in his violent aggression. Frank's last name, Booth, reminds us that Dorothy lives on Lincoln Street; and we remember that it was an actor named Booth who shot Lincoln, the liberator of the captives. Again, this has no connection to the intranarrative plot, but it adds another clue to our extranarrative conundrum.

As the abductor of Dorothy's husband and son, as the "owner" of Dorothy, and as the leader of the dark underground, Frank is an underworld god. In biblical mythology, he is Lucifer, the god of this age, the captor of the souls awaiting release. While abusing Jeffrey, he says to him, "I'll send you straight to hell, fucker!," as if threatening to invite him home. While pondering Frank's nature, we are given cinematic sounds and images of hellish growls, flames, and tormented faces. Frank's intake of what appears to be nitrous oxide is symbolic of his receiving air from above. As gas rises to higher levels and as Frank resides in the lower regions of the spiritual world, his receiving a gaseous substance from a higher level is fitting to his underworld nature. With his "Now it's dark" mentality, Frank is without question a god of darkness.

Along with his satanic role, Frank has the personality of an angry, frustrated artist. But his activity and attitude is one of destructiveness rather than creativity. Like Hitler, several of Hitler's top leaders, and other cult leaders of a similar nature, Frank is an angry artist who never came to be. He is an obsessive romantic, a syrupy sentimentalist, and a power-obsessed megalomaniac. As most artists are androgynous, Frank is so to a malignant extreme. His masculine assertion of his strength and power are obsessive, as he commands Jeffrey, "Feel my muscles!" His feminine romanticism is found in his gross sentimentality over songs like "Blue Velvet" and "The Candy Colored Clown," in his indulgence in lipstick, in his fondling of blue velvet, and in his admiration of his suave, feminized friend, Ben. Frank has the classic personality of an abused child who fancies himself a creative genius

220

As an underworld god, Frank receives air from above.

but who doesn't have the talent or discipline to bring it to pass. Thus, like Lucifer, and like Jim Jones, Idi Amin, and other self-deceived power-romantics, since he can't be the master creator, he becomes the master destroyer. Thus, by destroying (a reversal of creating) he gains a feeling of creating due to the surge of power associated with the act.

Frank cuts off Dorothy's husband's ear and tells her to stay alive for Van Gogh. Here we see an identification with a suffering artist, and the simultaneous destruction of a mock artist, as if he is jealous of real creators.

In his sexual abusiveness toward Dorothy, he apparently has a problem of premature ejaculation, which certainly would add to his need for omnipotence. In his sexual peculiarity Frank also vacillates between being a dominant, abusive man and a sniveling, sentimental baby. He calls Dorothy "Mommy," and he says, "Baby wants to fuck!," which signifies (similar to the abusive dentist in *Little Shop of Horrors*) a love-hate relationship with his mother, and a worshipful reverence for the mother principle.

221

PLACES OF SHADES

The Slow Club

Frank has two hangouts that we know of: the Slow Club, out on Route 7, and Pussy Heaven, the apparent abode of the romantic Ben and the fat ladies. The Slow Club is where Dorothy, after a slow introduction by the M.C., sings the slow song, and where Frank is enraptured with slow sentimentality over her singing. The Slow Club is a slow-motion time warp, with Frank in the center of this cosmic vortex.

There is another indication of time alteration in the mentioning of beers. Jeffrey, a young man, likes Heineken, an import beer of the eighties. Sandy's father drinks Bud, a domestic beer that was most popular in the seventies. The hip American beer of the sixties was Coors. But Frank's beer, is even farther removed. When he asks Jeffrey what kind of beer he likes, and upon hearing Heineken, Frank retorts, "Heineken?! Fuck that shit! Pabst Blue Ribbon!," his beer of choice, a beer of the fifties. We get the impression that Jeffrey and Sandra, as curious pilgrims, naturally want to progress into the future, looking forward to the day of revelation and redemption. Frank, on the other hand, as the satanic false creator, knows his time is limited, and therefore must slow time down, or even reverse it if possible, to delay his own prophesied demise.

Pussy Heaven

Another of Frank's hangouts is a place he calls Pussy Heaven, where Ben and some fat ladies apparently live, and where Dorothy's son, Donnie, Jr., is held captive. A small neon sign out front says, "This is it," as Frank announces to Jeffrey at their arrival. One gets the impression upon seeing the sign that it might be a bar. But upon entering, we see it clearly is not. Perhaps we might think it is a bordello, because it is a house, and there are some whorish looking women lounging about. But when we get a closer look at the ladies in question, we can't imagine them staying in business with their commodities. So what is this odd place?

We suspect that Ben lives at "This is it," Pussy Heaven. Before Frank arrives, the inhabitants don't seem to be doing anything in this purgatorial abode. They are not reading, watching television, playing, or doing any other normal activity that one would expect of people inhabiting a dwelling. When Frank pulls up front, Ben gladly announces "Frank is here!," and the place comes alive with Frank's penetration into Pussy Heaven.

In Frank's relationship with Ben, there is something odd and mysterious. Ben gives Frank money and drugs simultaneously, indicating that he is not giving him money for drugs, but for something else, perhaps for the privilege of sexually abusing little Donnie. If he is holding little Donnie, he might be the jailor of Donald, Sr. as well. This partnership of Frank and Ben is reminiscent of the dentist and patient in *Little Shop of Horrors*, figures of two underworld gods.

From mythology we remember that Poseidon, the god of the sea, is known for his viciousness, manipulation, and uncontrolled wrath, very much like Frank Booth, and like the sadistic dentist of *Little Shop of Horrors*. Poseidon's brother, Hades, is the jailor of the underworld, hungry for underground captives, and always in collusion with Poseidon for fresh victims. Of course the underworld is also the domain of the unconscious; it is the seat of Mother Earth, the chthonic maw of the world, and the tomb of the dead. Thus, Pussy Heaven is the opposite of Sky Heaven, the masculine abode of the male god. God's heaven is where redeemed spirits go; Pussy Heaven is where unredeemed shades are held captive. Ben, as the effeminate lip-syncher to "The Candy Colored Clown," and Frank, as the ambiguous macho-effeminate romantic, are both gods in this underworld heaven of the Great Pussy, the Terrible Mother. We are reminded also of Frank's worshipful, incestuous yearnings for his mommy, thus signifying ultimately whom he really serves.

ECO-FEMINISM

The three western religions have been perennially at war with the
mother religion. But wherever the vengeful side of her gets an opportunity to assert herself, we find her wrathfully getting back at agents of
the sky god, like Jeffrey.

Related to this we see what appears to be a directorial, environmental joke in the film. A scene of the downtown factory reveals ominous
shadows of large moving machinery and billowing industrial smoke.
The Lumberton radio station, WOOD, announces, "At the sound of
the falling tree, the time is . . . ," and, "It's a sunny, woodsy day in
Lumberton, so get those chainsaws out . . . . There's a whole lot of
wood waiting out there. So let's get going." Significantly, Dorothy's
husband is named Donald James Watts. James Watts of course was
Ronald Reagan's controversial director of the U.S. Department of the
Interior from 1981 to 1983. Donald James Watts gets his ear cut off
and is eventually killed, as if the director is consciously or subconsciously sending a message from an angry Mother Earth of Pussy
Heaven to the environmentally destructive business and political es-
tablishment.

IT'S A STRANGE WORLD

While Sandra and Jeffrey sit in his car, he asks her why there are
people like Frank in the world. Both of them comment how strange the
world is. Then she tells him her prophetic dream:

> There was our world. And the world was dark because there weren't
> any robins, and the robins represented love. And for the longest
> time there was just this darkness. And all of a sudden, thousands of
> robins were set free. And they flew down and brought this blinding
> light of love, and it seemed like that love would be the only thing
> that would make any difference. And it did. So, I guess it means there
> is trouble till the robins come.

As a background to this telling of the dream, we hear organ music coming from a church behind Sandra and Jeffrey. Again, we see a contrast between good and evil, light and dark. And here we seem to get the picture of a sweet and sentimental answer to the problem of evil. But the Lynchian telling of this dream, with the bookend ending of the film, closing with the sweet and innocent white-picket-fence image, leaves us suspecting that it really isn't that simple. Suspecting a parodist treatment of kitsch, we are safer in assuming that the filmmaker wants us to look at a deeper level. After all, the film shows us at the end that love robins do ugly things like eat bugs.

HEARING AND SEEING

Now, looking at *Blue Velvet* from a broad vantage, knowing that we are dealing with a grand contrasting scheme of light and dark, or revealed and concealed, we must have "ears to hear" the clues and eyes to see in the dark. We must remember that "just behind Vista [view] where we live," was found the first clue, the ear, a tool for hearing. We must join Sandy when she says, "I hear things."

We must also see, as Jeffrey says, "something that was always hidden." The blind man who can see tells us that it is possible to see the invisible; the ear found in the field is a clue that hearing is important in our investigation. Within the narrative Jeffrey is warned not to tell anybody about his find, nor to ask questions about the mystery. Of course, this is common advice that is traditionally given to seers by normal people lacking sight. But like Jeffrey, if we want to uncover the extranarrative enigma, we must press on, searching for the inaudible and invisible clues, until the "treasure hard to attain" is seen and heard.

SHADOWS

If we train ourselves enough to hear the inaudible and see the invisible, some of the most prominent things with which we will be confronted are shadows—those of others, of society, and most importantly, of ourselves. The contrasts of the hidden and revealed speak of these shadows behind most events and people. When we are living completely in the kitschish never-never land of light, we forget, like Peter Pan, our shadow. But our story will not allow such forgetfulness. The literal shadows of the machinery and smoke at the downtown factory are only symbols of more significant and invisible shadows.

Frank Booth, like the actor John Wilkes Booth, is a master of disguised personae, and thus, of shadows. He is similar to Moros, the Son of the Night, who, like his mother, operates in the shadows. Even Frank's words and phrases have double, occultic, shadowy meanings. To him, a "love letter" is a bullet, "fucking forever" is dying, and a kiss is an act of hatred.

As a result of her relationship with Frank, Dorothy's shadow manifests itself in sadomasochism. While performing, she wears a wig which looks exactly like her real hair, indicating a confusion of her revealed and hidden selves. Also influenced by Frank, she even becomes infected with shadow obsession, as she commands Jeffrey during her seduction of him not to look at her.

As a trickster, Jeffrey is willing to don an outward shadow persona as the bugman in order to get to the heart of the shadowy mystery. But what he struggles with internally as he gets closer to the center, is his own inner shadow. It takes Frank to remind him of his hidden side, when Frank says, "You're just like me!" His falling into the infectious trap of sadism with Dorothy also forces him to see this hidden and ugly side.

Contrasted with this illuminating shadow is Barbara, at Jeffrey's house, who while watching a robin eat a bug proclaims, "I could never eat a bug!" But of course she seems to be eating something equally as gross. Thus, in our extranarrative plot, some of us are confronted with our shadow by Frank, and we get it, and become more integrated persons by it. Others, like the intranarrative Barbara, and like the extranarrative filmgoers who leave the screening of *Blue Velvet* proclaiming that they could never eat a bug might not ever get it, because they don't have eyes to see in the dark shadow of their soul.

Some of us will see the shadows and, disliking what we see, will try to eliminate the dark side. But we must be reminded that blue, being a color between black and white, is an equilibrium that varies with tone. It is not a bugman's extermination of the shadows that brings peace and wholeness, but rather, an awareness and integration of their presence.

SANTA SANGRE

THE BLOODY ALCHEMY OF THE SOUL

Santa Sangre is a film made in Mexico, spoken in English, and produced by an Italian. Its director, Alejandro Jodorowsky, a Parisian resident, is a Chilean-born Russian Jew with a Spanish first name, born into a circus family. The seemingly international flavor of the filmic offering is just as varied in its combination of internal elements, as if it is a spliced version of a once dismembered body. These elements, heated as ingredients in an alchemical alembic, blend together in the mystical retort, producing a magical blend of opposites, and revealing special secrets to the human soul.

As a film of bloody mayhem, it is misunderstood by some as merely an exercise in senseless violence. One critic wrote the following diatribe against this film: "Jodorowsky swears that he is one of three living geniuses in the film world today, the others being Kurosawa and Fellini. Judging from his latest film, however, it's safe to say he belongs in a different crowd, like with Ted Bundy and Charles Manson. . . . To call this atrocity a film, or worse, a work of art, is akin to calling a mass murderer a folk hero" (Dubos).

Some entertainment critics will certainly diagnose the film as bad art, while overlooking the central leitmotifs of art and while missing the meaning of the film altogether. When taken seriously and explored symbolically, the film reveals itself as a mystical concoction of several themes blended together as one. It is:

an alchemical allegory,

a symbol of human consciousness,

the myth of Osiris,

the story of the phoenix bird,

the evolution of the self as found in the psychic development of the child, and

the psychic evolution of the filmmaker himself.

When all of these overlapping themes are seen side by side, they each reflect a different aspect of the same theme, for all of them are variations of the same story: in essence, the death and rebirth of the sacrificial self, which must overcome the obstacles of life, and yea, even death itself, to become whole and mature.

The story centers around our main protagonist, Fenix (Axel Jodorowsky as an adult, Adan Jodorowsky as a child), the son of circus parents. We are led back and forth between his childhood at the circus and his adulthood, where he is in a state of deep anguish. His childhood is a series of events that leave scars of abandonment, separation anxiety, and confusion. His adulthood is a series of angst-ridden attempts to exorcise himself of his childhood demons. While he finally resolves his childhood trauma in the end, he never leaves the world of the circus in his mind. For it is the circus, in which he was born and raised, that is his signifier of life, and thus, the analogy for his final resolution, because the *circus* (circle) is the symbol of original perfection to which our protagonist is aimed.

CHARACTERS

Fenix

Our main protagonist is appropriately named Fenix, signifying the legendary phoenix bird that rises from the ashes. When we first see him, as an adult, he is perched naked in the leafless stump of a tree in a hospital room. When offered fish, he swoops down to the floor and

The Phoenix perches in the *djed* tree, a symbol of Osiris.

eats it as a bird feeding from the water. He has a tattoo of an eagle on his chest, and in the dissolve to the next scene the face of an eagle replaces his on the screen, in exactly the same place and size. The eagle then flies to the circus, Circo del Gringo, where we are introduced to Fenix as a boy of eight.

Orgo

Fenix's father (Guy Stockwell) is a big fat ogre of a man—it is as if his name Orgo were derived from two Spanish words, *gordo* (fat) and *ogro* (ogre). He is given to drink, is unfaithful, and wields a patriarchal and hypnotic power over his wife. He drives a late 1940s pink American car, and he has both a white horse and a black one, the latter of which he uses for funerals. He is apparently the leader of this Circo del Gringo. He also has an eagle tattooed on his chest and he cavorts with the circus's tattooed woman (Thelma Tixau). We learn that he killed a woman in America, and he slits his own throat after his jealous wife throws sulphuric acid on his genitals and on his paramour, the tattooed woman.

Concha

Fenix's mother is Concha (Blanca Guerra), an intensely religious woman, devoted to a patron saint of her own canonization, a Saint Lirio. As a personification of engulfing femininity, her name, Concha (seashell), is a Latin American slang word for vagina. She swings by her hair on the flying trapeze. And she completely engulfs Fenix's life as a smothering *concha*.

Alma

A young deaf mute girl at the circus named Alma is the personification of her name, which means "soul." She is roughly the same age as Fenix. At some point in her childhood, her mother died and she was then put in the care of the tattooed woman, who treats her harshly, even

231

Fenix and Alma—spirit and soul—are separated in childhood to be reunited as adults.

cracking a whip while trying to force her to walk a burning tightrope. During a violent ordeal at the circus, after the sulphuric-acid attack, she is driven off in a Volkswagen van by her uncaring caretaker and separated from her childhood friend, Fenix. Later, in Alma's adult life, while still living with the tattooed woman, she is sold as a sex object to a drunken soldier. She escapes, spends the night on top of a red, white, and blue semi-truck cab, and returns to her house the next morning to find her adoptive mother gruesomely murdered.

Lirio

While Lirio is not a living character in the narrative, the name of the film (Holy Blood) is derived from her bloody baptismal font. Concha is the priestess of this armless saint, whose shrine is bulldozed by the owner of the land on which it stands. The name *Lirio*, of course, is Spanish for lily, the flower. The devotees of her sect hold lilies at her shrine. Concha tells what appears to be the local bishop the story of her patron saint. She says that on this site, some years ago, a little girl was attacked and raped. Her arms were cut off, and what she claims is a pool of blood at the shrine stands as a lasting testimony to her sainthood. Her name is possibly a derivative of Santa Lilioso, an actual ninth-century Spanish Christian martyr. The lily, of course, is used in Christian art to symbolize purity, and is often associated with the Virgin Mary, and with Easter Sunday. Certainly in the mind of Concha this signification is appropriate to her saint. But when we see the armless Concha in Fenix's adult life, we are reminded more of Lilith than of a lily. In Jewish lore, Lilith is the first wife of Adam, a personification of the Terrible Mother, who, like the Greek Hecate, makes demands for human sacrifice.

ALCHEMY

One way to look at this circus story is through the symbolism of alchemy, the ancient forerunner of modern chemistry. Being in a state of anguish, and unfortunate enmeshment with his all-consuming mother, Fenix must try a secret solution to his problem. Although it is never directly stated, the symbolism of alchemy is woven throughout the film. As an adult, Fenix walks into a mobile apothecary shop and picks up three elements he has ordered: mercury, sulphur, and boric trisulphate, a form of salt. These happen to be the three main ingredients used by the ancient alchemists.

Most people think of alchemy as a literal attempt to turn base metal into gold. The practice might have had that as a goal, but there is far more to it than that. Philosophic and spiritual gold are certainly goals, as are the uniting of philosophic opposites and rebirth.

In Fenix's experimentation he is literally trying to become invisible by drinking his magic potion. Since he is forced to be the hands for his armless mother, certainly invisibility would be a way out of his visible captivity. Having lost his childhood love, Alma, Fenix is left with his demanding mother. But besides being divided from his true love, he is also divided from his own soul. By becoming invisible to his mother (an act of separation) he can become united with his own soul. His alchemical experimentation is his attempt to find union of his opposites and to find spiritual gold.

The main tool used by the alchemical adept is the alembic, a crucible used to heat various elements with a gentle fire, called an *incendium amoris*. The *prima materia* (prime material), usually mercury (although sometimes sulphur) is the first ingredient heated. Mercury, considered the cold fire, represents spirit, changeability, and ambivalence, characteristics of the god Mercury (sometimes called Mercurius-Christ). Added to mercury is sulphur, considered the hot fire, which represents volatility, passion, desire, the active earthy element, and the body. The third main ingredient is usually salt, symbolizing the passive soul, and the reasoning intellect. The *magnum opus* (great work) is thought of as the making of a golden higher nature out of an earthy lower nature, all through purification by fire. The end product is the *lapis philosophorum* (philosopher's stone), called variously the red stone, the Bird of Hermes, the *elixir vitae*, the quintessence, or the gold of Mercury.

The alchemical process goes through three main stages, signified by three different colors: black, white, and red. Besides any physical attributes associated with the process of the *magnum opus*, each element and process also have spiritual, philosophic, or psychological meaning.

The first, or black stage is the purgational period, metaphorically connected to the human triad of body, soul, and spirit. Just as the elements are burned into black powder, so too is human nature thought to be scorched in the act of separation and purgation. The *prima materia* is often seen as in a state of *nigredo*, or blackness, even before the firing, although sometimes blackness occurs through the application of fire, wherein separation and putrefaction of the elements takes place. At this stage, a union of opposites may produce a death of sorts, known as *mortificatio, calcinatio,* or *putrefactio*.

The second, or white stage in the *magnum opus* symbolizes illumination. At this point a washing (*ablutio* or *baptisma*) leads to a whitening (*albedo*) of the elements. This stage is equated with the release of the soul (*anima*) at death, which later reunites with the body, effecting a resurrection. This whitening leads to the one white color that contains all other colors (*omnes colores*). This white *albedo* stage is the first goal of the work. It is the silver or moon condition.

The third and final stage of the work is the red (*rubedo*) stage, associated with union and perfection. By raising the heat in the retort to its most intense level, the union of red and white produces the union of the opposites. This is the gold of the great work, just as the burning red sun is seen as gold. Here the metaphoric royal *chymical* wedding takes place between *Sol* and *Luna*. The solar king and lunar queen are fused together into a golden union. The *sponsus* and *sponsa* are united in royal incest in the *nuptiae chymical*, the *hieros gamos*, or the *mysterium coniunctionis*, as it is variously called.

Besides the mixing and heating of elements in the adept's cauldron, various schemas diagram the philosophic and spiritual interactions of the alchemical metaphors. The favorite of these schematics is the quaternity, essentially a quartered mandala in which the four elements (fire, air, water, and earth) or the four directions are plotted in opposition to each other in order to work out the logistics of reconciling the opposites. Since four is a number of completion, and the circle is the symbol of the golden sun, and since the alchemist seeks to reconcile opposites, the quaternity is a fitting symbol of uniting opposites into a synthesized whole.

There are clear indicators of alchemical involvement in Fenix's life. The prominent colors worn by our cinematic alchemist are black, white, and red. In the first childhood sequence, we see Fenix in black and white. When he performs magic (which is related to alchemy) he has a touch of red added to his black and white formal wear. During the elephant's funeral procession, all of the circus people wear black except Fenix, who wears the red gown of Santa Lirio. While the black-dressed circus people stand on one side of the canyon watching the elephant's coffin drop into the ravine, the poor people from the shantytown across the divide are all covered in white powder. Alma is the only funeral processant with whiteface. In the end, just before Fenix's salvation, she again puts on whiteface, this time while wearing black. When Fenix buys his elements from the apothecarist he is dressed completely in black. His first victim is dressed first in black and white, then in white, until finally we see her bleed red.

After placing his victims in backyard graves, he paints them white. When they come out of their graves to haunt him, they are all in white. His last victim, the world's strongest woman, is dressed in black and white until she is then covered in red blood. Just before his final release from his emotional hell, Fenix's terrible mother, Concha, shows up in her red Lirio gown. He is dressed in black and white at this time, until he also gets stained in red blood. The pattern of these color combinations all indicate the three stages of alchemic firing.

The three elements of alchemy: mercury, sulphur, and salt, can be seen in the personages of three characters. Fenix, besides being the alchemist in our *magnum opus*, is also mercury, the prime material, the changeable, ambivalent cold spirit, seeking, as Mercury, to reconcile opposites. Concha is representative of sulphur, known to the alchemists as the active, passionate, hot, volatile, desireful, earthy substance equated with the body. It is appropriate that as sulphur, she pours sulphuric acid on her husband. Alma is the passive, reasoning intellect, the salt thought of as the soul.

Fenix's quaternity is seen in several places. First of all there are four main characters, two male and two female, all equally divided from one another. Then there are four clowns, who on more than one occasion make a circling motion around a central axis. At the burning of the Concha and Lirio dolls, which can be seen as the culmination of the *magnum opus*, they all dance clockwise around the fire, indicating the completion of the great work. There are also four Down's syndrome inmates with whom Fenix is associated at his convalescent residence. The doctor in charge of the facility brings more inmates into a circle dance around the garden fountain. There are also four musicians in white surrounding two drunken dancing soldiers outside of the tattooed woman's apartment. All of this symbolism of fours and oppositions among the fours and encircling of the fours represents the quaternities associated with Fenix's unspoken alchemy. Completion, perfection, and reconciliation are inevitable in such signification.

ROSARIUM PHILOSOPHORUM

An ancient text of alchemical philosophy, the *Rosarium Philosophorum* (1550), contains eleven illustrations that coincide roughly with the *magnum opus* of alchemy and with the story of Fenix in *Santa Sangre*. A look at this set of illustrations will give us another angle from which to view Fenix's story.

Figure 1 (see page 238) depicts a fountain signifying the *aqua permanens*, or divine water, also known as the mercurial fountain, and also as the uterus in which the symbolic *foetus* is gestated. On two separate occasions in our film we see such a fountain, one in the middle of the court outside the tattooed woman's apartment (where the four musicians play music for the dancing drunk soldiers), and in the center of the garden at the hospital (around which the inmates circle). According to C. G. Jung, "the treasure in the sea, the companion, and the garden with the fountain are all one and the same thing: the self.

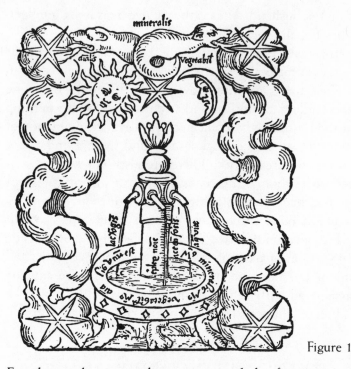

Figure 1

For the garden is another *temenos*, and the fountain is the source of 'living water' mentioned in John 7:38" (Jung 1953, 118). In alchemical philosophy, Mercury glides between the burning alembic and the baptismal font, promising ultimate reconciliation. The fountain in Fenix's psychic journey is his birth and early development, at the outset of his horrendous ordeal.

The second illustration of the *Rosarium* depicts a royal couple giving their left hands to one another (Fig. 2). The left hand indicates the sinister side of life, as opposed to right-handed orthodoxy. The mythology of such a left-handed royal couple is either mother-son or brother-sister incest, engaged in a broken taboo reserved for royalty.

In *Santa Sangre*, hints of this incestuous pairing are found in several places. We witness Fenix and his controlling mother sleeping in the same bed and kissing one another as two lovers would. Concha forces this pairing against Fenix's will. In another more hidden instance, there is the possibility that Fenix and his childhood sweetheart are actually brother and sister. We are told that Fenix's father, Orgo, killed a woman in America. We are then told that Alma's mother died, provoking the question that perhaps the women are actually one and the same. It takes royal incest, like that between the Babylonian Tammuz and Semiramis, to set up à divine opposition-conjunction continuum. In order for ultimate reconciliation and perfection to be achieved, ta-booed transgression must perforce be instituted at the highest social level. For it is through the extreme transgression and redemption of the royal pair that the land is fructified.

The third illustration of the *Rosarium* shows a naked royal couple standing side by side each extending a flower to one another, with a third flower brought down by a heavenly dove (Fig. 3). They are no longer touching left hands, but at this point are holding the flowers. We are reminded that in the beginning of the film, Alma offers a flower to Fenix. Toward the end of the film, Fenix offers a flower to the strongest woman in the world. The flowers in Fenix's alchemy are a

Figure 2

Figure 3

promise of union. After final reunion, we can say that the Bird of Hermes brings the *Flores Mercurii* to the reunited couple.

The fourth illustration shows the royal couple immersed in the mercurial fountain (Fig. 4). We are reminded that Fenix is snared in the depths of his mother, Concha (seashell/pussy). Descending into the maternal sea is a night sea journey, a nocturnal descent into the abyss of the subconscious.

In Figure 5a, the sea has enveloped the naked royal couple in their act of *coitus*. It would seem that a conjunction is taking place here. But the conjunction we witness is between the Terrible Mother and her victim son. The sea is the raging chaotic state of *massa confusa*.

Figure 5b shows the king and queen still in the sea, but they have now sprouted wings. In this stage, called the *fermentatio*, the couple are developing more of the spiritual element in the alembic fire. In their childhood, deaf Alma signs to Fenix with her graceful hands a bird

Figure 4

flying from his chest into the heavens, as if to suggest that a bird will spring from his burning or drowning.

Figure 6 shows the couple blended together as one, but they are dead and lying in a sarcophagus. We see a picture of this with the image of Fenix on top of one of his victims in the grave. The *Rosarium* calls this stage the *conceptio*, which equates coitus with death. The royal love-making has produced the death of the participants. The secret behind the French term for orgasm, *la petite mort*, is that the masculine spiritual seed implanted in the womb of the feminine earthy body is integrally connected to the agricultural cycle of death and life, which is the core of both spirituality and corporeality. The incestuous son must suffer an inevitable death in his *hieros gamos* with the mother goddess. Thus Fenix, in his relationship with the great pussy, is doomed to his alchemical *putrefactio*.

In Figure 7, the soul leaves the putrefaction and ascends into the heavens. In our cinematic rosarium, this happens at the circus. While the young magician Fenix wears his tuxedo of black, white, and red, he puts Alma into a glass box and causes her to disappear, only to be replaced by Concha, the devouring motherly sea of chaos. In the very next scene we witness the sulphuric acid attack on Orgo and the

Figure 5a

tattooed woman, after which Alma is driven away for good. While
Fenix is locked in his father's trailer, looking despondently out the
window, he sees little Alma looking out the back window of the van
being driven away, as the spirit and soul are separated from one
another. Fenix the spirit is left with the body, his sulphuric mother, an

Figure 5b

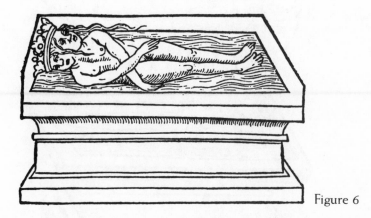

Figure 6

inequitable union at best, a tortured marriage at worst. Then the chaos really begins.

Figure 8 shows the blended couple still dead in the grave with dew dropping from heaven. In alchemy, this is the *ablutio*, whitening, or purification. Living without his soul, Fenix, as the masculine part of the

Figure 7

243

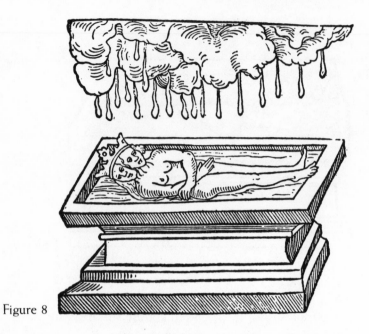

Figure 8

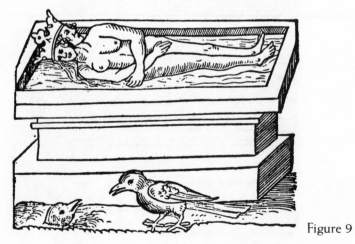

Figure 9

Figure 10

coniunctio, is required to furnish dew for the motherly earth. This dew, true to the myths of the hungry mother, is found in the blood of victims. After they are each killed and in the grave, Fenix paints their bodies white, indicating the second stage of the alchemical process and the eighth stage of the *Rosarium*, both of which are the illumination, the bright secret behind the black horror. The alchemist would say, "Despise not the ashes, for they are the diadem of the heart."

Jung reminds us that the king and queen, as spirit and body, are not complete without the soul (Jung 1954, 243). Thus, Alma (soul) is needed to make the picture perfect. Figure 9 shows the return of the soul. This is where Alma comes back into Fenix's life at the end of the film. Alma's reappearance gives Fenix the strength to fight his way out of the uteral tomb.

Figure 10, a number of completion, shows a new, blended, resurrected couple with outstretched wings. In the film, we see Alma and

Fenix stretch out their arms in glad release from Fenix's fiery Gehennah. The *Rosarium* pictures the royal couple standing on the moon, signifying conquest over the enmeshing aspect of the feminine principle and their identification with the solar principle of gold, the end result of the *magnum opus*.

THE EVOLUTION OF CONSCIOUSNESS

Now that we have seen Fenix as a self-administering alchemist in search of the philosopher's stone, and as a tripartite being evolving in the figure of the hermetical *Rosarium*, we shall now view him in light of the evolution of consciousness, which is essentially the same evolution told in a different language. Psychoanalyst Erich Neumann's *Origin and History of Consciousness* affords us another vantage from which to view Fenix's evolutionary maturation, from scared little circus boy to tormented mental patient to liberated ex-captive.

Santa Sangre originates, appropriately, at a circus, which of course means circle. The circle, as a symbol of the sun, is also original perfection, around which all of life revolves and to which all of life seeks its centeredness. Neumann suggests that human life is primevally ensnared, as a victimized child, in what is called uroboric incest. The uroboros is most often represented as the serpent biting its own tail. While at the apothecarist's shop, Fenix, dressed completely in black, hallucinates wrestling with a large serpent, indicating the terrific struggle in which he is bound, while caught in his incestuous relationship with his mother.

The Terrible Mother, as the hungry maw of the earth, clamors for fertilization, of which blood sacrifice is the only suitable kind. Here, the incestuous son, caught in the snares of the mother, provides for her voracious sacrificial appetite. In his struggle for individuation, the male caught in this feeding frenzy divides into a destructive/constructive, or an anti-creative/creative polarity. Here we find Fenix as a creative artist, as a showman, his only outlet of life-affirming expression.

Involution of the self in enmeshment with the Mother.

Simultaneously we see him as a destroyer of life, sending women to their premature deaths.

One of the early events found in the myths of consciousness is the separation of the world parents. Typically this is seen in creation myths depicting the severance of the sky and earth. In Fenix's life, his parents seem to be psychologically divided from the beginning and the division intensifies with the exposure of the father's unfaithfulness to the point of a literal physical separation. In creation myths, it is light that divides the world into opposites of day and night. Myth-opoetically, it is elucidation that divides the darkness of the soul.

The mythical hero is born of the world parents before their separation. But as in most hero myths, he must go through a horrific ordeal

247

before the virtues of heroism are conferred upon him. Some form of castration is often the prescribed form of initiation into the stage of heroism. In rites of passage, a circumcision is symbolic of this humiliation. Sometimes a cutting of the hair, as with Samson, is allegorical for this cutting of the flesh. In Fenix's case, his beard (a symbol of male virility) disappears after he leaves the hospital and cleaves to his mother. We are reminded that Achilles is dressed as a female by his mother Thetis. Male novices in primitive initiation ceremonies are often dressed as women, and Shakespeare's macho hero Coriolanus is psychologically emasculated by his mother. Also, like Samson weaving at the loom while in captivity, we see Fenix knitting as his mother's vicarious arms. This temporary loss of male power, symbolized by one's linkage to the distaff, is the mother's attempt to keep the son in her long-reaching clutches.

In the evolution of consciousness, and thus in the hero's struggle for freedom, a fight with the androgynous uroboros ensues. The uroboros represents the great round of the unconscious, the *massa confusa* of the dark, preenlightened, preliberated consciousness. Fenix's uroboric struggle, as we have seen, is symbolized in his hallucinated serpent fight. At this time, he sees a promotional procession for the strongest woman in the world. Knowing that he is powerless against his mother's psychic, murderous, misogynic power, he picks this strong woman to bring home, hoping that she will be strong enough to fight off the incestuous corporation which might break the bond of the matriarchate. The strong woman (obviously played by a man in the film) signifies androgyny, on one hand harkening back to the uroboric chaos of preconsciousness, on the other hand pointing toward a future androgynous blending of the royal brother-sister union.

Eventually a slaying of either or both of the parents is the springboard from which the solar patriarchal revival can be ushered in by the son. In the case of Orestes, he kills his mother to avenge his father's death, thus replacing matriarchal, preindividual unconsciousness with patriarchal, solar consciousness. Fenix fulfills this mythic mandate by finally stabbing his unquenchable mother.

The dragon fight of mythology is often accomplished with the help of an enlightened female figure. Whether through Medea, Ariadne, or Athene, the hero often has a wonderful female compatriot in the eternal struggle for freedom. This heroine is hostile to the devouring mother archetype. In Fenix's case, his heroine, of course, is Alma, who, instead of becoming another victim of the mother's jealous rage, helps Fenix finally put the bloodthirsty monster to rest. With Alma's assistance, the slaying of the matriarchal serpent is Fenix's resurgence into enlightened consciousness and individuation.

OSIRIS

The story of Fenix, especially in its resurrectional aspect, is also the story of Osiris, King of Eternity, Ruler of Everlastingness, as found in *The Egyptian Book of the Dead*, and in Plutarch's "On Isis and Osiris." Osiris was originally found in two manifestations, as the God of the Underworld, the Ruler of the Dead, living in the West, and as the Lord of Heaven, known as Ra, in the East. These two deities eventually synthesized into the double soul of Osiris. Centuries later, alchemists identified Osiris's black complexion with the black powder of their *magnum opus*. This blackness, thought to possess magical qualities, is considered a source of life and power. Osiris represents unmanifest deity in the dark potentiality of *in*volution as well as deity in its resurrected *e*volution. As in alchemy, the Osiris principle is the lower nature (dark earth) giving birth to higher nature (solar gold). The black ore of earthy ignorance is transformed into the illuminating gold of wisdom.

Two brothers and two sisters are involved in the Osirian story, all from the same incestuous royal family. Osiris and Isis form one pair, and Set and Nephthys the other. Osiris, as the brother and husband of Isis, is bamboozled into lying down in a chest prepared for him by his evil brother Set and his confederates. Set nails down the lid of this chest, insuring Osiris' death. The chest is then cast into the Nile, where it floats down to the sea. It then lodges in a tamarisk tree, and is postsequently sawn out and made into a pillar in the house of the king of Byblos, where Isis recovers it. The earliest symbol of Osiris is the *djed*, a tree trunk with branch stumps projecting to either side at the top. The shape of this dismembered tree is very much like that of the dismembered Osiris, and like that of Concha and Lirio physically and of Fenix psychically.

Isis puts the chest in an unfrequented location, where it is accidentally found by Set, who then dismembers the body into fourteen parts and scatters them over the fields, where they serve as fertilization. As the antagonist of Osiris, Set represents evil and darkness. His emblem is the flint knife, the instrument of dismemberment and death. He represents the matriarchal destructiveness against which Osiris is fighting. Isis, in her search for the scattered body parts, erects a tomb at the site of each found piece. But the phallus is missing. When found, it is embalmed and saved for future fertilization. It is through this dismembered phallus that Isis conceives Horus, the bird-god of the sun, depicted as a king with the head of either a falcon or a hawk. Horus conquers Set and brings together the scattered body parts and restores life to Osiris. With his death and resurrection, Osiris becomes the ideal to which mortals strive for everlasting life. As one who is scattered over the fields, he is a vegetation god. As one who conquers death, he is the Ruler of Everlastingness.

Fenix's blackness alluded to earlier brings to mind the blackness of Osiris in his underworld aspect, and the first (black) stage of alchemy. The quaternity of the four incestuous brothers and sisters of the Osirian myth is found in the main characters of the film, with Fenix, as the double-souled Osiris, filling the two male parts of both Osiris and Set. He is Osiris as the psychologically dismembered and resurrected brother; he is Set in his evil, murderous complicity with the matriarchate. Fenix's mother, Concha, is analogous to Nephthys, the wife and sister of murderous Set. Alma, the one who helps Fenix in his reintegration, is Isis in her search for a dismembered Osiris. Fenix in relation to Alma is Osiris in relation to Isis. But Fenix in relation to Concha is Horus in relation to Nephthys and Set.

The analogy to Osiris's coffin is Fenix's trailer, into which he is locked by his mother. Fenix's flotation down the matriarchal sea is his

Nile voyage. In the beginning of the film, we see Fenix perching like a bird in a dismembered tree, matching the description of the *djed*, the emblem of Osiris. The only two chests or coffins in the film are that of the dead elephant, and that of Concha, where she is dressed as an Egyptian queen. Here she orders him (as Set) to dismember yet another vegetation offering to fertilize the land.

The elephant plays a significant part in this Osirian arcanum. It represents the qualities that Fenix hopes to attain, given a natural opportunity of evolution: strength, fidelity, sagacity, and gentleness to friends. We know that Fenix closely identifies with this creature. As a child, he cries at its funeral, and later, as a man, he visualizes himself as the dying elephant, with a bleeding nose like that of the animal. Fenix identifies with the creature because the elephant is a type of Osiris, in the dismemberment and scattering of its body parts in the ravine. Fenix's dismemberment is found mainly in his own psychic severance, but also, very importantly, in the dismemberment of Concha. Here, in his total enmeshment with Concha, Fenix loses control over his own body parts. His hands are merely the tools for his bloodthirsty mother. Severed from his own self, his dark Settian half feeds the earth mother her food of human flesh. Also, the themes of noses, ears, and hands indicate dismemberment—for instance, when the strange man in the street pulls his ear off and terrorizes Alma with it. Set and his emblematic flint knife are found dramatically in Fenix's nefarious use of knives. Osiris's missing phallus is strikingly paralleled in Fenix's emasculation. From Osiris's embalmed phallus is born Horus, the bird god, avenger of Osiris. In Fenix's story, we see the picture of this as Fenix finally develops enough strength to overpower Concha, as a new man, as Horus, the sun god manifested as the resurrected bird. Isis's searching for the scattered body parts is represented in Alma's receiving the picture of Fenix's hands at the theatre, in her apparent search for her dismembered love.

Horus avenges his father's death, like Orestes of Greek tragedy, and like Fenix of circus tragedy. Fenix strongly identifies with his father, Orgo, in his choice of knife-throwing practice and costume, in his hypnotic abilities, and in his possession of the same paternal brand of drink. Such identification forces Fenix to revenge his father's death. Thus, the patriarchate and matriarchate perennially try to win the favor of the ambivalent self. And if the self evolves successfully, the mythic boon is not far away.

The story of Fenix, as the story of Osiris, is the self in search of consciousness. It is the story of masculine spirituality and feminine corporeality in conflict, wherein, as with alchemy, that which is earthy becomes airy, and the two unite as one.

THE PHOENIX

As we follow Osiris/Fenix in his evolution from dismembered no-where man to resurrected bird man, the picture of the phoenix—fitting the name Fenix—is the most appropriate symbol of this resurrection. The phoenix is a mythical bird about the size of an eagle and graced with certain features of a pheasant. Its feathers are partly red and partly golden. When it sees death draw near, it nests itself in sweet-smelling wood and resins, which it exposes to the sun's rays, thus burning itself into ashes. Then it transforms itself into a new phoenix rising from the ashes.

According to Saint Jerome, the eagle is the emblem of the ascension and of prayer. The image of the eagle in *Santa Sangre*, besides being connected to the phoenix, is also symbolic of loftiness and masculine spirituality, soaring above the chthonic plane of feminine corporeality.

Osiris is also identified with the phoenix: "I am that Great Phoenix which is in Heliopolis. I am the ordering of all that is and exists" (Herodotus, *History* 2:73). After painting one of his victims ash white, Fenix sees a light emanating from the grave, to illumine a white bird rising from the corpse, an apt symbol of the phoenix motif. In another instance several of his victims rise from their graves, with one of them even leading a white horse, symbolic of Pegasus, the winged horse that springs from the decapitated trunk of the Gorgon. This horse, like the phoenix, represents a freeing from the chthonic tomb of earth and a release into spirituality. From the beginning, where we see the face of an eagle juxtaposed on Fenix's face, through the middle of the story, where Orgo tattoos an eagle onto Fenix's chest and where Alma makes the sign of a bird flying from his tattoo, to the end, where Alma again makes the sign of the flying bird against the backdrop of the flames, Fenix is unquestionably the phoenix. When the Concha doll is thrown off the balcony, a bird flutters away. After Fenix kills Concha, the film cuts back to his childhood, as we see him being released from his trailer. Shortly thereafter, back to the adult sequence, Alma leads Fenix out of his dark cavernous abode. Alma lifts her hands up in surrender to the police. Fenix follows her lead as he exclaims, "My hands! My hands! My! hands!," feeling for the first time a spiritual rejoining of his severed parts. This is Osiris's release from his coffin and dismemberment, and the phoenix's renewal from the ashes. In this respect, he is also the alchemical bird of Hermes. In essence, he is the philosophic gold brought about through the alembic fire. He is the spiritual nature raised from the putrifaction of the corporeal nature.

THE INVOLUTION AND EVOLUTION OF THE SELF

The life of Fenix is the involution and evolution of the self, from childhood trauma, through adult uteral regression, to eventual individuation. Fenix's story is told in two stages of his life, one at a certain age in childhood, the other as an adult. The trauma inflicted upon him as a child has no doubt left him in a state of psychic regression as an adult. It is not revealed to us until the end of the film that Fenix's adult relationship with his mother is merely hallucinatory. In this illusionary state, instead of moving toward a healthy evolution of consciousness, he regresses into an extremely complicated and entangled mother-involvement. His sidekick as an adult is the circus dwarf from his childhood, who disappears with his other hallucinatory figures at his point of resurrectional individuation. The dwarf, as a small person and as a childhood friend, symbolizes his involution back to childhood. The disappearance of the dwarf (who was the last hallucinatory figure to disappear) symbolizes his final stage of evolution. The child motif in Fenix's story is preconsciousness, it is the self lost in the dark abyss of amniotic chaos before the evolution of elucidated consciousness. But while the child motif represents preillumination, it also is futurity and the potentiality for independence. So while we see Fenix perched in the *djed* tree in a seemingly psychotic state of ambivalent confusion, the emblematic bird stance itself points toward the resurrectional future. Birds frequently symbolize human souls, and sometimes also thought, imagination, and spirituality—attributes practically absent in Fenix's temporary state of involution.

But it is not so easy to break the spell of the maternal enmeshment. Attis, due to Cybele's motherly-enmeshed jealousy, undergoes self-castration, madness, and death. Orestes is cursed with insanity by the furies for his matricide. And Fenix is on the very precipice of insanity in his psychic enslavement.

The implied incestuous relationships that Fenix has with his mother and with Alma (who may be his sister), form another sign of individuation. According to Jung, incest symbolizes "the longing for union with the essence of one's own self, or, in other words, for individuation" (Jung 1954, 218).

With the seed of the phoenix inside of him, Fenix, in his preconscious state, hopes to turn death into life. With the strong woman as his audience, he promises to turn the mummy in the coffin into one hundred flying birds. Instead, he fails, and he envisions himself in cruciform with one hundred or so chickens dropping down around him—a picture of humiliation and death instead of hope and resurrection.

The fountain in our chronicle, around which the circle turns, besides representing birth, is individuality, strength in adversity and centroversion—the essence of the self fulfilling its mission. Rotation around the point of divine space, the *axis mundi*, like the spinning of a top, with paradoxical centrifugal and centripetal forces, projects the self simultaneously into a vortex and a reverse vortex, claiming all of the space necessary for maturation.

In order to be complete, the self must leave the force of the primary parents. As the alchemists believe, that which remains in the retort never reaches the stage of red stone, the transformation into gold. To *involve* is to get stuck in uroboric incest. To *evolve* is to transcend the uroboros and sprout wings. But a mere killing of the mother is not what is called for. Neither will a mere soaring in the masculine world of universals do. A rescuing of the *inner* maiden and a complete union of the opposites is necessary for the attainment of the self's golden treasures.

ALEJANDRO JODOROWSKY

Alejandro Jodorowsky has talked openly about his life in numerous interviews. From these candid self-revelations, we can easily find parallels between the filmmaker and his cinematic Fenix. He also certainly has the right background for such numinous filmmaking. He was born of circus parents, an absent father who hung by his hair in a circus act and a dominating mother, by his own account. Jodorowsky has degrees in philosophy, mathematics, and physics from the University of Santiago. He studied mime under Marcel Marceau at the age of twenty-five. And he has studied Zen Buddhism among other subjects in his varied and heavy reading intake. He writes stories for comic books and runs a psychoanalytic school and clinic based on the Tarot near his home in Paris.

In a *Penthouse* interview (June 1973) Jodorowsky recalls a childhood memory about a friend who showed him a bucket containing a man's penis which had been cut off of a sailor by a prostitute. The children buried the penis in a little grave they had made in a cemetery. (Recall the emasculating elements in Fenix's life, and the missing phallus of Osiris.) No doubt such memories contribute to conscious and subconscious aspects of his filmmaking.

Jodorowsky also remembers being ridiculed as a boy for having a large nose. (Recall Fenix's identification with the elephant and the filmic references to Fenix's nose). Many such elements in *Santa Sangre*

are no doubt directly or indirectly from the life of Jodorowsky himself:
the circus, the mime act, the absent father, the dominating mother,
dismemberment, the mother-son enmeshment and so on.

Jodorowsky says that, "Life is like a circus. It's a circle where God is
laughing. When you accept that, you start to dance. I waltz with
death" (Wolper). Certainly this is what he is doing in *Santa Sangre* in the
circus of the great cosmic round.

Regarding his creative process, Jodorowsky says, "My ideas come
like dreams . . . suddenly. And when it happens, I say 'Thank you!' to
my unconscious" (Wilmington). Perhaps this method of creating as-
sures greater freedom for the muses of the collective unconscious.

Jodorowsky says that he hated his enmeshing mother. A small
obituary in the November 15, 1973 issue of *Variety*, reporting his
mother's death in Lima, Peru, would seem to indicate his distance from
her. The article says that her filmmaker son "has not been located by
the family, now living in Peru, and [he] is believed to be somewhere in
Europe."

Having had six wives, he metaphorically says that he murdered
women all his life. When asked by Claudio Argento, the producer of
Santa Sangre, to make a quick crime film, Jodorowsky wrote a story
inspired by a man he met in a bar. This man was an infamous Mexican
serial killer, Goio Cardenes, who murdered thirty women and buried
them in his garden. After spending a decade in prison and in an
asylum, Cardenas emerged with no apparent memory of his crime
spree. He later married and became an attorney and a writer. Jodorowsky says that *Santa Sangre* "is not about that man, but he motivated
me to write a story about redemption" (Wolper). Indeed, Jodorowsky
has made a story of sacrificial redemption, perhaps in more ways than
he is aware. Having hated his mother and women all his life, Jodorowsky's art is not only the story of Fenix's redemption, but also of the
filmmaker's, and of an audience hopefully perceptive enough to participate in his alchemical opus.

HOLY BLOOD

While the only mention of holy blood is found at the shrine of Santa Lirio, there are copious amounts of the gushing fluid throughout the film. While the bishop finds Santa Lirio's pool of blood to be paint, the blood of the numerous victims is indeed real. Young Fenix clings adhesively to his desperate mother, Concha, as she clings adherently to the armless statue of Santa Lirio. His attachment to this religious fanatic is deeper than physical, for the rest of the story concerns a constant shedding of blood. We see Orgo cutting off Concha's arms and chickens drinking her blood. Orgo cuts his own throat and the blood spurting from his neck is lapped up by dogs. Fenix kills various women and buries them in his backyard, as spatters of blood stain his clean white shirt.

The central theme of the Lirio cult is obviously blood. As a grown man Fenix can not escape this obsession. His armless mother, as a figure of the Terrible Mother, demands blood for the fructification of the land. Blood is thought of mythically as the rain or dew that guarantees fruitfulness for Mother Earth. In the same way that a literal womb is thirsty for impregnating seed, so too the earth is thirsty for fertilizing blood. While alchemy is thought of as something earthy becoming airy, blood is the reverse: something divine manifested on the lower planes. The most violent of cults demand blood, and of course even those religions that seem the most antiseptic, such as those of the West, are usually bloodier than we would care to realize. *Santa Sangre* is the bloody alchemy of the soul, where sacrifice is the central motif in this religion of individuation. As we trace this theme from our various vantages, we can see a blood-stained scarlet cord threaded through each section.

In the alchemical tradition, we see that the final stage leading to the philosopher's stone stands for bloody sacrifice. For it is only in the shedding of blood that the adept of the heart can attain ultimate consecration. As the scriptures attest, "Without the shedding of blood, there is no remission of sins."

In the illustrations of the *Rosarium Philosophorum*, we see that the royal couple have to die before they can be reborn. The union of their two bodies into one in the midst of their coital deaths brings to mind the folkloric belief that sperm is a form of sacrificial blood. When the man's seed is planted in the womb of the woman, it is considered a sacrificial death that will bring forth fruit. Thus, two coming together as one is a figure of a vegetation god dying and being buried in the womb of the earth, that fruit may arise.

In our study of evolutionary consciousness, we see that myth, as an analogy of consciousness, necessitates blood from the hero in order to satisfy the cyclical demands of the great uroboric incest. As a symbol of gaining consciousness, the hero sheds the blood of the world parents, thus breaking the old uroboric incest and starting a new era of existence. His own blood is also shed in his heroic mission.

The story of Osiris is a story of bloodshed and dismemberment, the precursor to renewal. The Arabic saying "Blood has flowed, the danger is past," which is the central idea of all sacrifice, is the appropriate dictum of the story, which is the insurer of peace in human interaction.

The phoenix willingly sacrifices itself, shedding its own blood, in order to become new life. The three stages of the phoenix, first as the original burnt offering, second as the whitened ashes, and third as the reborn golden Bird of Hermes, besides paralleling the three stages of alchemy (black, white, and red), are also analogous to the three stages of the sacrificial hero; the commissioned warrior, the buried skeleton, and the decorated resurrection man.

In the psychology of the self, we all know that the child, unlike the phoenix, is usually the last one to want to sacrifice itself. It is only when the child learns the secret of sacrifice, such as in the scarification of initiation rites, that he or she can think maturely and independently. Modern children deprived of such "primitive" rites are usually denied the most important secret of adult transition, the most important ingredient of maturity and wisdom, which is sacrifice.

In his enslaved servitude to the mother, Fenix is certainly sacrificing others, which any child can do. But in his intimate participation with sacrifice, he never learns the concept of self-sacrifice until Alma comes back into his life and he becomes reunited with his feminine soul. Of all of his potential victims, she is the only one who willingly submits to his murderous designs. When Concha tells him to cut off her arms, Alma, unlike all the others, holds them up for the cutting. Here, rather than pushing the sacrificial pendulum in the same tired direction toward resistant victimization, Alma's mysterious behavior effects an enantiodromianic reversal of opposites in Fenix's confused heart. Instead of killing Alma while immediately behind his mother, he stabs his mother instead, as if killing the Terrible Mother within him. (His mother previously and erroneously warns him, "You'll never be free of me, I'm inside of you!")

Hints found throughout the narrative point toward the necessity of sacrifice which, in its proper spirit, is an act of grace. As it is written, "Where sin abounds, grace more abundantly abounds." In Concha's theatrical hand act, with Fenix as her hands, she acts out the creation story of Genesis, where sin beckons gracious sacrifice: "God created the heavens and the earth, fish, and land, and trees, yielding fruit, and birds flying above the earth. And God created man and woman. Then the serpent came with temptation, and he offered fruit, and then, they knew sin—universal, universal sin."

In a microcosmic sense, this creation story is the story of *Santa Sangre*. All of the elements contained in this stage production are the elements of the film itself, all the way from Fenix eating the fish in the beginning of the story through the wrestling match with the serpent to the awareness of universal sin. Concha, obsessed with this sin, constantly reminds Fenix (or, we should say at this point that Fenix reminds himself in the form of his hallucinated mother) that he is integrally connected to sin. She tells him at one point that he cannot atone for his sins with nightmares. Elsewhere she tells him that the stage dancer has defiled him with lust and that he is too weak to resist temptation—all pointing toward a yearning for the remedy for sin, which is sacrifice.

The fruit in our story has an ambiguous meaning. On one hand, it is the temptation to inner knowledge, which is connected to sin. On the other hand, fruit contains the seed that will redeem sinfulness. For it is in the sacrificed seed that fruit is brought forth and it is in the fruit that the seed of future fruit is contained. Moreover, it is in sacrificial blood that the womb of the earth produces fruit. In the filmic narrative there are two significant appearances of fruit. As a child magician, Fenix pulls fruit from the air and gives it to Alma. It is only after she receives this fruit that she is able to walk across the burning tightrope which she was too frightened to negotiate before. In Fenix's convalescence at the hospital, the doctor brings a large bowl of fruit and offers it to the Down's syndrome inmates as they circle around their fountainal *axis mundi*. In both cases, the seeds of spiritual fructification are found in sacrificial giving. So while sin and death abound by blood, so too does the seed of fruit and life abound by sacrifice.

In his identification with his father and with the elephant, Fenix carries the fruit-bearing seed of sacrificial redemption. We remember that his father, Orgo, kills himself: in a sense, a self-sacrifice. We also remember that Fenix visualizes himself bleeding from the nose, an identification with the dying elephant. The stage dancer victim mysteriously says to Fenix, "I like your nose," signifying that the identification with a dying, bleeding, and eventually dismembered creature is more than just pet friendship. When we put these seeds together with the image of Fenix in agonizing cruciform, we suspect that all is not lost after all. His *in*volution into the psychic womb of Concha as sacrificial fruit is a necessary precursor to his evolution as the new fruit brought forth from sacrifice. His *e*volution of consciousness is now complete, as the filmmaker indicates with the sacrificial psalm on the screen: "I stretch out my hands to thee: my soul thirsts for thee like a parched land. Teach me the way I should go. For to thee I lift up my soul" (Psalm 143:6, 8).

Thus the story of *Santa Sangre* is truly the story of holy blood. It teaches us that spiritual gold, as embodied in the phoenix, is found in self-sacrificial giving rather than in the sacrificing of others.

PART 4

UNORTHODOX MESSIAHS AND SEEING

While the previous sections on masculine and feminine monsters show various types of heroes in mortal combat with their respective dragons, this section focuses on a particular type of hero—the unorthodox kind. We see in these films that an alternative, minority vision is needed to redeem a dragon-dominated world.

At this juncture in the history of Western culture, when institutions that once carried torches of enlightenment have turned into draconian butchers themselves, seemingly crazy, prophetic voices suggest, as they have always suggested in prerevolutionary times, that the redeemers of society are not to be found in the conventional, the institutional, and the traditional, but in the eccentric, the prophetic, and the revolutionary.

RUMBLE FISH

THE MOTORCYCLE MESSIAH

D espite its initial financial failure, *Rumble Fish* is a film of significant worth. Adapted by S. E. Hinton and Francis Ford Coppola from Hinton's novel, it is a story of following and leading, fighting and ceasing to fight, wisdom and ignorance, freedom and captivity, all set within an ever present vicious continuum of time and moved by the musical rhythm of Stewart Copeland with a cameo performance by Queen Ida and her Zydeco Band. There are many hints of mystical transcendence in this movie which go beyond the obvious, such as Rusty James' out-of-body experience and verbal references to Greek mythology.

CHARACTERS

The Motorcycle Boy

Bits of graffiti all over town saying "The Motorcycle Boy Reigns," testify to the reverence attached to the hero's stature by the community youths. Color-blind and partially deaf, this twenty-one-year-old local idol (Mickey Rourke) has spent an extended time away, looking for his mother in California. Like many mythic heroes, he is quiet, mysterious, speculative, and pensive. He seems to have ridden in from nowhere, as if sent from God as a divine deliverer. When confronted by the blackhearted cop, he does not speak, as if he knows his fate is integrally tied to this enforcer of doom, like a lamb led to the slaughter.

Rusty James

Contrasted with most of the other characters in the story, Rusty James (Matt Dillon) is less perceptive to the meaning of life and the deeper issues of human interaction. His smarter friend Smokey (Nicolas Cage) steals his girlfriend from him with more adept social skills. Rusty James, puzzled by the conversations of his intellectual brother and father, is not wise enough to keep himself out of trouble, physically or socially. Though he does not understand his older brother, he looks up to him with religious devotion.

The Cop

A symbol of law, authority, limits, and death, the cop (William Smith) is obsessed with the Motorcycle Boy, intent on his destruction. Almost every time the cop enters the picture, his shadow precedes him, as if his shadow were more prominent than his actual figure.

The Father

The philosophic, alcoholic father (Dennis Hopper) of the Motorcycle Boy and Rusty James maintains a welfare-supported household short on furniture but long on books. What this derelict lacks in personal and social responsibility, he makes up for in literary and philosophic understanding.

Cassandra

A nice looking young lady in love with the Motorcycle Boy, Cassandra (Diana Scarwid) has a penchant for heroin and an attachment to the same books read by the Motorcycle Boy. Her role, seemingly insignificant at face value, is more meaningful in its mythic import, as Cassandra of classical mythology.

Benny

The billiard room proprietor, Benny (Tom Waits), is a hip, off-the-cuff philosopher, a divine timekeeper. He speculates: "Time is a funny thing. Time is a very peculiar item. You see, when you're young, when you're a kid, you got time. You got nothing but time. Throw away a couple of years here, a couple of years there—it doesn't matter. You know, the older ya get, you say, Jesus, how much I got? I got thirty-five summers left. Think about it—thirty five summers."

Benny's words are accented by periodic cuts to time-lapse photography, clocks, and more references to time. Each time we see a clock, it is progressively set at a later hour, reminding us of time speeding by.

Steven

Rusty James's tagalong buddy since kindergarten, Steven (Vincent Spano) is a timid and loyal, albeit reluctant, follower of Rusty James's tumultuous leadings. This bespeckled devotee takes notes on all important events and is a detached observant recorder.

MYTHIC DRAMA

Rumble Fish opens at Benny's Billiards, the address of which is number thirteen, befitting the unlucky scenario of the street-smart saga. After Rusty James orders a cup of hot chocolate, he gets the bad news that Biff Wilcox is looking for him. He is to meet his opponent at ten o'clock behind the pet store. From then on, premonitions of shadowy trouble threaten to dominate the atmosphere and our characters are left to their own coping mechanisms sans a messiah.

As Rusty James and his friends make plans for the evening's fight, they walk past the pet store, where they see colored fish in this black-

and-white film. Rusty James gets sidetracked by the sight of his girlfriend Patty (Diane Lane). He falls asleep on her couch at her side and wakes up at 9:45, fifteen minutes after he is supposed to meet his friends for the nocturnal rumble. Finally meeting up with his friends, Rusty James asks about his absent sidekick Steve, as if his passive buddy were a good-luck charm to protect him from his own precariousness. Rusty James suggests, "maybe he's late," connecting his friend to the mortificational harshness of time.

The scene of the planned fight is in what appears to be a combination of subway platform and abandoned warehouse interior, a subterranean scene of anticipated antagonism. While looking for Biff Wilcox and his rival faction, Rusty James surmises, "It looks like we're going to have to fight ourselves, huh?" One of his compatriots comically slaps himself—an obvious clue to the meaning of the rumble fish. A shadow of a cat passes by, a wino stirs, and finally the rival gang appears from the hidden recesses of the ominous cavern.

Rusty James and his opponent fight, only to be interrupted by the sudden appearance of his majesty, the Motorcycle Boy. All eyes turn in obeisance to the rolling throne, to hear the worshipped one quietly ask, "What is this, another glorious battle for the kingdom?" His ironic sarcasm speaks of his kingdom being of another world, perhaps one without rumbles. As a prince of peace, when his kid brother mentions that he thought the Motorcycle Boy was gone for good, our philosopher king answers, "I thought we had a treaty."

Rusty James gets badly cut, the masterful man of mystery saves the day, and suddenly the shadow of the cop appears, and again, the rumblers hush in respectful silence. They seem to give this sinister policeman as much reverence, or at least fear, as they do the legendary Motorcycle Boy. Here, we suspect that we are witnessing two grander rival factions, grander than the rumblers of the time-bound streets, and grander and more spiritual than the small factions of the time and space limitations.

The cop says to Steve in a stern, fatherly manner, "It's a little bit late for you, isn't it, Steven?," again reminding us that passive observers of the cosmic drama are ruled by the harsh dictates of Father Time. He

The Motorcycle Messiah sees a truth in the rumble fish that is hidden to all others.

adds, "You know, I'd watch the company I keep, if I were you," referring to the Motorcycle Boy. His severe countenance and threatening gestures give us an indication that his presence is more than that of a cop, but rather, something of a predestined executioner, a Grand Inquisitor, an evil prince and spiritual counterpart to the returning hero. Speaking of the target of his obsession, our enforcer of chthonic law laments, "You know, I really thought he left for good," only to be sharply answered by Rusty James, who shouts, "Yea, well maybe you miss truth too much. Maybe he had to come back just to see you!" Rusty James doesn't realize the fuller meaning of his own prophetic statement. Now addressing his spiritual adversary directly, the inquisitor verbalizes his dark wishes: "You know, we'd all be better off if you'd just stay gone," revealing more of his monomaniacal intent.

After the fight, Steve and the Motorcycle Boy tend Rusty James's battle wound. While the prince doesn't seem to be too concerned over the state of woundedness, Steve demands that he do something, reminding us of Jesus' contemporaries, who demanded miracles, and political action as a sign of his deity.

Talking about his time away, Rusty James asks the living legend how the ocean was. But the Motorcycle Boy never got to the ocean, as he says, because California got in the way. Here we get some of our first glimpses of the Motorcycle Boy's mission. Unlike the cop, who is fixated on time and law, the Motorcycle Boy is fixated on water. The recurring pictures of time-elapsed clouds, puddles of water in the streets, and the ocean are part of the destiny of this cyclical cycle boy. We eventually learn that glittery California is a stumbling block on the way to a greater glory.

The clock in their apartment says that time is in the eleventh hour. The Motorcycle Boy walks off to another corner of the apartment in

True to her mythic role, Cassandra the prophetess is not believed by Rusty James.

rapt meditation, as if contemplating his fate, while the two younger boys talk admiringly about him.

The next day, Rusty James runs into Cassandra, a pretty heroin user in love with the Motorcycle Boy. She descends a fire escape, signifying her Dante-esque descent into lower regions of the spiritual world. Like everybody else, she talks much about the Motorcycle Boy. She tells Rusty James, who despises her, "I thought he was gone for good, and I was wrong." Then she changes her mind and says, "But I was right." Suspecting prophetic insight, maybe there is a deeper meaning to his being "gone for good." But like his friend Steve, Rusty James cannot handle a metaphorical messiah. As with the Roman-hating unbelievers in the gospel account, only a militant regent will do. Rusty James yells at Cassandra, "No, no, no, no, no. You were wrong! You're wrong man! He's back! Always talking crazy."

Later, when Rusty James talks with his brother and their father, he reports that Cassandra said she wasn't hooked. The Motorcycle Boy says, "Yea, well I believe her." "You do?" asks an incredulous Rusty James. The older brother expounds further, "Sure. You know what happened to the people who didn't believe Cassandra?" Before Rusty James has a chance to respond, the father answers, "Yea, the Greeks got 'em. You know what I mean?" We remember that the Greek Cassandra's prophetic nature is double-edged. Whatever she prophesies comes true but nobody believes her. Thus, the Motorcycle Boy and his mythologically connected father know enough not to fall into the anti-mythic trap of disbelief, even if the belief might be a prophecy of the Motorcycle Boy being "gone for good".

But unfortunately, Rusty James is not so hip. In his state of mythic denial, he says, "Man, what the fuck do the Greeks have to do with anything, huh? You think I care about the Greeks? No, I don't care. I don't give a shit about the Greeks!"

At the pool hall, Benny delivers his monologue on time at this point. This night Rusty James, Smokey, and a few of their friends break into a house up by the lake and have an orgy, the news of which gets back to Patty, Rusty James' girlfriend. She rejects him. He gets suspended from school for too many messups, and he acts like he doesn't care.

Still unaware of the hidden secrets to which his brother and father are privy, Rusty James has a conversation with the Motorcycle Boy about the leader's role as a pied piper. The Motorcycle Boy shows his brother a picture in a magazine that was taken of him and his motorcycle while he was in California. But, in Jesusian fashion, he warns his brother not to tell anybody about it. Rusty James tells his brother that the boys would have followed him anywhere. The Motorcycle Boy sarcastically replies that they would even follow him to the river and jump in, adding, "You know, if you're going to lead people, you have to have somewhere to go." Obviously, there is a connection between the monarch and the river. At this point, the two brothers run across the draconian cop standing in front of a mammoth handless clock. Thus, a dark angel from beyond time vents more of his hellish invective toward his familiar target of hatred. We suspect that a cosmic collision between these two timeless forces is inevitable. The descending sun casts quickly moving shadows over the salvational fire escape. That evening, the two brothers and Steve cross the river to have some fun, but not before stopping at the bridge to pay homage to the flowing symbol of eternity. The Motorcycle Boy says in his typical ambiguous fashion that the river "goes all the way to the ocean," leaving his poetic words a mystery.

Across the river is partyland. Bars, whores, pool halls, flashing lights and laughter beckon Rusty James toward his typical search for El Dorado. But it does not impress the Motorcycle Boy. There is another world more important than this land of illusion. Knowing that the older brother is color-blind and partially deaf, Steve asks him what all of this exciting glitter looks like to him. The philosopher says, "Black-and-white TV with the sound turned off." The enlightened one's sensory limitations are indicative of his clearer and more intense inner senses. He knows too well the deceptive nature of a Californiaesque temporal illusion. He says to his kid brother, "You know, it seems to me that I can remember seeing colors. It was a long time ago. . . . You know, I stopped being a kid when I was five." His words echo the Apostle Paul: "When I was a child, I spoke as a child, I understood as a child, I thought as a child; but when I became a man, I put away childish things. For now we see in a mirror darkly; but then, face to face; now I know in part, but then shall I know even as also I am known" (I Corinthians 13:11–12).

The Motorcycle Boy tells his brother that he saw their mother while he was in California. She's living with a movie producer, a master of illusion. Like Saint Augustine in *The City of God*, he deplores a temporary kingdom in his parable about California: "California's like a beautiful wild girl on heroin, who's high as a kite, thinking she's on top of the world, not knowing she's dying—even if you show her the marks." He is like a messiah speaking to his disciples, "in parables, because they seeing, see not; and hearing, they hear not, neither do they understand. And in them is fulfilled the prophecy of Isaiah, which saith, By hearing, ye shall hear and shall not understand; and seeing, ye shall see and shall not perceive. . . . But blessed are your eyes, for they see; and your ears, for they hear" (Matthew 13:12–14, 16).

At the pool hall, a black guy attests to the illumined one's nature: "He's a deep mothafucker, you know? . . . He's a prince. . . . You know what he's like? He's like royalty in exile."

Our prince then suddenly disappears. Rusty James and Steve get mugged on their way home, and while he is either knocked out or dead, Rusty James has an out-of-body experience, wherein he gains insight into some of the lessons his would-be redeemer has been trying to teach him. His spirit comes back into his body, and His Majesty shows up in time to beat up the muggers.

Rosy-fingered Dawn appears and we see the master and his disciples at the river's bank, with poor Rusty James battered from his brush with death. Steve, a doubting Thomas, is angry that Rusty James' trouble comes from his wanting to be like his brother. He yells at the master, "I wonder why somebody hasn't just taken a rifle and blown your head off?" But the Motorcycle Boy, in his patient omniscience, answers, "Well, even the most primitive society has an innate respect for the insane," again, speaking in parabolic ambiguity. If he were merely insane we could dismiss him as a derelict mind with unusual powers. But the insanity he speaks of is not of the clinical variety. There is something divine about this madness.

This stirs something in Rusty James's mind. While sitting at Benny's Billiards in deep contemplation for the first time in the story, he is asked by the older and wiser Benny, "What's the matter with you? I ain't never seen you sit still so long." He asks Benny for some advice: "How do you know when someone's crazy?" To add to his consternation, Rusty James finds his brother over at the pet store, obsessing about the fish and mumbling esoterically. The older brother explains that the Siamese fighting fish will even try to fight their own reflection in a mirror. The cop comes in and tells the Motorcycle Boy he is crazy. The crazy one responds with more odd words: "But they belong in the river. I don't think they'd fight if they were in the river." Incensed, the cop says, "Someone oughta get you off the streets." The odd one retorts, "Someone oughta put the fish in the river." The Motorcycle Boy leaves the pet store when it closes and the kid brother continues to tag along like a naive puppy dog.

The boys run across their father in a bar, and Rusty James asks if his mother is crazy, by this time unsure of a lot of things. To be expected, the father answers with more abstract words: "Rusty James, every now and then a person comes along who has a different view of the world than the usual person. It doesn't make 'im crazy. I mean an acute perception—that doesn't make 'im crazy. However, some times, it can drive you crazy—acute perception."

Rusty James complains of not understanding again, and the father continues, "Your mother was not crazy. And neither, contrary to popular belief, is your brother crazy. He's merely miscast the play. He was born in the wrong era—on the wrong side of the river."

Rusty James slowly begins to have a slight change of faith. He confesses, "Man, I feel like I'm wasting my life waiting for something."

Just a few minutes before midnight, the Motorcycle Messiah tells his brother his crazy plans. He says he's going to put the fish in the river and he instructs Rusty James to get on the cycle at that point and follow the river all the way to the ocean. Without understanding all of this craziness, Rusty James confusedly follows his elder brother back to the locked pet shop. After the boys break in, the camera pans a stuffed wolf, eerily signifying the hour of the wolf. The Motorcycle

The authoritarian cop wants to steal the Motorcycle Boy's time.

Boy releases most of the birds and animals and carries the colored rumble fish toward the river. Suddenly the shadow of the cop appears. We hear a gunshot. The Motorcycle Boy is on the ground and the cop puts his smoking pistol back in his holster and lights a cigarette in post-orgasmic satisfaction. Rusty James completes his dying brother's mission by picking up the fish from the ground and putting them in the river. Two cops begin to arrest Rusty James. He sees his colored reflection in the cop car window, and he socks it. The killer cop lets the kid go. The Motorcycle Boy dies. The father silently walks off. Steve takes notes. And Rusty James rides the cycle all the way to the ocean.

Now the cycle is completed. Like Socrates, Jesus, and others with "acute perception," the Motorcycle Messiah is accused of being crazy, and is predestined to suffer his tragic fate. Beyond the obvious allegory of the rumble fish as a microcosm of the rumbling kids, and the rumbling kids as a microcosm of our rumbling human world, is the allegory of the Motorcycle Boy's messianic mission. Only through this

273

preordained death can Rusty James be set free from his own self-destructiveness. The clouds in the story arise from the ocean and drop water on the land, which flows into the river, which flows back to the ocean. So too has Rusty James finally learned from the parables of the ambiguous *cycle* boy.

TAXI DRIVER
THE MAD MESSIAH OF HISTORIC CHRISTIAN ART

W hen art imitates life we are not surprised, and rarely shocked. When life imitates art we sometimes have a different reaction. Some critics of *Taxi Driver* wanted to ban the film after they learned that it had inspired John Hinckley, Jr.'s attempted assassination of President Ronald Reagan in 1981. Interestingly, the story was originally loosely based on the life of Arthur Bremer, the 1972 attempted assassin of Governor George Wallace. Hinckley, obsessed with Jodie Foster in her portrayal of the young prostitute in this film, planned to kill Reagan to impress her, in much the same way Travis Bickle plans to kill Senator Palantine in the film.

In an era when assassinations have become a media phenomenon, as they have for Travis, and as they have in the decade following the film's 1976 release, there have appeared a punk group named The Dead Kennedys, and yet another named Jodie Foster's Army. After being victimized by Hinckley's obsessive harassment, Jodie Foster went on to play a victim of gang rape in a later film based on a true incident, *The Accused* (1988). Yet another incident of life imitating art may be found in the case of the 1980s subway vigilante, Bernard Goetz, being lionized in the same way that Travis Bickle is in the film.

Taxi Driver was made on a budget of $1 million, a doubling of the original budget, but still a minuscule amount by film industry standards. When the original budget was given by Columbia, neither Martin Scorsese, nor Paul Schrader, nor Robert De Niro had made significant names for themselves, but in the months of preproduction waiting, it was decided that these three talents could be banked on for the higher amount.

When asked about the potential banning of *Taxi Driver*, screenwriter Paul Schrader said, "You ban all portrayals of psychopaths, you've taken them away from art, and therefore from society. But the problem is, you lose *Crime and Punishment*, but you still have Raskolnikov. . . . Society will lose art, and still have the psychopaths" (Mankin).

It is also Schrader's opinion that society is actually healthier with the viewing of such sociopaths in art, as he reasons, because some of them will be helped by seeing their sickness. He has mentioned that if Hinckley's parents had seen *Taxi Driver* as many times as Hinckley did, there probably would not have been an attempted assassination on Reagan's life.

Director Martin Scorsese grew up in a poor neighborhood in Little Italy, near the Bowery, in a strict Catholic environment, where he learned as much religion in the streets as in church. According to Scorsese, after growing up seeing fights and blood everywhere in his neighborhood, he learned the morality that violence is very often used to right wrongs. Paul Schrader grew up in the Midwest in a Reformed Calvinist background. Before trying his hand at screenwriting, he wrote film criticism, analyzing *film noir*, among his other interests. His 1972 book, *Transcendental Style*, argues that the filmmakers Ozu, Bresson, and Dreyer are prime examples of a style he considers highly religious. This transcendental style is surely at the core of his own style, as exemplified in *Taxi Driver*.

TRAVIS BICKLE, A PSYCHOLOGICAL PROFILE

Taxi Driver centers on Travis Bickle (Robert De Niro), a Marine Corps Vietnam veteran from the Midwest. An insomniac, he gets a job driving a taxi from 6 P.M. to 6 A.M., six days a week, sometimes seven, earning from three hundred to three hundred and fifty dollars per week. He is disgusted by the baseness of the people of the night. As he says, "All the animals come out at night: whores, skunk, pussies, buggers, queens, fairies, dopers, junkies. Sick. Venal." He narrates much of the film through his diary, heard in voice-overs. The more he writes, the more we see into his mind, and the more we see that his sanity is deteriorating. More than his trouble sleeping and his frequent headaches, he suffers from an obsession with the "scum" of his world. As he drives through the rain, we hear his diary voice-over saying, "Someday a real rain will come and wash all this scum off the streets." While applying for his taxi job he mentions that his driving record is clean, "like my conscience."

The more time he spends having to wipe semen and blood off the back seat of his cab, the more obsessed he becomes with the venality of the city's scum. He even mentions to his one celebrated fare, Senator Charles Palantine, a presidential candidate, "I think the president should just clean up the whole mess here. He should just flush it right down the fucking toilet!"

With more sleeplessness, headaches, and disgust, he feels progressively more lonely and without purpose. He suffers from possible hypochondriasis, suspecting himself of having stomach cancer. He spends his spare time watching television and going to porno movies. His social life is limited mainly to interactions with crass cabbies who share vulgar stories of sexual exploits and dirty jokes. Nonetheless, he searches for transcendence over the literal and human garbage of his city streets and over his increasing feelings of emptiness.

Displaced Sexuality

Although he frequents porno moviehouses, Travis appears to be almost asexual. He doesn't fit into the sexual talk of his fellow cabbies. His porno watching doesn't seem to be of a masturbatory intent. And he doesn't seem to be having a dating life, as much as he might want to. He watches romantic soap operas, and "American Bandstand," with slow-dancing couples, as if wishing he could connect with someone himself; yet his awkward attempt to flirt with the concession clerk at a porno theatre is forthrightly rebuffed. Such frustrated sexuality must find an avenue of expression; in Travis' case, he displaces it into a religious mission, as will be shown.

Psychological Devolution

Overburdened by the scum of the streets, and lonely, Travis finds a young woman to whom he can direct some of his obsessional feelings. Pretty, sweet, and seemingly untainted by the pervasive societal scum, Betsy, Senator Palantine's political volunteer (Cybill Shepherd) is the perfect candidate for Travis's puritanical tastes. He constantly watches her from a distance before walking into her campaign headquarters office to ask her out. He projects his own feelings onto her, suggesting to her that she is lonely, and that she "needs something," like maybe him and his protection. During their first time together, he wastes no time trying to convince her of the negative attributes of her male fellow campaign worker. Failing to pick up on this clue to Travis's nature, she accepts a date with him, which shortly turns out disastrously. As if it were the commonly acceptable thing to do, Travis takes her to a dirty movie on their first date. She leaves the theater and rejects him, and he is naively surprised by her actions.

Her rejection devastates him. His headaches get worse and he falls into deeper depression, with accompanying fears of cancer. His statement to himself, "You're only as healthy as you feel." reveals the precarious state of his condition. More violence in the streets adds to his insecurity, and paranoid ideations begin to infiltrate his mind. He says, "Loneliness followed me everywhere. . . . there's no escape." In his isolation and increasingly murderous feelings, Travis picks up an angry fare (played by Martin Scorsese) who talks of shooting his adulterous wife "in the pussy with a .44 magnum."

Travis begins to compensate for his feelings of worthlessness. He says in his diary, "I believe that someone should become a person like other people." Seeking solutions to his sinking feelings, he confides to fellow cabby, "the wizard," "I just wanna go out and really do something." He confesses to the wizard that he has some bad ideas in his head, and receives some completely irrelevant counseling. Without support or direction, he breaks from reality, signified by his breaking of the romantically tuned television set. He is now clearly psychotic, ruled by paranoid ideations, obsessed with a murderous mission, and unable to sort out the natural laws of cause and effect. In his words, "My life has taken another turn. Suddenly there is a change." He buys several handguns and plans to assassinate Senator Palantine, apparently to impress Betsy, among other psychotic and largely unknown reasons. His preparation for his mission is reminiscent of Lee Marvin's mental and physical conditioning in *Cat Ballou*. Now, as a man with a mission, he says, "Here's a man who would not take it anymore." He has decided that the killing of Palantine will somehow clean up some of the dirtiness in his sullied world. At least it will revenge some of the imagined powers controlling the rejecting Betsy.

He saves a wrinkled twenty-dollar bill given to him by a pimp (Harvey Keitel) who abuses his whore in his cab, and eventually hands it back to the pimp's partner for a paid conversation with Iris, the abused preteen prostitute (Jodie Foster).

It is as if Travis has redirected his awkward sexuality into violent aggression. Working himself into a state of climactic inevitability, leading to his attempted assassination of Palantine, he has an overwhelming urge to implant a silver seed into a victim of his psychotic rage. When his original attempt is foiled and he is forced to leave hurriedly in a state of psychological *coitus interruptus*, he must imbed his seed into another worthy recipient. He drives madly to the pimp's place deciding that this Matthew (called Sport by Iris) is just as worthy a target. So he kills him and two of his partners, setting the young prostitute free from her bondage.

TRAVIS'S TRANSCENDENTAL STYLE

Martin Scorsese said in an interview that the whole idea in making *Taxi Driver* was "to make a story of a modern saint, you know, a saint in his own society, but his society happens to be gangsters" (Powell).

The Undefiled One

Travis thanks God for the rain, because it helps wash away the garbage, a symbol in his mind of the human garbage filling the streets. Cleanliness, as he attests about his conscience, and as he believes about his sexuality, is of the traditional cliché variety, being next to godliness. At one point he drives his cab through the spray of a gushing fire hydrant, as if he and his cab are receiving a spiritual cleansing from the venal filth surrounding him.

The Antichrist

We are told that Travis works all night, from six to six, six days a week. Thus, Travis's exposure to the metropolitan demons of the night inspire within him righteous indignation, as if the beastly antichrist of his town must be dealt a mortal blow.

The Madonna-Whore Split

Coming from a Christian background (as do his cinematic creators), Travis manifests a variation of the traditional madonna-whore split. On one hand, he idolizes the madonna in Betsy, who dresses mostly in white and is believed by Travis to be pure and undefiled. He writes of her that she is alone, and that "they can not touch her," as if placing her on a throne as the Mother of God. On the other hand, he mentally fucks the whore via his viewing of pornographic movies. Yet when confronted with a real whore, Iris, his mission is to rescue her—the sign, in his brand of spirituality, of a true believer.

280

The Prophet

In their stilted conversation, Travis and Betsy don't get one another's jokes, and she says he reminds her of some Kris Kristofferson lyrics: "He's a prophet and a pusher. Partly truth, partly fiction. A walking contradiction." True to his puritanical nature, he takes offense over the word pusher, as he does later, when the gun fence tries to sell him some drugs, and when Matthew the pimp accuses him of being a cop. However, he doesn't take offense at the word *prophet* because he is beginning to see himself as one, even lamenting, "I'm God's lonely man," almost as if to say "I'm God's only man." Not long after meeting Betsy, he even starts acting like a prophet. During her initial rejection of him, he tells her, "You're going to die in hell like the rest of them!"

Sacred Prostitute

Iris has dozens of what appear to be votive candles lit in her apartment, turning her house of prostitution into a religious shrine. She talks of astrology, and in response to Travis's offer of help, she offers to help him and begins unzipping his pants, acting as a sacred fire woman of an ancient shrine. But Travis is not so easily swayed with such temple help. He has a higher plan in mind, from a different religion.

Calvinist Crusader

After his anointing of psychotic transcendence, Travis takes on the role of a true prophet with a mission. Contrary to his former lamentations, with the planned assassination now in mind he surmises, "I see it clearly now. Now my whole life is pointed in one direction. I see that now there never has been a choice for me." Here, elements of Schrader's Calvinistic influences are evident. In his book on the transcendental style, Schrader talks about the theological paradox that one becomes free by choosing one's predestined fate. And so Travis's theology of predestination pushes him ever onward toward his divine task, which is designed to bring freedom for himself and for either Betsy or Iris, or perhaps both of them.

Religious Rituals

In preparation for his divine mission, Travis's behavior now takes on ritualistic overtones. He develops a routine of calisthenics. He holds his hand over a flame. He spit-shines his cowboy boots. He sharpens his knife. He burns the withered flowers that were rejected by Betsy. He target practices with his guns. He designs a sliding sleeve ejectory for one of his pistols. And he practices psychological intimidation and fast-drawing in his mirror. He even happens upon a real-life practice shot by shooting an armed robber in a food market.

Religious Regression

While we see Travis deteriorate into rageful psychosis, he simultaneously undergoes a unique religious devolution. In the beginning of our story, we see Travis with generalized righteous indignation. His midwest religious background gives him a general disgust of his surroundings. But his religion steadily devolves into a more primitive brand of zeal.

The name Travis is linguistically connected with traveling and travailing, signifying his role as a religious pilgrim in search of his ultimate work, his calling in life. He has the sight and zeal of a true believer; the only thing he lacks is a calling, until he finds it. As if believing that the protection of the madonna is his preordained mission, he worships the lady of purity, like the chivalrous troubadours of yore.

When the goddess spurns his love, his logical next move, true to the behavior of religious paranoiacs, is to commit tribal patricide. So here, in his new mission, we see him regressing from Christianized Maryolatry, to pagan regicide. He must destroy the head of the totemic tribe, as he says, "so that all of the king's men will not be able to put it back together." Of course, the killing of the father god, the dominator of the madonna, will put the killer on the throne in the king's place. Travis sees Palantine, promising salvation to the people, as a false messiah who must be destroyed so that the true messiah may reign.

Here, as is common with paranoid psychotics, Travis's religious grandiosity reveals itself. He tells Iris that he is doing some work for the government and he eats a eucharistic meal of bread and brandy, symbolic of the body and blood of the savior with whom he begins so intimately to identify.

Besides committing totemic patricide, Travis, the religious traveler, also feels destined to rescue the whore. Here, in his own messianic mission, like Christ with the woman caught in adultery, instead of desecrating this victim of the flesh trade, he must save her. This twelve-and-a-half-year-old prostitute, Iris, represents to him innocence corrupted by the perpetrators of his sick world.

Whether from pimp or politician, the maiden must be rescued from patriarchy.

Her name, besides being the name of a flower, means rainbow. We are reminded that the rainbow is given as a sign after Noah's flood as a promise that God will not judge the world by water again. Rather, the prophecies point to fire as being the next judgment. While Travis earlier prays for rain to wash away all of the sin, we now see him preparing to rain down fire on the sinners.

In his religious devolution, just as in his psychological devolution, we see Travis moving backwards, toward a more primordial devotion. The symbolic precursor to this time regression is found in the street drummer, who demonstrates for his audience a stylistic throwback to Gene Krupa, after which he again regresses, as he says, "forty years back, to Chick Webb." This is our religious pilgrim's clue to travel back in time himself—to religious cosmogonic time (although in Travis's case, it is more like demonic time). First, he is a self-righteous Midwestern puritan. Then, while he prepares himself for his mission of judgment, he takes on a more fanatical militaristic stance, as a soldier of fortune preparing for holy war. In the meanwhile his hair gets shorter. When he meets Matthew the pimp, he is called a cowboy (which is ironic, since it is Matthew who sports a hat). This transition from soldier to cowboy signifies his time regression. The second time he meets Sport (Matthew), Travis is called an Indian (while Matthew wears a headband), a signifier of further time regression. Sport tells him, "Go back to your fucking tribe, before you get hurt." Travis sports a mohawk haircut by this time, showing his religious identification and the intensity of his holy war. When he runs out of bullets in his murderous rampage he uses his knife, a final symbol of regression. Mircea Eliade writes of such religious regression:

Regression to chaos is something literal—as, for example, in the case of the inititiatory sickness of future shamans, which have often been regarded as real attacks of insanity. There is, in fact, a total crisis, which sometimes leads to disintegration of the personality. This psychic chaos is the sign that the profane man is undergoing dissolution and that a new personality is on the verge of birth (Eliade 1957, 196).

Thus, Travis must regress to primitive religious chaos in order to be born again.

The Passion of the Prophet

In his passionate need to save Iris, Travis is willing to die for her, and even pulls the trigger on himself after murdering his foes (but he has run out of bullets by this time). After the sacrificial bloodbath, the camera angle gives us a direct overhead shot, with the arms of the wounded Travis stretched out in messianic agony, a view quite similar to Dali's surrealistic painting of the crucified Christ.

After the prostitute is saved and her parents send him a loving thank-you letter, Travis, our religious madman, becomes a celebrated media hero. Betsy wants back into his life, but now that his mission has been accomplished, he no longer has a need for her. She praises him for his heroic ordeal and hints strongly of wanting to be with him. But this is the juncture in the gospel narrative where after the death and resurrection, yet before the ascension, Jesus commands Mary Magdalene, "Touch me not; for I am not yet ascended to my father." The resurrected and purposeful Travis just smiles and drives off in his clean, redeemed, taxicab.

THEOLOGICAL AND ARTISTIC MERIT

Considering that there have been critics who would ban such films as *Taxi Driver*, how should we evaluate the film? Perhaps *Taxi Driver's* theological and artistic worth can be seen in the theological questions or aesthetic inspiration it provokes.

In keeping with the Judeo-Christian tradition, the film depicts a religion of violence, a story of killing as a means of redemption— blood sacrifice as a means of psychological and spiritual release. Like the gospels, the film shows a person considered a madman who saves a victimized sinner. *Taxi Driver* forces us to ask what madness really is, and what a prophet is. It forces us to look closer at our seemingly sane

Who is more dangerous—a murderous madman or a popular politician?

political and religious messiahs. A movie about a modern psychotic saint brings up questions about the fine line between saintliness and insanity, or spiritual sight and psychosis. It provokes us to question the state of modern Western religion, and the relation of sexuality to spirituality. And, of course, the controversy surrounding the film forces us to question our concepts of censorship.

In our age of self-appointed political and religious prophets, such a film could actually help decrease the likelihood of dangerous people seizing power. It can do this by causing us to look closer at the messages of the lunatic fringe, compared to those in power. While Senator Palantine in the film is not painted as a bad guy, a juxtaposition between the politician (as a figure of those in power) and Travis Bickle, can help us in our sociopolitical discernment. The juxtaposition between Palantine's potential victimization and Travis's psychotic victimizing forces us to question the difference between that which is promising yet pernicious, and that which is "pathological" yet prophetic. In other words, who is more dangerous to society, a crazy Travis Bickle who kills two or three, or a seemingly sane politition who kills thousands or millions?

If the filmmakers have succeeded in provoking such questions, they have succeeded in making fine religious art, despite modern moralists who religiously campaign, as Travis would say, to "flush all of this down the fucking toilet." *Taxi Driver* is certainly not an irresponsible exercise in promoting senseless violence as some would presume. Rather, it is a legitimate artistic depiction of historic Christianity that can actually help quell violence in more ways than we would guess. Travis, Senator Palantine, and the censors of such art all have a mad mission. But many of the Palantines and censors do not recognize their own madness.

REPO MAN

A PROPHET OF TIME TRAVEL

W ritten and directed by Alex Cox and produced by Michael Nesmith, *Repo Man* (1984) is a frenetic exercise in rhythmic craziness that makes a great deal of sense in a nonsensical way. The neutron bomb, extraterrestrials, government agents, criminal punkers, a lobotomized nuclear scientist, and automobile repossession men searching for a 1964 Chevy Malibu make for an entertaining film of disjointed meaningfulness. The story moves in lickety-split timing, progressively speeding up throughout, which is part of the beauty of this psychic offering of driven pursuit.

The main character, Otto (Emilio Estevez) gets fired from his stock clerk food market job, where it seems only generic brands are sold. His girlfriend dumps him for their mutual friend. Desperate for money, and failing to get any from his dope-smoking, born-again, hippie parents, Otto stumbles upon a job as an auto repossession man, where the boss links his name to *auto*. He meets Leila, who works for the United Fruitcake Outlet and who is searching for the 1964 Chevy Malibu that supposedly has extraterrestrial aliens in the trunk. She in turn is evading government agents who are also looking for the same car, driven by a lobotomized nuclear scientist. When a twenty-thousand-dollar bounty is placed on the car, Otto and his fellow repo men enter the frantic search. But they must compete with their rivals, the Rodriguez brothers. Robberies, torture, vomiting, hospital shootouts, high-speed chases, government wiretapping, neutron disintegration, belief in the book *Diuretics*, and lunatic prophecies make up the hurried plot.

KITSCH

Throughout the narrative we are invited to a superb outlay of American kitsch. The path of Otto's satirical landscape is littered with generic food, singing commercials, a televangelist, car deodorizers, generic statements such as "I blame society for what I am," and "Don't you think it's time we settled down?" In addition, the Circle Jerks, posing as a tuxedoed lounge act, sing "When the Shit Hits the Fan."

This cinematic canvas painted in tones of kitsch is further colored by digs on commies, Christians, televangelists, cholos, UFO aficionados, winos, millionaires, Scientology, and even Gypsy dildoes and normal persons. This satiric venue of schlocky Americana provides a perfect backdrop for a story that suggests a transcendence of such a world.

REPO CODE

Otto learns from Bud (Harry Dean Stanton) about the Repo Man Code. There is a whole list of dos and don'ts to which the repo man must adhere; as Bud says, it is a sacred trust, "that's what this country was founded on." The only problem with Bud's moral code is that it ignores the interests of anyone but the repo man. Bud thinks he is above the punkers robbing stores, when in reality his behavior is just as sullied. Bud represents rigidity, drivenness, hypocrisy, fundamentalism, and a tightly-closed system of control.

DRIVENNESS

The theme that propels this drama hastily into the speedy future is the concept of drivenness. The mad car chases, the fierce competition with the Rodriguez brothers, the obsessive need to find the Chevy Malibu, and the frantic subplots and counterplots around the pursuit of the hot car all point toward dashing drivenness. Among the lessons Otto learns from Bud is that the repo man takes speed, and that while normal people avoid tense situations, the repo man gets into them.

Otto's materialistic black partner hints that since he found the book *Diuretics: The Science of Matter over Mind* in a Maserati in Beverly Hills, the book will change one's life, indicating a push toward accelerated materialism. But Otto intuitively rejects the book, having a different sort of life-changing experience ahead of him. This partner of Otto's is so driven his ironic oversight causes him to toss out a packet of money left in a repo car.

The Repo Man with a code: postmodernity with speedy avarice.

Twice in the film we see a political poster advertising a candidate named Harry Pace running for city controller, signifying that the driven characters have elected such a breakneck velocity.

Aldous Huxley once said that an eighth deadly sin should be added to the original seven—the sin of hurry. This Harry Pace with which our characters whoosh and zoom is the demonic time of postmodernity.

Erich Fromm also had some things to say about this savage addiction to speed. Writing about the Futurist Manifesto of 1909, he says: "Here we see the essential elements of necrophilia; worship of speed and the machine; poetry as a means of attack; glorification of war; destruction of culture, hate against women; locomotives and airplanes as living forces" (Fromm 383).

THE CRAZIES

Miller

Contrasted to this sense of obsessive drivenness, and the rigid repo code, is Miller (Tracy Walter), the sci-fi philosopher at the repo yard. This oddball presents an alternative attitude—a poetic, contemplative, seemingly nonsensical, etherial, and non-rigid existence.

Besides learning from the repo men, Otto also sits under Miller's tutelage. As the two of them burn clothes in a barrel, Otto throws a copy of *Diuretics* in the fire, signifying his rejection of the rushed mode of materialistic existence and his openness to an alternative view, however crazy. Miller shares his philosophy:

> MILLER: A lot of people don't realize what's really going on. They view life as a bunch of unconnected incidents and things. They don't realize that there is this, like, lattice of coincidence that lays on top of everything. For example, suppose you think of a plate of shrimp. Suddenly somebody will say, like, "plate," or "shrimp," or "plate of shrimp." out of the blue. No explanation. No point in looking for one either. It's all part of the cosmic unconsciousness.

I'll give you another instance. You know how everybody's into weirdness right now? Books in all the supermarkets about Bermuda triangles, UFOs, how the minds
invented television, that kind of thing?

OTTO: I don't read them books.

MILLER: Well, the way I see it, it's exactly the same. There ain't no
difference between a flying saucer and a time machine.
People get so hung up on specifics, they miss out on seeing
the whole thing. Take South America for example. In South
America thousands of people go missing every year. Nobody knows where they go. They just, like, disappear. But
you think about it for a minute, you realize something.
There had to be a time when there was no people. Right?

OTTO: Yea I guess.

MILLER: Well, where did all these people come from? I'll tell you
where—the future. Where'd all these people disappear to?

OTTO: The past?

MILLER: That's right! And how'd they get there?

OTTO: How the fuck do I know?

MILLER: Flying saucers, which are really—yea, you got it—time
machines. I think a lot about this kinda stuff. I do my best
thinkin' on the bus. That's how come I don't drive, see?

OTTO: You don't even know *how* to drive.

MILLER: I don't wanna know how. I don't wanna learn, see? The
more you drive, the less intelligent you are.

Here, in the midst of all of the zooming craziness, from the mouth
of what seems to be one of the looniest of all, are the keys to *Repo Man*.
The lattice of coincidence, which C. G. Jung would call synchronicity,
operates throughout the film. For example, when Otto leans over a
bridge to vomit, he happens to see the Chevy Malibu for which he is
searching. "Accidental" circumstances seem to work toward a mysterious purpose.

Miller's "cosmic unconsciousness" sounds like a combination of cosmic consciousness and Jung's collective unconscious. While ministering to Otto's wounds Miller chants as a native American, indicating that he is perhaps connected to a more primeval force, removed from the modern world of American darting kitsch.

While the driven people look only at the unconnected specifics, Miller sees the connected big picture. His emphasis on thinking and intelligence suggests quiet contemplation, something glaringly lacking in all of the others. Yet others see him as an acid burnout, disconnected to the hurried world of rigid repo codes and normal kitchish logic.

The Scientist

The other crazy in the story, the lobotomized nuclear scientist from Los Alamos, talks about being driven mad by working on the neutron bomb (one of the crown jewels of zipping postmodernity). He is so driven he literally drives incessantly with no apparent direction.

While seeming similar, this meshuga is much different from Miller. While Miller's seeming lunacy has an outward rhythm of brainsickness, the scientist's dementia is lacking the benign flavor of Miller's; for the scientist's monologue actually promotes the neutron bomb, lobotomies, and nuclear radiation. As one deranged by nuclear work, he is the end result of postmodernity, and he is the one everybody is following. Miller's philosophy, by contrast, while seeming unhooked to the normal person in the land of Kitsch, is actually valuable ancient wisdom.

CONVERSION

Otto, as the main protagonist, is caught in the middle of various worldviews among which he must choose. Otto has a falling out with his repo associate Bud upon hearing Bud berate the slow unfortunates on Skid Row. In discouragement, Otto "coincidentally" happens upon the much-valued Chevy Malibu. The lobotomized driver mysteriously stops and lets Otto in. When Otto asks to drive the car, lo and behold, the scientist *coincidentally* falls over the steering wheel, and the car is Otto's. So he dutifully drives the car back to the repo yard and subsequently joins the repo men for a party at Miller's house. But he is mysteriously changed. Instead of succumbing to the fast temptations offered to him by the repo wives, he seems to be less driven, more relaxed, more in tune with another dimension.

THE FINAL CHASE

Meanwhile, while the repo men party at Miller's, Bud, who has recently been fired, breaks into the repo yard and steals the Chevy Malibu. But, alas, he is too driven, and not worthy of such a car. He ends up in the hospital, possibly from radiation poisoning. The chase heats up with ever more passionate speed. Machine gun fire is ex-

Otto, the soul, is drawn toward the time machine by Miller the prophet.

changed with warnings over the hospital intercom to be quiet in the stairwell. All of the swishing racers eventually converge at the repo yard. The Malibu is glowing a bright blue-green. The government agents try touching the car, but some mysterious force emanating from the popular vehicle prevents them. The television preacher and a rabbi show up for the action but their faith is seemingly impotent against the strange power. A bolt of lightening ignites the preacher's shielding Bible. Watching all of the action, one of the agents says he loves his job. "In fact, it's more than a job. It's a calling."

When it appears that all are overwhelmed by the car, crazy Miller casually walks over to the glowing wonder and gets in. Otto reminds him that he can't *drive*. But Miller just smiles and motions for Otto to join him. Leila tries to hold Otto back with a kitschish reminder about their "relationship." But here, Otto's conversion is complete. There is no holding him back. He gets in the car. Miller turns something on the dash board and the car ascends. It hovers for a while, then jets off, flying over downtown Los Angeles with the greatest of grace and speed. Otto exclaims, "Wow! This is intense!" Miller says, "The life of the repo man is always intense."

TIME TRAVEL

The driven people in our story are all whooshing speedily into the future, mainly in driving machines, as if Kitschville infects them all with rabid competition. Opposed to these bullet-like harriers, Miller talks about the past. As someone lacking speed, codes, and style, he is ignored by postmodernity like the pack of money tossed in the street. While the driven world of the repo man symbolizes a society devoid of contemplation, the prophet seems to suggest that a repossession of bygone days is needed—a time devoid of the harry pace. Since Miller believes that UFOs are time machines, and since he is certainly not a
. driven person, he takes his new disciple Otto to this primordial past.

Before his conversion Otto was ensared in the Big Hurry. His life was a metaphor for accelerated postmodernity, slipping into the future of generic materialism. Otto (auto), as Miller's passenger to golden time, is the vehicular collective soul. In such a pilgrimage of human consciousness he can choose either panicked, kitschish whooshiness or relaxed, timeless contemplation. In the soul's choice, it is certainly easy enough to distinguish between the postmodern, zippy world of repo and the tranquil, thinking world of Miller. But discriminating between the craziness of the scientist and Miller is not so simple for those of generic discernment. Miller would tell us, however, that the contemplative life gives one the ability to decipher between radiated kitsch and illuminated wisdom.

FIELD OF DREAMS

SEEING THE INVISIBLE

*F*ield of Dreams (1989), based on W. P. Kinsella's novel *Shoeless Joe*, is a story rich in emotional appeal and human sensitivity. It concerns a man who, by all clinical standards, could be diagnosed as psychotic. He hears a voice, sees people that others do not see, and bases his life's actions on his questionable and highly erratic perceptions.

The message and moral of *Field of Dreams*, a popular mainstream film, are rather obvious and on the surface. Unlike most of the films discussed in this book, it does not contain a great deal of hidden mythology. Consequently, this essay differs from its companions in that it is not concerned primarily with elucidating the film's mythic content. Instead, this essay attempts to address the complaints of those critics of *Field of Dreams* who find the notion of building a baseball diamond in a cornfield less than compelling. While appreciating the father-son reunion, but discounting the craziness of Ray's vision, some viewers still say they don't "get it." It is precisely such complaints that warrant the making of such films.

NORMALCY

While Ray Consella (Kevin Costner) and his family participate in something that is quite abnormal and illogical by their own admission, they are contrasted with the masses that fit in the middle of the bell-shaped curve. The farmers at the feed store are quite concerned that Ray is "hearing voices." They are more disturbed and even amused by his seemingly foolish act of plowing under his money-producing crop in order to build a baseball field in the middle of his farm.

If we assume that the norm is the ideal, as do Ray's skeptical neighbors, and as do some of the film's critics, we accept the standards of the majority as the mark to which seekers of perfection should strive. But the standards of the majority in this *reel* life are dominated by the herd instinct. The people in the film's PTA meeting easily follow the instigator of book banning, but when a new voice is heard, that of Annie, Ray's sixties-oriented wife (Amy Madigan), they are just as easily swayed by her. It is no wonder that Jesus of Nazareth calls the masses sheep in search of a shepherd.

Alexis de Tocqueville, George Orwell, Aldous Huxley, Eric Hoffer, Irving Janis, Michel Foucault, Hannah Arendt, Noam Chomsky, and many others have given us insightful volumes on the pernicious "tyranny of the majority" (to use de Tocqueville's words) and on the despotic force of "groupthink," to use Irving Janis's term. The majority in our narrative come close to burning "subversive" works such as *The Diary of Anne Frank*, a true underground account of militant majority oppression, and *The Wizard of Oz*, which in reality is a subversive populist political satire of the sham of the big government/big business partnership of its day.*

The majority in the narrative, just as the majority in society, follow the majority. While the majority believes it follows the leadership of the majority, the leadership actually follows the majority in its use of majority sentiments to manipulate majority actions to further the ends of the elite minority. Unfortunately, the majority often cannot tell the difference between the selfish designs of the elite minority and the

* The Wicked Witch of the West represents banks. The Tin Man stands for industrial workers, the Scarecrow for farmers, the Lion for William Jennings Bryan, the Wizard for the president of the United States, and Dorothy is the average person. Oz is symbolic of gold, the emerald city of money; and of course the yellow brick road represents the promise of wealth. When Dorothy sings about a place "over the rainbow," she is hoping for a redemptive heaven better than government owned railroads and big business economics.

uninformed will of the majority. It is exactly this consigned majority assent that outlaws thinking dissent, which in turn perpetuates the tyranny of the majority, sometimes resulting in the wholesale slaughter of the minority, or a holocaustal genocide of a neighboring tribe.

The thinker, Terence Mann, in our story represents a lone voice of dissent in a vast sea of assenting majority rule. Calling Terence Mann (James Earl Jones) a pervert and a commie, the PTA mob is easily led to herd anger by the voice of "reason." Mann is accused of promoting promiscuity, godlessness, the mongrolization of the races, and disrespect to high ranking officers of the U.S. Army. They jeer him as a menace to society. They want to ban his novel *The Boat Rocker*. Guessing from its title, the book is no doubt an allegory of his life as one opposed to the crowd. Ray discovers that Mann, having given up his writing, has lost hope of finding a thinking minority. Confronted with the extremes of the dissenting minority and the apathy of the majority, he looses faith in his ability to help people think for themselves. Ironically, he is lifted up from his discouragement by two of the people he previously helped think, Ray and Annie Consella. In fact, these two take on his once fervent stand for insightful truth against the unthinking majority.

ABNORMAL PERCEPTION

Ray says he had never done anything crazy in his life until he heard the voice. Then he risks losing his entire income, property, and family by listening to this dangerous voice of abnormality. As children of the sixties, Ray and his wife, Annie, have not lost sight of the value of questioning authority, of abnormal perception, of independent thinking, and of expecting the extraordinary. Hearing a voice revives his countercultural penchant for the different and mystical. His decision to obey the voice sets him apart—beyond just eccentricity—for a divine mission. The protests of the uninitiated majority, challenge, and, ironically, perfect his and his family's faith, setting them closer to the camp of the lunatic fringe. Even Ray begins to doubt his own

The man of faith wrestles with his doubt.

sanity when he can't figure out the purpose of the voice. We hear a Willie Nelson song, "Crazy," and a John Sebastian song, "Daydream," and we see a clip on television from the film *Harvey*, about a six foot rabbit. In anger, Ray turns off the television and tells his disappointed daughter that that man—Jimmy Stewart—is crazy. But upon further reflection he submits to the crazy voice and reaps the bounty thereof.

Ray and his family provide examples of religious faith, in the tradition of a long line of faith-prophets. When Noah hears God command him to build an ark, he is exposed to the militant doubts of the majority. But the promise given him is that belief will save him and his family from the wrath prescribed for the unbelieving masses. Abraham, Moses, David, and an entire host of voice-hearers choose to obey the extraordinary rather than join the ranks of normal doubters. Besides just obeying the voice (the first step of faith) the believer also sees the invisible. Elisha prays that his normal fearful companion can see what he sees, and the young man's eyes open to see chariots of fire and a great heavenly host encompassing them (2 Kings 6). Shakespeare's Duke Theseus in *A Midsummer Night's Dream* suggests that the lunatic, the lover, and the poet, unlike normally sighted people, all see alike—in reality, they see the invisible.

The fact that the majority of the observers of Ray's baseball field can not see the ball players is a picture of what normally happens in an all-too-normal society. Their lack of sight signifies spiritual blindness in the same way that Job's "friends" are blinded by the mindset of a "moral" majority, and in the same way that the prophets' audiences often cannot see the truth of salvation right before their unbelieving eyes. Ray slowly learns the truth of spiritual illumination, that "the just shall live by faith" (Habakkuk 2:4).

INSANITY AND INSPIRATION

The difference between insanity and inspiration is sometimes indistinguishable, for both states depart from the norm. The insane are rarely thought of as inspired, but the inspired are often thought of as insane. Like Ray, the prophets of old exhibit thoughts and behavior that could easily be diagnosed as highly neurotic and even psychotic. Take for example the prophet Hosea, who is commanded to marry a prostitute as a picture of the adulterous behavior of the nation. Then there is Jeremiah, who is commanded by God to hide his dirty underwear under a moist rock by the Euphrates until they become moldy and to use them as an illustration of how God will spoil the pride of Judah. Many of the prophets were like ancient crazy performance artists, exaggerating reality in order to deliver a pithy point to a hardened audience. John the Baptist, wearing sheepskin, eating locusts and wild honey, and preaching repentance, is certainly a candidate for psychopathologic diagnosis. Then, Jesus of Nazareth was also considered insane by his contemporary skeptics.

The inspired one sees the world through the most penetrating lenses. To share this vision with normal people is to invite ridicule, if not outright banishment from the kingdom of normalcy. Ray's brother-in-law, Mark (Timothy Busfield), talking about Ray to Annie, complains, "He used to be so normal," signifying that Ray has broken out of the confining bonds of normalcy and into another world of inspired sight.

William Blake said, "If the doors of perception were cleansed, everything would appear to man as it is, infinite." And indeed, Ray, the seer, in this tale of infinity, has the ability to pierce far beyond the mundane existence of finite normalcy, into a world of unbelievable dream time.

It is certainly understandable that an inspired seer would be thought of as crazy, considering that those with normal sight are in almost unanimous agreement with what they believe to be the truth. This is why it is so easy for nations to devastate other nations in mass military destruction, because the will of the herd seems all the more truthful when strengthened by numbers. And this could be why some seers go insane—because the strength of numbers can overwhelm the lone voice of spiritual sight.

Naturally, with its fictional characters of sight, *Field of Dreams* employs second sight in an exaggerated form. The filmmakers assume an extra dose of suspended disbelief within the audience. But still, for many normal viewers, the exaggeration is too much. They join the intranarrative in-laws and the skeptical farmers in discounting this craziness, indicating that there will always be those who will never "get it." Then, some viewers seem to like the film a great deal, and in conversations about the film never once mention the major juxtaposition between majority and minority thinking. While their lives are committed to normal majority sight, we again see an indication that many simply do not "get it."

Concerning the inspired seeing mind, Aldous Huxley has this to say: "The mind is its own place, and the places inhabited by the insane and the exceptionally gifted are so different from the places where ordinary men and women live, that there is little or no common ground of memory to serve as a basis for understanding or fellow feeling. Words are uttered, but fail to enlighten" (Huxley, 13).

DREAMS AND VISIONS

While most people are not seers in the mystical sense, most people do dream and have visions. The writer and director of *Field of Dreams*, Phil Alden Robinson, says that the film is "about the power of love to make dreams come true." Before accepting the voice, Ray Consella worries that he might end up like his father, one who must have had dreams but who never realized them—one who "never did a spontaneous thing in his life." Ray's vision and his allegiance to it sets in motion the wonderful blessing to others. He is given only one part of the vision at a time, which keeps him fervently in anticipation of the next surprise.

Possibly the main difference between the seer or genius and the normal person is that the seer has willingly suspended his or her disbelief more consistently and permanently, risking potential negative fallout from the surrounding army of unbelievers. Charles Baudelaire in 1863 said in *The Painter of Modern Life* that "genius is nothing more nor less than childhood recovered at will."

The prophet Joel, speaking for God, had this to say about seeing dreams and visions: "And it shall come to pass afterward, that I will pour out my Spirit upon all flesh; and your sons and your daughters shall prophesy, your old men shall dream dreams, your young men shall see visions" (Joel 2:28). The only problem with his prophecy is that most people are not willing to believe it. Such has always been the case with societies of normal sighted people. Normal people have dreams and visions, but prophets chance those dreams and visions with faith, risking their reputations and lives for the inner witness of spiritual truth. We need to remind ourselves that "faith without works is dead" (James 2:17). As if listening to such voices, or to Morpheus, the god of dreams, Ray acts on faith.

CONVERSION

Terence Mann has lost his faith in his ability to convert others to the life of sight. A Pulitzer Prize–winning novelist, and a pioneer in the civil rights and antiwar movements, he is said to have been the finest satirist of his time. But he has lost his voice. It takes the passion of his previous convert, Ray, to reconvert him. After regaining his faith, he no doubt finally sees, as the novelist Conrad saw, that the task of the novelist is "above all to make you see."

Then there is Mark, Ray's spiritually blind, unbelieving brother-in-law. He tries with all his might to get Ray to change his mind about his crazy vision, even going so far as to work out a deal for him to sell the farm to save his family from financial ruin. Then, true to all classic conversion experiences, like Saul on the road to Damascus, Mark has a sudden surge of faith. Perhaps in a state of prayer for Ray's injured daughter, Karen (Gaby Hoffman), Mark's eyes open enough to see the miracle of the resurrected Doctor Graham (Burt Lancaster) come to the rescue. Suddenly he asks, "When did all of these ball players get here?," and his sister Annie breaks out laughing. After being the prime voice of normal "reason" for so long, in his conversion mode Mark now says to Ray, "Whatever you do, don't sell the farm." Again, as with Saul of Tarsus, that against which Mark fought the hardest overcomes him.

HEAVEN

In his first meeting with Ray at the baseball field, Shoeless Joe Jackson (Ray Liotta) asks if this is heaven. "No. It's Iowa," Ray tells him. Later, John Consella (Dwier Brown), Ray's father, asks the same question and gets the same response. Overjoyed to be playing baseball again, John says, "I could have sworn it was heaven." Ray then asks him, "Is there a heaven?" John answers, "Oh yeah. It's the place dreams come true." Then Ray, thinking of the many fulfilled dreams on his farm, remarks, "Maybe this is heaven." Ultimately, when all is dreamt and seen, when dreams and visions reach their apex, the human spirit sees heaven, the place where dreams come true.

In Nahuatl, the language spoken by the Aztecs and still spoken in many parts of Mexico, the word for "dream" is *temichli*, literally "the edge of death." When Terence's faith revives, he gets an invitation to walk beyond this edge of death into the other side, where his lost gift of writing is restored, along with his faith. For it is in the dream of the beyond that a portion of heaven is manifested in the here and now.

THE VOICE

The three messages given to Ray are: "If you build it, he will come," "Ease his pain," and "Go the distance." While Ray helps to fulfill the dreams of others through his own visions, he doesn't realize that one of his own dreams is about to be fulfilled as well: that of resolving the estranged relationship between him and his dead father. Ray thinks the first two messages refer first to Shoeless Joe Jackson, then to Terence

Sight is the reward for those who follow their dreams.

Mann, and then to Doc Graham. It is not until his walk of faith that he finally sees that the messages refer to his father. Each blessing leads to another. Ultimately Ray discovers that the voice was his own, and that the messages bring blessings not only to others but also to himself. For in seeing far enough to bless others, one is also blessed.

CHOOSING TO SEE

Just at the point where Ray almost loses his faith, his daughter Karen tells him, "Daddy, we don't have to sell the farm. People will come." Terence Mann joins in by suggesting that the people who come will feel like they are dipping in magic waters. Then Mark argues, "Sell, Ray," with the threat that the bank will foreclose in the morning if he doesn't act today. But the voice of "unreason" resounds through his fellow seers: "They'll come, Ray." Thus, one who sees will be torn between the two sides of vision—between a herd call toward tyrannical normalcy and a minority-based, sagacious truth from someplace beyond. The choice will determine if truth and wisdom will be bestowed upon a society desperately in need of these lost veritable treasures.

EPILOGUE

During the Middle Ages, cathedrals were commonly built over temples and ruins of temples of the Goddess—a gesture symbolic of the conquering patriarchy. Another medieval practice of domination was the holocaust of women believed to be witches, or followers of the Goddess. Within a period of two hundred years, through the authority of the *Malleus Maleficarum* ("The Hammer of the Witches," 1486), more than nine million people, ninety percent of whom were women, were exterminated for being associated with the feminine principle. These gynocidal victims included seers, midwives, herbalists, and other intuitive practitioners of the healing arts who were in competition with the male-dominated enterprises of religion and medicine.

Today, rather than declaring official war on women, we go straight to the source and make war on Mother Earth. Since 1951 the United States government, while denying the serious repercussions, has exploded more than seven hundred nuclear bombs under the Nevada desert, from two to eleven times bigger than the one that destroyed Hiroshima. With trillions of dollars spent annually on weapons of mass destruction, patriarchal institutions such as the Pentagon and war contractors are entrenched in an ultramasculine destructive mode of human and environmental biocide. The regents of the Hard-on Club convene in their ideological circle jerks as they compare the size of their privy members disguised as wars on drugs, wars on crime, and wars on the Saddam Husseins of the world. In reality, the patriarchate has declared wars on the poor, the feminine, the competition, the earth, and to their own ironic unknowing, their own ailing biosphere. But the military-industrial-media complex is only the official (but whitewashed) side of this mass slaughter. Our nuclear-chemical-consumer complex is the mass complicitous side of the destruction, in which we all play a part.

We don't need cinemyths to tell us of an imbalanced mythic ideology between the masculine and feminine; we need only see what is clearly happening. Nonetheless, films like *Little Shop of Horrors* show us that the eternal battle of the sexes is an analogy for the battle between the greater principles of masculinity and femininity, or that between the God and the Goddess. Other ancient myths in addition to the Greek Gigantomachy speak of this great partition. Native British Columbian tribes, for example, tell of an original war between the Sky People and the Earth People. Such polarization can be found not only in world mythology, but within the individual hearts of each of us. But the issue is not merely one of a battle of the sexes. It is far more complex and critical than that. Our very survival on this planet is integrally dependent on how we resolve this imbalance—within our own personal psyches, and further, within our collective geopolitical divorce.

But the great bifurcation is extensive. Besides a separation of the masculine and feminine within film itself, we can even see this same chasm within film theory, in the intellectual world outside of film narrative. This opposition can be illustrated thus:

MASCULINE	FEMININE
formalism	realism
structuralism/semiology	phenomenology

As we saw in the Introduction, the school of formalism saw film as essentially something to be constructed out of basic building blocks, as a montage machine designed to propagate an ideology. As such, film is masculine technology in the service of propaganda.

The realist school is in essence a feminine reaction to masculine construction. Rather than seeing film as a set of building blocks, the realists see cinema as a lens through which to radiate the glories of a beautiful and feminine earth.

While having some significant influence, the realist school was soon overshadowed by two scientific, and thus masculine methods of film analysis—structuralism and semiology. Semiology especially emphasizes a strict, masculine, scientific approach to dissecting film art, sign by minute sign.

Like the realists, the school of phenomenology also reemphasizes the feminine principles of experience, sense, and an unveiling of the natural beauty as found in nature.

In addition to film and film theory, the grand severance is evident within cultural groups. Through ruling Western patriarchy, the feminine principle has been molded into various shapes in each of the Western religious cultures. For example, in some Islamic cultures, especially in their more fundamentalist manifestations, the feminine is prominently repressed to where a lack of basic human rights for women is glaringly evident. In some forms of Christian culture the feminine principle becomes severed in the classic madonna/whore split. In Jewish culture, the feminine principle reacts (as seen in *Little Shop of Horrors* and *Santa Sangre*) by ironically producing creative messianic sons.

But let us not forget another major western religion—Marxism. Seeing patriarchal capital oppressing victimized labor, Karl Marx, as a creative messiah, developed what was essentially a new feminine religion. Despite Marx's opinion of religion as the opiate of the people, his practical followers knew too well the religious and opiative power of Marxist indoctrination. In idea, Marxism is essentially the revivication of the feminine, with the emphasis on the earth, the oppressed, and a rebalancing of the economic power structure away from masculine over-dominance.

Two classic Russian revolutionary films by two of the genre's masters, Pudovkin and Dovzhenko, illustrate this feminine principle of Marxist ideology. Pudovkin's *Mother*, a cinematic version of a Gorki novel, is the story of a drunken father who is overthrown and killed, after which the mother is exalted in his place. Dovzhenko's *Earth* depicts the proverbial "boy and his tractor" motif of the genre, again, uplifting the earth or feminine principle, to a typically propagandistic degree. Unfortunately, phallocracy stole the idea of Marxism, and reformulated it into yet another destructive tool to dominate the feminine earth and the passive masses.

Besides seeing the grand division of heaven and earth in film, film theory, and religious culture, we can also easily see this divorce manifested in other sociocultural phenomena. The dynamics of environmentalism, feminism, the new age movement, and the gay and lesbian movement are all feminine reactions against Western paternalism. Environmentalism, a welcome and necessary attempt to rescue an abused Mother Earth, is a natural outcry of a centennial of industrial rape. Within feminism, especially ecofeminism, there is a literal revival of the ancient Goddess religion, which of course is also closely linked to environmentalism. Within the new age movement, apart from its connection to environmentalism, there is also a revival of the earth principle of ancient old time religion. The gay and lesbian movement is a natural political outcry against a masculine, homophobic political and social hierarchy.

In one way or another, if one principle dominates its polar opposite for too long and too oppressively, the oppressed will eventually raise its rebellious head to stand up for its rights. Just as the French Revolution demanded liberty, equality, and fraternity to replace submission, hierarchy, and paternity, so too will the feminine raise her voice in various other movements. Anytime there is an overabundance of penile dominance, there inevitably comes a reaction against this dangerous phallocracy. But does this mean we merely replace phallocentrism with gynocentrism?

We know from our cinemyths that extreme femininity can be just as

310

destructive as masculinity. We are reminded that many of the healthy solutions found by our cinematic heroes strike a balance between the polar opposites. George and Mary in *It's a Wonderful Life* bring the forces of heaven and earth together in order to combat an evil force of extremity. Likewise, Seymour and Audrey in *Little Shop of Horrors* manage to break free from the hammers and vortices of their sexist war to find a free and peaceful balance.

Like Antonius Block in *The Seventh Seal*, the soul will often attempt to approach reality with masculine science (or knowledge), which will always yield some fruit; but without feminine wisdom, of the sort Antonius Block practically stumbles upon, the soul cannot have a complete and balanced picture of existence. Likewise, without the masculine principle, feminine reality is also incomplete. Life itself, after all, results from the blending of sexual opposites.

Since we are presently stuck in the masculine side of our cosmic split, it is inevitable that the Goddess will continue to assert herself in various forms. Feeling polluted, raped, and pillaged for too long, Mother Earth demands her just rights. When the conquering rod of erected regal capitalism (or masculinized communism) has taken advantage of the passive elements of existence for too long, the mother religion arises in angry fury to throw off the shackles of this phallocratic slavery.

There are increasingly prophetic voices being spoken to the Erection Society. Besides those in social movements, such voices can be heard in significant cinemyths such as Peter Greenaway's *Drowning by Numbers* (1988), Paul Schrader's *The Comfort of Strangers* (1991), and Ridley Scott's *Thelma and Louise* (1991), in each of which the angry Goddess takes revenge on the patriarchate. Brandon French has pointed out in her book *On the Verge of Revolt* (1978), that the precursors of the 1960s women's movement can be seen in American films of the 1950s. Likewise, films today reflect the current state of affairs and things to come. The Goddess is saying through her prophets, that there must be a change or the consequences will be severe. In listening to these voices, in addition to possibly saving the planet, we might still be able to redeem the feminine virtues of truth, beauty, wisdom, mercy, grace, nurturance, and peace. As it is now, we operate mostly under their masculine polar opposites: propaganda, kitsch, knowledge, law, force, conditioning, and war. If we wait too long, we will all lose. The environmentalists tell us that nothing short of revolutionary change will save the earth, and thus, human life. It is up to us to pay attention to the prophecies and then to act with expeditious wisdom.

REFERENCES

BOOKS

Agel, Henri and Amédée Ayfre. *Le cinéma et le sacre*. Paris: Editions du Cerf, 1961.

_____. *Poetique du cinéma*. n.p.: Edition du Signe, 1973.

Andrew, J. Dudley. *The Major Film Theories: An Introduction*. New York: Oxford University Press, 1976.

Arnheim, Rudolf. *Film as Art*. 1932. Berkeley and Los Angeles: University of California Press, 1960.

_____. *Art and Visual Perception: A Psychology of the Creative Eye*. 1954. Berkeley and Los Angeles: University of California Press, 1974.

Ayfre, Amédée. *Cinéma et mystère*. Paris: Editions du Cerf, 1969.

_____. *Le cinéma et sa vérité*. Paris: Editions du Cerf, 1969.

Barthes, Roland. *Writing Degree Zero*. Translated by Annette Lavars and Colin Smith. 1953. New York: Noonday Press, 1968.

_____. *Mythologies*. Translated by Annette Lavers. 1957. New York: Noonday Press, 1972.

_____. *Elements of Semiology*. Translated by Annette Lavers and Colin Smith. 1964. New York: Noonday Press, 1967.

Bataille, Georges. *Eroticism: Death and Sensuality*. 1957. San Francisco: City Lights Books, 1986.

Bazin, André. *What Is Cinema?* Translated by Hugh Gray. Berkeley and Los Angeles: University of California Press, 1967.

Bergman, Ingmar. *Four Screenplays of Ingmar Bergman*. Translated by Lars Malmstrom and David Kushner. New York: Simon and Schuster, 1960.

Biró, Yvette. *Profane Mythology: The Savage Mind of the Cinema*. Translated by Imre Goldstein. Bloomington, Ind.: Indiana University Press, 1982.

Braudy, Leo. *The World in a Frame: What We See in Films*. Chicago: University of Chicago Press, 1976.

313

Budge, E. A. Wallis, trans. *The Book of the Dead.* 1960. New Hyde Park, New York: University Books, 1968.

Butler, Ivan. *Religion in the Cinema.* New York: A. S. Barnes and Company, 1969.

Campbell, Joseph. *The Hero with a Thousand Faces.* 1949. Princeton, N.J.: Princeton University Press, 1968.

_____. *The Masks of God: Primitive Mythology.* New York: Viking Press, 1959.

_____. *Renewal Myths and Rites of the Primitive Hunters and Planters.* Eranos Lecture. 1960. Dallas: Spring, 1989.

_____. *The Masks of God: Creative Mythology.* New York: Viking Press, 1968.

_____., ed. *Man and Time: Papers from the Eranos Yearbooks.* Bollingen Series 30:3. 1957. Princeton, N.J.: Princeton University Press, 1983.

Campbell, Richard H., and Michael R. Pitts. *The Bible on Film: A Checklist, 1897–1980.* Metuchen, N. J. and London: Scarecrow Press, 1981.

Cooper, C., and Carl Skrade. *Celluloid and Symbols.* Philadelphia: Fortress Press, 1970.

Dinesen, Isak. *Babette's Feast and Other Anecdotes of Destiny.* 1953. New York: Vintage Books, 1986.

DeNitto, Dennis, and William Herman. *Film and the Critical Eye.* New York: Macmillan, 1975.

Eberwein, Robert T. *Film and the Dream Screen.* Princeton, N.J.: Princeton University Press, 1984.

Eisenstein, Sergei M. *Film Sense.* Edited and translated by Jay Leyda. New York: Harcourt Brace, 1942.

_____. *Film Form: Essays in Film Theory.* Edited and translated by Jay Leyda. 1949. New York: Harcourt Brace Jovanovich, 1977.

_____. *Film Essays and a Lecture.* Edited and translated by Jay Leyda. New York: Praeger, 1970.

Eliade, Mircea. *Cosmos and History: The Myth of the Eternal Return.* 1954. New York: Harper & Row, 1959.

_____. "Time and Eternity in Indian Thought." In *Man and Time: Papers from the Eranos Yearbooks,* vol. 3. 1949. Princeton, N. J.: Princeton University Press, 1983.

_____. *The Sacred and the Profane: The Nature of Religion.* 1957. New York: Harcourt Brace Jovanovich, 1959.

Ferlita, Ernest, and John May. *Film Odyssey: The Art of Film as Search for Meaning.* New York: Paulist Press, 1976.

_____. *The Parables of Lina Wertmuller.* New York: Paulist Press, 1976.

Feuer, Jane. *The Hollywood Musical.* Bloomington: Indiana University Press, 1982.

French, Brandon. *On the Verge of Revolt: Women in American Films of the Fifties.* New York: Frederick Ungar Publishing, 1978.

Freud, Sigmund. *Leonardo Da Vinci: A Study in Psychosexuality.* 1916. New York: Vintage Books, 1947.

Fromm, Erich. *The Anatomy of Human Destructiveness.* Greenwich, Conn.: Fawcett, 1975.

Frye, Northrop. *Anatomy of Criticism: Four Essays.* 1957. Princeton, N.J.: Princeton University Press, 1990.

————. *Fables of Identity: Studies in Poetic Mythology*. New York: Harcourt Brace Jovanovich, 1963.

————. *The Great Code: The Bible and Literature*. New York: Harcourt Brace Jovanovich, 1982.

————. *Words with Power: Being a Second Study of "The Bible and Literature."* New York: Harcourt Brace Jovanovich, 1990.

Gabbard, Krin, and Glen O. Gabbard. *Psychiatry and the Cinema*. Chicago: University of Chicago Press, 1989.

Gibson, Arthur. *The Silence of God*. New York: Harper & Row, 1969.

Girard, René. *Violence and the Sacred*. 1972. Baltimore: Johns Hopkins University Press, 1989.

————. *Things Hidden since the Foundation of the World*. Translated by Stephen Bann and Michael Metteer. Stanford, Calif.: Stanford University Press, 1987.

Grant, Michael, and John Hazel. *Who's Who in Classical Mythology*. New York: Hodder and Stoughton, 1979.

Greenberg, Harvey R. *The Movies on Your Mind: Film Classics on the Couch, from Fellini to Frankenstein*. New York: Dutton, 1975.

Hall, C. *The Meaning of Dreams*. New York: McGraw-Hill, 1966.

Heidegger, Martin. *Being and Time*. Translated by John Macquarrie and Edward Robinson. 1926. San Francisco: Harper & Row, 1962.

Hesse, Hermann. *Narziss und Goldmund*. 1959. London: Peter Owen, 1977.

Holloway, Ronald. *Beyond the Image: Approaches to the Religious Dimension in the Cinema*. Geneva: World Council of Churches, 1977.

Homer. *Odyssey*. Translated by Butcher and Lang. New York: Macmillan, 1935.

Hurley, Neil P. *Theology Through Film*. New York: Harper & Row, 1970.

Huxley, Aldous. *The Doors of Perception* and *Heaven and Hell*. 1963. New York: Harper & Row, 1990.

Janis, Irving. *Groupthink: Psychological Studies of Policy Decisions and Fiascoes* (2nd ed.). Boston: Houghton Mifflin, 1982.

Joyce, James. *A Portrait of the Artist as a Young Man*. 1916. New York: Penguin Books, 1981.

Jung, C. G. *Collected Works*. Vol. 5, *Symbols of Transformation*. 1952. Princeton, N.J.: Princeton University Press, 1976.

————. *Collected Works*. Vol. 12, *Psychology and Alchemy*. 1953. Princeton, N.J.: Princeton University Press, 1968.

————. *Collected Works*. Vol. 16, *The Practice of Psychotherapy*. New York: Pantheon Books, 1954.

————. *Collected Works*. Vol. 15, *The Spirit in Man, Art, and Literature*. New York: Pantheon Books, 1966.

————. *Collected Works*. Vol. 13, *Alchemical Studies*. 1967. Princeton, N.J.: Princeton University Press, 1976.

Kawin, Bruce. *Mindscreen: Bergman, Godard, and First-Person Film*. Princeton, N.J.: Princeton University Press, 1978.

Kirk, G. S. *Myth: Its Meaning and Functions in Ancient and Other Cultures.* Cambridge: Cambridge University Press, 1970.

Koestler, Arthur. *The Act of Creation: A Study of the Conscious and Unconscious Processes of Humor, Scientific Discovery, and Art.* New York: Macmillan, 1964.

Kracauer, Seigfried. *Theory of Film: The Redemption of Physical Reality.* New York: Oxford University Press, 1960.

Kris, Ernst. *Psychoanalytic Exploration in Art.* 1952. New York: International Universities Press, 1979.

Lacan, Jacques. *Ecrits: A Selection.* Translated by Alan Sheridan. New York: Norton, 1977.

Lévi-Strauss, Claude. *Structural Anthropology.* Translated by Claire Jacobson and Brooke Grundfest Schoepf. New York: Basic Books, 1963.

_____. *The Raw and the Cooked: Introduction to a Science of Mythology.* 1969. Translated by John and Doreen Weightman. Chicago: University of Chicago Press, 1983.

Lévy-Bruhl, Lucien. *How Natives Think.* London, 1926.

McCarty, John, and Mark Thomas McGee. *The Little Shop of Horrors Book.* New York: St. Martin's Press, 1988.

McLuhan, Marshall. *Understanding Media: The Extensions of Man.* New York: McGraw-Hill, 1964.

Malinowski, Bronislaw. *Myth in Primitive Psychology.* London, 1926.

Malone, Peter. *Movie Christs and Antichrists.* New York: Crossroad, 1988.

Martin, Thomas M. *Images and the Imageless: A Study in Religious Consciousness and Film.* London: Associated University Press, 1981.

May, John R. and Michael Bird, eds. *Religion in Film.* Knoxville: University of Tennessee Press, 1982.

Maynard, Richard A. *The American West on Film: Myth and Reality.* Rochelle Park, N.J.: Hayden, 1974.

Mead, Margaret. *Male and Female: A Study of the Sexes in a Changing World.* New York: William Morrow, 1949.

Merleau-Ponty, Maurice. *Sense and Non-sense.* Translated by Hubert Dreyfus and Patricia Dreyfus. Evanston, Ill.: Northwestern University Press, 1964.

Metz, Christian. *Film Language: A Semiotics of the Cinema.* Translated by Michael Taylor. New York: Oxford University Press, 1974.

_____. *The Imaginary Signifier: Psychoanalysis and the Cinema.* 1975. Bloomington: Indiana University Press, 1982.

Moffett, Thomas. *Helth's Improvement.* 1600.

Mosley, Philip. *Ingmar Bergman: The Cinema as Mistress.* London: Marion Boyars, 1981.

Munsterberg, Hugo. *The Film: A Psychological Study.* 1916. New York: Dover, 1970.

Neumann, Erich. "Art and Time." In *Man and Time: Papers from the Eranos Yearbooks,* vol. 3. 1949. Princeton, N. J.: Princeton University Press, 1983.

_____. *The Origins and History of Consciousness.* 1954. Princeton, N.J.: Princeton University Press, 1973.

_____. *The Great Mother: An Analysis of the Archetype.* 1955. Princeton, N.J.: Princeton University Press, 1974.

REFERENCES

Parks, Rita. *The Western Hero in Film and Television: Mass Media Mythology*. Ann Arbor, Mich.: UMI Research Press, 1982.

Pettazzoni, Raffaele. *Miti e leggende* (vol. 1, p. v) Turin: 1948.

Ray, Robert B. *A Certain Tendency of the Hollywood Cinema, 1930–1980*. Princeton, N.J.: Princeton University Press, 1985.

Robbins, John. *Diet for a New America*. Walpole, N.Y.: Stillpoint Press, 1987.

Sarris, Andrew. "Notes on the *Auteur* Theory in 1962." In *The Primal Screen: Essays on Film and Related Subjects*. New York: Simon & Schuster, 1973.

Sawyer, Ruth. *The Way of the Storyteller*. 1942. New York: Penguin, 1986.

Schrader, Paul. *Transcendental Style: Ozu, Bresson, Dreyer*. Berkeley and Los Angeles: University of California Press, 1972.

Shang Yang. *Book of the Lord Shang* (I:8 & 10–12) (trans. J.J.L. Duyvendak) London, 1928.

Sklar, Robert. *Movie-Made America*. New York: Random House, 1975.

Stewart, K. "Dream Theory in Malaya." In *Altered States of Consciousness*, edited by C. Tart. New York: Wiley, 1969.

Stokes, Henry Scott. *The Life and Death of Yukio Mishima*. New York: Ballantine Books, 1974.

Sun Tzu. *The Art of War*. Translated by Samuel B. Griffith. Oxford: Oxford University Press, 1963.

Tocqueville, Alexis de. *Democracy in America*. 1840. New York: Knopf, 1946.

Tyler, Parker. *The Hollywood Hallucination*. (pp. vii, 141, 203, 237) New York: Simon & Schuster, 1944.

————. *Magic and Myth of the Movies*. New York: Simon & Schuster, 1970.

van der Leeuw, Gerardus. *Sacred and Profane Beauty*. New York: Holt, Rinehart & Winston, 1963.

Wall, James M. *Church and Cinema*. Grand Rapids, Mich.: Eerdman's Publishing Co., 1971.

Warshow, Robert. "Movie Chronicle: The Westerner." In *The Immediate Experience*. 1946. Garden City, N.Y.: Doubleday, 1962.

Wolf, William. "The Genius of Bergman." In *Landmark Films: The Cinema and Our Century*. (pp. 230ff) New York: Paddington Press, 1979.

Wolfenstein, M., and N. Leites. *Movies: A Psychological Study*. New York: Atheneum, 1970.

Wood, Michael. *America at the Movies*. New York: Basic Books, 1975.

ARTICLES

"Alejandro Jodorowsky: Filmmaker." *Penthouse*, June 1973, p. 6.

Alpert, Hollis. "*The Graduate* Makes Out." *Saturday Review*, 6 July 1968, pp. 14–16.

Brown, Joseph Epes. "All Time is Present." *Parabola* 15, no. 1 (Spring 1990): p. 38.

Carpenter, Ronald H., and V. Seltzer. "Nixon, Patton, and a Silent Majority Sentiment about the Viet Nam War: The Cinematographic Bases of a Rhetorical Stance." *Central States Speech Journal* 25 (Summer 1974): 105–10.

Champlin, Charles. "*Sailor* Sinks in Translation." Review of *The Sailor Who Fell from Grace with the Sea. Los Angeles Times,* 18 May, 1976.

Dawson, Jan. Review of *The Graduate. Sight and Sound* 38, no. 1 (Winter 1968/69).

Day, Barry. "It Depends on How You Look at It." Review of *The Graduate. Films & Filming* 15, no. 2 (November 1968).

Dempsey, Michael. Review of *Taxi Driver. Film Quarterly* 29, no. 4 (Summer 1976).

Dooling, D. M. "Focus." *Parabola* 7, no. 2 (Spring 1982): p. 2.

Dubos, David. "*Santa Sangre,* Sicka Cinema." *Village View,* 30 March–5 April 1990, p. 12.

Farber, Stephen, and Estelle Changas. Review of *The Graduate. Film Quarterly* 28 (Spring 1968).

Floyd, Nigel. "Jodorowsky." *Timeout* (London), April 11–18, 1990, p. 6.

Gallo, William. Review of *Taxi Driver. Film Heritage* 11, no. 3 (Spring 1976).

Gow, Gordon. Review of *Taxi Driver. Films & Filming,* September 1976.

Hibbin, Sally. Review of *Crimes of Passion. Films & Filming,* October 1985.

Hoberman, J. "Carless in Gaza: *Repo Man.*" *Village Voice,* 17 July 1984, p. 49.

Jones, Alan. "The Lost Ending: *Little Shop of Horrors.*" *Cinefantastique,* September 1987.

Kael, Pauline. Review of *Repo Man. The New Yorker,* 6 August 1984, pp. 72–73.

Kinder, Marsha. "The Adaptation of Cinematic Dreams." *Dreamworks* 1 (1980): 54–68.

Lane, John Francis. "Jodorowsky Shoots Back to Form." *Screen International,* June, 1988, p. 12.

Levy, Shawn. "Alejandro Jodorowsky's Visionary Passion." *Boxoffice,* February 1990, p. 26.

Mankin, Eric. "*Taxi Driver* and the Question of Psychopathy." *L.A. Weekly,* 16–22 July 1982, p. 26.

Mann, Roderick. Review of *The Sailor Who Fell from Grace with the Sea. Los Angeles Times,* 25 January 1976.

Michener, Charles. Review of *Taxi Driver. Film Comment,* March–April 1976, p. 4.

Milne, Tom. "Shape of the Universe: *Insignificance.*" *Sight and Sound* (Summer 1985), p. 218.

Murphy, Mary. "Director Makes Waves in Debut." Review of *The Sailor Who Fell from Grace with the Sea. Los Angeles Times,* 12 May 1976, part 4.

Obituary of Sara Prullansky Jodorowsky. Variety, Nov. 15, 1973.

Powell, Ann. "Scorsese and His Saint." Review of *Taxi Driver. Millimeter,* March 1976, pp. 30–32.

Rayns, Tony. Review of *The Sailor Who Fell from Grace with the Sea. Monthly Film Bulletin,* August 1976.

Rose, Brian. "*It's a Wonderful Life*: The Last Stand of the Capra Hero." *Journal of Popular Film* 6, no. 2 (1977).

Rosen, Marjorie. "Critics and the Politics of Superlatives." *Millimeter,* April 1976, p. 26.

Sallitt, Dan. "Suburbia and *Repo Man*: Sympathy for the Rebel." *L.A. Reader,* 11 May 1984.

Sarris, Andrew. Review of *The Seventh Seal. Film as Film,* 18 October 1958.

————. Review of *The Graduate. Village Voice,* 28 December 1967.

Silverman, Kaja. "Male Subjectivity and the Celestial Suture: *It's a Wonderful Life*." *Framework* (Spring 1981).

Stumbo, Bella. "From Horror to Hope." *Los Angeles Times Magazine*, 21 April 1991, p. 8.

Valenti, Peter. "The Theological Rhetoric of *It's a Wonderful Life*." *Film Criticism* 5, no. 2 (Winter 1981).

Ventura, Michael. "Down Coppola's Dream Streets." Review of *Rumble Fish*. *L.A. Weekly*, 21–27 October 1983.

————. "The Significance of *Insignificance*." *L.A. Weekly*, 2–8 August 1985.

Wall, James M. "The Best Film of 1986: Probing the Depths of Evil." Review of *Blue Velvet*. *The Christian Century* 7–14 January 1987.

Westerback, Colin L., Jr. "Beauties and the Beast: *Seven Beauties/Taxi Driver*." *Sight and Sound* 45, no. 3 (Summer 1976): 136.

Wilmington, Michael W. "Jodorowsky Looks at Himself and Uncovers Santa Sangre." *Los Angeles Times*, April 14, 1990, F4.

Wineapple, Brenda. "The Production of Character in *It's a Wonderful Life*." *Film Criticism* 5, no. 2 (Winter 1981).

Wolper, Carol. "Director A. Jodorowsky." *Premiere*, May, 1990.

Wood, Robin. "Ideology, Genre, Auteur." Review of *It's a Wonderful Life*. *Film Comment*, January–February 1977.

Young, Colin. Review of *The Seventh Seal*. *The Prompter*, Santa Monica, February 1959.